"*International Student Mobility to and from the Middle East: Theorizing Public, Institutional, and Self-Constructions of Cross-Border* investigates internationalization in the region through new lenses. It critically analyses the concepts of mobility, focusing on TNE and program mobility, and of international students, focusing on student agency, both from a theoretical and practical point of view. It also shows the diversity and inequality present in the region."

Giorgio Marinoni, *Manager, HE and Internationalization International Association of Universities, Paris*

"This book is an excellent much-needed addition to the scholarship of international higher education. It gives a unique insight into the perspectives, experiences, and paradigms surrounding international students mobilizing to and from the Middle East. Researchers, stakeholders, and leaders in higher education will benefit from reading the research-driven thought-provoking and informative chapters."

Carly Armour, *Research Graduate Assistant, Office of the Provost, University of Iowa, USA*

"*International Student Mobility to and from the Middle East: Theorizing Public, Institutional, and Self-Constructions of Cross-Border Students* provides critical insights into international student mobility in comprehensive contexts of international, transnational, and interregional education in policy, system, culture, and strategies. The significant debates about internationalization, regionalism, and regionality with higher education from the global perspectives of the authors also offer practical implications for stakeholders, including policymakers, education managers and practitioners, and international students. I would like to congratulate the editors: Aneta Hayes and Sally Findlow for this excellent publication."

Li Wang, *Dr Tech, University of Sydney, Australia*

"This book proposes unique problems and potential solutions facing international higher education in the Middle East. From the topic of international branch campuses to the complex experiences of international students, this is a must-use resource for instructors working with international students or teaching global higher education courses."

Molly Harry, *Doctoral Candidate, University of Virginia, USA*

"This is an invaluable book that is relevant and important to the study of international student mobility to and from the Middle East and Arab Gulf. This timely book calls for a better understanding of the cross-border student population and their community."

Xi Lin, *Assistant Professor of Adult Education, East Carolina University, USA*

"This book provides comprehensive and interdisciplinary discussions on up-to-date issues of students' mobility in the Middle East and Arab Gulf, which is a unique and strategically important region. I highly recommend this book."

Benny Lim, *Director of the M.A. in Cultural Management programme, Chinese University of Hong Kong, HK*

"A timely book dedicated to the importance of international students gaining transferable skills and the focus of establishing resources that open doors to the new and interesting employment market. Readers will grasp the need for cross-cultural communication as a crucial qualification for individuals who live and/or study abroad."

Leslie Ekpe, *Graduate Student Senate President, Texas Christian University, USA*

"If you are seeking to expand your understanding of how internationalization is conceived and student mobility is perceived, then this book is for you! The book presents internationalization discourses and educational policies that either reflect or obscure priorities and realities and highlights unique experiences, assumptions, and constraints of international students in diverse contexts."

Caroline Wekullo, *Research Scientist, Masinde Muliro University of Science and Technology, Kenya*

"This pivotal book postulates how binary views of "international" students can threaten systematic efforts which attempt to improve diversity and equity work across global higher education. Supporting internationalism, as addressed by these authors, leaves the reader with the concept of how we can evaluate our social footprints of multicultural/multilingual education across the world."

Allison Silveus, *Instructional Designer, University of North Texas Health Science Center, USA*

"In this volume, *International Student Mobility to and from the Middle East: Theorizing Public, Institutional, and Self-Constructions of Cross-Border Students,* the editors have arranged a thoughtful compilation of chapters that challenges and complicates our understanding of "cross-border" mobility. These new conceptualizations, seated in observations of students "to and from the Middle East" are nevertheless widely relevant to broader notions of globalization and internationalization in universities, particularly as we enter uncharted post-pandemic and virtual spaces of higher education."

Eric W. Layman, *Doctoral Candidate, Indiana University-Bloomington, USA*

"The book provides real insight into international student mobility, embedded in less-noticed education systems. Students, higher education management, and stakeholders all over the world can enrich their current understanding by engaging dialogues with authors on these context-specific topics."

Hang Tran, *Lecturer and Vice Head of Information Technology and Communication Center, Da Nang University of Economics, Vietnam*

"This collection of research studies highlights the importance of diversity and inclusion in an international higher education context. The selection of topics welcomes new ways of knowing as the authors share personal identities and journeys into their research."

Juan Manuel Niño, *Associate Professor & Co-Coordinator of Urban School Leaders Collaborative, University of Texas at San Antonio, USA*

International Student Mobility to and from the Middle East

This volume investigates how international students in and from the Middle East are constructed by nations, institutions, other students, and themselves. Making a valuable contribution to understanding the nuances and complexities of educational politics and priorities affecting these constructions, the text considers the broader impacts of discourse on internationalisation.

Offering a unique combination of critical analysis of educational policies combined with empirical contributions through authors' own research, chapters highlight intersections between politics, the internationalisation of higher education, and the construction of mobile learners. Emphasising variation and nuance in the internationalisation of policies in the Gulf Cooperation Countries, and other Middle Eastern countries, the volume offers a theoretical framework to help understand the political, educational, and ethical implications of emerging constructions of international students and their comparison across the Middle East.

This timely volume will benefit researchers, academics, and educators with an interest in higher education, international and comparative education, as well as the Middle East more specifically. Those involved with educational education policy and politics, specifically related to the Middle East, will also benefit from this volume.

Aneta Hayes is Senior Lecturer in Education and Internationalisation Director in the School of Social, Political, and Global Studies, Keele University, UK.

Sally Findlow is Senior Lecturer and Director of Professional Doctorates in the School of Social, Political, and Global Studies, Keele University, UK.

Routledge Studies in Global Student Mobility

Series Editors: Krishna Bista and Christopher Glass

Routledge Studies in Global Student Mobility offers a scholarly forum for original and innovative research which explores, explains, and increases understanding of issues and opportunities relating to international student mobility in K-12, higher education, and beyond. Consisting in peer-reviewed authored and edited volumes, the series advances theoretical understanding and identifies best practices for educators and professionals involved in study abroad.

As an interdisciplinary scholarly venue, the series showcases new ideas and fresh perspectives relating to international student mobility, study abroad, exchange programs, student affairs from the US and around the world, and from a wide range of academic fields, including student affairs, international education, and cultural studies.

This series is produced in collaboration with the CIES SIG Study Abroad & International Students, STAR Scholars Network, and Open Journals in Education (OJED).

Books in this series include:

Impacts of COVID-19 on International Students and the Future of Student Mobility
International Perspectives and Experiences
Edited by Krishna Bista, Ryan M. Allen, and Roy Y. Chan

International Student Mobility to and from the Middle East
Theorizing Public, Institutional, and Self-Constructions of Cross-Border Students
Edited by Aneta Hayes and Sally Findlow

For more information about this series, please visit: https://www.routledge.com/go/routledge-studies-in-global-student-mobility

International Student Mobility to and from the Middle East

Theorising Public, Institutional, and Self-Constructions of Cross-Border Students

Edited by Aneta Hayes
and Sally Findlow

Routledge
Taylor & Francis Group
NEW YORK AND LONDON

First published 2022
by Routledge
605 Third Avenue, New York, NY 10158

and by Routledge
4 Park Square, Milton Park, Abingdon, Oxon, OX14 4RN

Routledge is an imprint of the Taylor & Francis Group, an informa business

British Library Cataloguing-in-Publication Data
A catalogue record for this book is available from the British Library

Library of Congress Cataloging-in-Publication Data
A catalog record for this title has been requested

ISBN: 9780367686581 (hbk)
ISBN: 9780367686598 (pbk)
ISBN: 9781003138457 (ebk)

DOI: 10.4324/9781003138457

Typeset in Sabon
by KnowledgeWorks Global Ltd.

Contents

Figures

Tables

Foreword

I've thought for some time now that the 'official' narratives around the movement of international students in higher education have been dominated by a rather fixed and pared back view of student flows; as broadly coming from the East to the West, with the 'west' busying itself in setting up branch campuses in strategic locations, including in the Middle East. The official narrative tends to go something like this.

In 2000, around 99.4 million students around the globe were enrolled in higher education. The OECD, in its annual *Education at a Glance* shows that in the 1990s, around 1.3 million students were enrolled outside of their country of citizenship. Fast forward to 2015, and the figure is now more than three times that number – with around 4.5 million students now studying in another country (OECD, 2014, p. 342). By 2030, some 414.2 million students were forecast to be enrolled (Calderon, 2012, p. 1). By anyone's reckoning, this is a very large population on the move, and all the more remarkable because by 2008, 24.4% of this population of international students came from just three countries – China, India and Korea – with the largest population by far being China (14.9%).

In policy circles in the destination countries of the 'west', increases in access to higher education continue to be justified by government policies calling for greater investment in advanced knowledge and skills to create competitive knowledge-based 'magnet' economies (Jessop, 2008). Mobilizing the 'brain power' of a nation or region or attracting global 'talents' via international student recruitment leading to skilled retention visas – is viewed as critical to the economic health of nations – because it is the creativity of this 'brain power' that will ostensibly drive new knowledge creation leading to innovation, patents, other forms of intellectual property and new firms (OECD, 1996; Robertson, 2008). These arguments draw from agendas and projects driven by governments, international agencies – such as the Organisation for Economic Cooperation and Development (OECD) and The World Bank (WB), and regional organisations, such as the European Union (Jessop, 2008).

It's not that this official narrative is untrue, as this collection of chapters on inter/national students in the Middle East makes clear, but it does not help make visible the multiplicities and complexities that best describe students and their likely experiences in the Middle East or indeed that of their universities. Take, for example, an international branch campus, for instance in Abu Dhabi or Qatar, that enrols both national and international students. The student body might now be comprised of students from within the UAE, and those students who enrol in their university programme in the United States, but who take up their place in the branch campus. As this fragment of an example suggests, what we need are a range of ways of capturing the complexities of who moves where and why; which institution's fabrics are stretched out into global and regional spaces and what are their effects on places; what moves – ideas, people of institutions – or all three; whose movements are forced, precarious, and dangerous; and what narratives at the level of the individual, institution and government better capture this world in motion?

And what of contraflows, such as those becoming more and more apparent among the rising powers and eager global players – in this case, China and Singapore – not as major sending countries as they once were, but as increasingly important destinations. The rise of China as a global power and its economic strength in comparison with the United States has resulted in 'study abroad' programmes for American students seeking to acquire some understanding of China and engagement with Mandarin as a potential contender to English (UNESCO, 2014). The Chinese government has also funded many scholarship holders from around the globe to study in China, while China's Belt and Road Initiative has sought to attract students both too and from the Middle East as it casts its net in the direction of higher education.

And now a global pandemic – COVID-19 – which brought the world to a stop in 2020–2021, whose rapid spread from one global city to the other has been aided by a world in motion, including higher education students and faculty, whose movements have been stopped and stalled, and what new forms of movement – albeit virtually/ideationally – have been facilitated, using the new infrastructures that have kept us moving while suspended in place?

There is, I would argue, not just a space for, but an urgency about, a more nuanced, close-up look at the worlds of higher education and inter/national students in the Middle East. This edited collection with its rich tapestry of chapters does just that. In the tradition of Fahey and Kenway (2010) or Hannan et al., (2006), whose conceptual grammar on movement invited new fresh ways of understanding movement, editors Hayes and Findlow, and the various authors in this book, invite us to think with the phrase – both/and that movements can be multiplicities of ideational and material resources that taken together construct new worlds.

- Susan L. Robertson is Professor of Sociology of Education at the University of Cambridge, UK. Her research focuses on education policy and politics, transformations of the state, rescaling governance and social justice. Susan has written extensively on the political economy of higher education, including emerging regionalisms around the globe. She is also founding editor and editor in chief of the journal *Globalisation, Societies and Education.*

References

Calderon, A. (2012). Massification continues to transform higher education. *University World News*, 2nd September, 2012, Issue 237, Retrieved June 21, 2015, from http://www.universityworldnews.com/article.php?story=20120831155341147

Fahey, J., & Kenway, J. (2010). International academic mobility: Problematic and possible paradigms. *Discourse: Studies in the Cultural Politics of Education*, 31(5), 563–575.

Hannan, K., Sheller, M., & Urry, J. (2006). Editorial: Mobiliites, immobilities and moorings. *Mobilities*, 1(1), 1–22.

Jessop, R. (2008). A cultural political economy of competitiveness and its implications for higher education. In B. Jessop, N. Fairclough, & R. Wodak (Eds.), *Education and the knowledge-based economy in Europe*. Sense Publications.

OECD. (1996). *The Knowledge-Based Economy.*

OECD. (2014). *Education at a Glance 2014.*

Robertson, S. L. (2008). Embracing the global: Crisis and the creation of a new semiotic order to secure Europe's knowledge-based economy. In N. Fairclough, R. Wodak, & B. Jessop (Eds.), *Education and the knowledge-based economy in Europe*. Sense.

UNESCO. (2014). *The international mobility of students in Asia and the Pacific.*

Acknowledgements

This book is based on research conducted by the authors who contributed the chapters to this volume. Without their contributions it would have not been possible to complete this project. We would therefore like to sincerely thank them for sharing their knowledge with us. We appreciate the time they have spent working on the chapters and for their patience and commitment to this volume.

We would also like to thank our reviewers for supporting the authors, as well as each other towards publication. We are greatly indebted to all of you.

Finally, we would also like to thank the Series Editors, Krishna Bista and Chris Glass for accepting our book proposal. We feel humbled to be part of your book series and hope we have made a valuable contribution.

Editorial

Constructions of (Inter-)National(-ised) Students in the Middle East: Comparative Critical Perspectives

Aneta Hayes and Sally Findlow

This book is intended as a contribution to understanding how educational policies and priorities travel, or don't, how 'internationalisation' discourses either reflect or obscure local priorities and realities, and on a deeper level how 'the global' impacts on the particular and vice versa. To do this, it presents diverse accounts of 'international' higher education policy in and around the Middle East and Arab World, with a focus on how 'internationalised' students are portrayed – by policy, nation-states, by other students and by themselves. The portrayals emerging from specific national contexts included in the book are contested around the world and in the region itself. The purpose of this book is to bring these accounts together, showing how they are thoroughly contextualised in local terms, and how these contextualisations gain extra significance for our understandings of regionalism and regionalisation when considered, critically, together. There is no right or wrong contextualisation here and the purpose of this volume is not to dispute or support the accounts and analyses presented by our authors; rather, the purpose is to bring them together to theorise movement of what we refer to as international*ised* people by presenting, as noted in the foreword by Susan Robertson, multiplicities of ideational and material resources discussed in individual chapters.

There is broad acknowledgement that the reputational benefits of highly 'internationalised' universities (in terms of global rankings and recruiting high numbers of international students) come at the cost of (mis-) representations of globally mobile learners. While there are encouraging examples of countries where this influence has been challenged by pluriversal approaches to internationalisation, wherein international students are constructed as political, social and intellectual equals (Wiers-Jenssen, 2019), there is also evidence suggesting that the politicisation of 'internationalisation' through rankings competition legitimises the logic of intellectual, social and political domination of host countries over international students. In the United Kingdom, the United States and Australia, for

DOI: 10.4324/9781003138457-1

instance, international students have been represented as economic objects and supplicants of the prestigious education systems of receiving countries (Marginson, 2012; Hayes, 2017; Lomer, 2014), leading to their betrayal with respect to the promises of a 'truly intercultural' academic and social experience and security (e.g., Forbes-Mewett & Nyland, 2008; Tran & Pham, 2016; Yu & Moskal, 2019). The politicisation of internationalisation is also associated with geography, especially when issues of intellectual equality for international students are concerned, because the global education system is hierarchical, privileging a certain 'gaze', depending on where the students come from and where they travel to study (Mignolo, 2011).

It is to add local colour to these more abstract arguments that we called for contributions from the Middle East. The Middle East is a region where approaches to internationalisation have been argued to be commonly linked to individual countries' economic development (Findlow & Hayes, 2016; Hayes & Findlow, 2020; Hayes & Al'Abri, 2019). Yet, despite this common link, the cultural, political and economic diversity of the region has 'demanded' varying approaches to internationalisation in individual Middle Eastern nations, enacting different constructions of *who* the 'desired' international student is (ibid). Additionally, some of the Middle Eastern nations are affected by protracted conflict; a situation which has shaped a special relationship between internationalisation and, for instance, 'management' of the refugee crisis, ensuring protection from persecution or/and building peace and sustainable livelihoods (Hayes et al., 2019). Simultaneously, increased investment in international branch campuses in some Middle Eastern countries also affects home students. There is evidence suggesting that home students attending overseas universities in the Middle East are often approached in the same way as international students in those universities' countries of origin (e.g. Holden, 2018).

These and other implicit inequalities, inconsistencies and silences around how higher educational 'internationalisation' is conceived, and how 'international' or mobile students are viewed, was the driver for this edited volume of first-hand accounts. When we reviewed the outstanding individual contributions, we found we had something slightly different: a critical interrogation of how educational policies and priorities travel or don't, how 'internationalisation' discourses either reflect or obscure local priorities and realities, and how 'the global' impacts on the particular and local and vice versa.

The diverse accounts of 'international' higher education 'policy' in and around the Middle East and Arab World seemed more than anything else to interrogate a number of prevailing assumptions: that there is any such thing as 'policy' (as distinct from geopolitically networked responses to shifting markets); that 'international' and 'internationalised' mean anything consistent; that it is meaningful to attach the term 'mobile' to students rather than institutions or policy/marketing strategies. Each of the local accounts in this edited volume questions these assumptions in different ways. Working conceptualisations of internationalisation in the Middle East, their consequences for 'internationally' mobile learners against a precarious socio-political context, often silenced and unproblematic, are examined across chapters that ask, 'What does "international" mean in this context?' and, 'Who, or what, is "mobile"?'. Overall, the book presents an idiosyncratically 'regional' story of different but connected countries' approaches to 'internationalisation', that simultaneously challenges, underscores and develops established work on (higher-)educational (inter-)nationalisation, regionalism and localism.

The book is organised into two parts:

Part I: 'Theorising 'Internationalised' Students: Points of Departure for Macro-Level Analyses' presents constructions of ('internationalised' or mobile) students at macro-level, that is at the level of national policies and socio-political contexts across the Middle East and Arab Gulf. These contributions represent a set of 'points of departure' against which the empirical case studies in Part II are analysed. In their problematisations of international higher education in the Middle East and Arab Gulf, the five chapters in Part I shed light on habitual silences around troublesome concepts, demographic complexities, and different stakeholder motivations for international mobility or 'trade'.

The first chapter, by Jason Lane and Christine Farrugia, presents four problematisations that together ground many of the later discussions. First, the authors challenge the idea that it is (always or most significantly) students rather than institutions that 'cross borders'. With a focus on the international higher education and 'branch campus' trade in the United Arab Emirates (UAE), they discuss the 'various combinations of both institutional and student mobility'. Second, in terms of how these students are subjectified, the authors draw attention to monolithic 'international student experience' policies that position students, often with high levels of intercultural capital, as outsiders, needing special treatment. Third, flowing from the first two problematisations, they suggest that the policy and analytical focus could more meaningfully shift towards consideration of the *relationships* between institutions and students, and the internationalised nature of these. Fourth, they set the scene for further chapters to develop the important argument that categorisations, of 'national' and 'international' are themselves problematic. The specific example they cite, in the context of the Arab Gulf, is that of 'stateless' residents, who through accident do not have legal citizenship. While the Gulf instance may be unique in some ways, it is easy to find comparables with other international contexts; Lane and Farrugia point out that across the world, such categorisation depends on 'who is doing the counting'.

The second chapter, by Giulia Marchesini and Holly Ann Johnstone, takes up the baton by further problematising the 'international' *trade* rather than the students. Marchesini and Johnstone focus on the ways this trade, or competition, leads institutions to concentrate on positioning themselves in terms of 'attractiveness', losing sight of the ethical, societal, intercultural and *learning* rationales for internationalisation. Citing proponents of this rationale, 'to learn from the world and not just teach the world what the institution already knows in order to satisfy some ... economic motives' (Hawawini, 2011), the authors thus present the 'problem' as a conceptual one in the first instance. With reference to this trade in the MENA region, they further explore ways that definitions of student mobility are themselves inadequate. For instance, drawing on NGO statistics, they point out that what is seen as the 'weak attractiveness' of the region's tertiary institutions is predicated on the number of international partnerships, which drive not learning but economic links. The reasons for this weak attractiveness, they suggest, are to do with incompatible ideals of educational 'quality' which can be rooted in cultural traditions, 'worries regarding academic freedoms', quality assurance, as well as divergent levels of centralisation or institutional autonomy; the latter being associated with 'improved performance' measured by international scales. However, taking up another problematisation offered by Lane and Farrugia, they point out that this notion of 'attractiveness' is also inadequate, grounded as it is in a very narrow working definition of 'international' or 'foreign'. While Lane and Farrugia highlighted the limitation in categorising students based on their legal status, Marchesini and Johnstone show that narrow definitions and categorisations also neglect the vibrant *intra-regional* student mobility in the Arab Gulf. The *shades* of international and intra-regional mobility are revealed in easily accessible statistics, which headline calculations and problematisations simply ignore: '... more than half of the inbound students come from the region itself: 45% from the Middle East and 10% from North Africa'.

The third chapter, by Clare Walsh, builds on these various problematisations by developing a concern with the contestability of terms such as 'international' and 'mobility'. Echoing Marchesini's and Johnstone's focus on intra-regional mobility, Walsh considers issues of standards and international and intra-regional comparability. Walsh also picks up the idea of rationale, or motivations, from the perspective of the provider, for international trade. Tapping into the 'identity' motivation, she points out that in the Arab Gulf context, higher education has always been a soft-power catalyst, blending and moving between the goals of economic development (and international and intra-regional competition), regional identity and political collaboration, and national identity. The third way Walsh problematises academic mobility in and around that Arab Gulf is by revisiting some of the older literature around regionalism, regionalisation and 'new regionalism' (Robertson, 2008). Her discussion approaches the strong regionalism of the Arab Gulf on two levels. First, she makes a case for 'regional' sets of expectations and motivations, as distinct from expectations a decade and more ago that we would see the proliferation of regional higher education *policies*. But second, she points out that despite the documented emergence of national, intra-regional competitive forces in the Gulf, what has also undeniably emerged are several mechanisms for regional quality assurance (Arab and GCC), which she presents and discusses as key 'mobility mechanisms'.

The fourth chapter, by Omer Caliskan and Hilal Buyukgoze, moves to the Middle East proper to discuss the international student phenomenon in Turkey but also adds to the argument developed in the preceding three chapters that despite global statistics indicating otherwise, 'international' mobility *is* alive and kicking in the Middle East, as evidenced in Turkey's case with 'almost one-third of those students com(ing) from nearby Middle Eastern countries'. Caliskan and Buyukgoze highlight the under-acknowledged role, or influence, of shared 'historical, cultural, racial and political proximities' in shaping intra-regional, international academic mobility. In keeping with this theme of cultural origins, the authors then highlight the socio-economic differences (and consequent expectations) between mobile students from different countries; they point out that students from wealthier Gulf countries tend to travel to the United States or Europe, while those from Middle Eastern countries like Syria and Palestine tend to opt for the cheaper and presumably less risky destination of Turkey, which is nonetheless 'more modern' than many in the surrounding region. Such regional nuance to patterns of mobility is rarely discussed. Finally, the authors apply this same cultural heritage lens to the motivations of Turkey as a host country to host internationally mobile students. Tapping into the 'soft power' discussions of the previous two chapters, they explain the political and diplomatic rationales for prioritising internationalisation in the form of generous scholarship programmes.

The final chapter in Part I, by Sulaiman Mouselli, develops Caliskan and Buyukgoze's discussion of student motivations for overseas study by looking at international mobility in, to and from Syria during and since the recent period of conflict, and highlighting some notable silences. The first thing the author does is problematise the prevailing assumptions of agencies that facilitate much of this mobility, focusing on some resulting inequalities of opportunity. First, while commending the work of EU and global agencies in facilitating higher education access to Syrian refugees through scholarships, Mouselli notes that 'Syrian students inside Syria, however, have no access to such scholarships'. Mouselli explains that the motivations, for both institutions and students in Syria, for seeking to participate in international mobility programmes are predominantly economic and competitive, but that this also blends with longstanding traditions of intercultural knowledge generation. This context adds poignancy to a number of other lost mobility routes, which he notes have largely passed un-remarked on. These include Syrian students no longer being able to travel overseas to get doctorates and qualify as university lecturers, in order to feed back into an 'internationalised' national cultural repository. And he notes that the higher education trade in Syria has suffered invisibly as the inbound traffic from the United States, Europe and globally to study subjects such as religion and Arabic has also dried up, further reducing Syria's role in higher educationally mediated transnational and intercultural communication. Individually and combined, these represent macro-economic, personal socio-economic, and cultural losses to both Syria and the world.

Part II: Representations of internationally (and intra-regionally) mobile students in and from the Middle East draws on empirical findings to interrogate the complexities and nuances in the public, peer, social media representations and self-constructions of ('internationalised' or mobile) students in and from this region. They develop Part I's analysis of local 'mobility' markets, trends and policies by showcasing connections between internationalisation (understood mostly as student mobility) rationales and human capital development. The chapters in this section make unique conceptual contributions by, for instance, offering critical comparisons between the actual voice of the students and the type of 'exteriority' that speaks for them.

Reading Annette Bamberger's chapter through this lens helped us understand how the genealogical emergence of representations of international students in Israel as that of diaspora 'family' were made intelligible because of Israel's historical, economic, political and social influences. Our premise that policy cannot get to work without first problematising its territory is strongly supported by what Bamberger reveals about the relationship between that representation and its territory in the context of the two Israeli universities considered in her chapter. She shows how the social media campaigns of the two universities to attract a particular type of international student are made 'legitimate' because of the connection between the campaigns' representations of international students and the contextualisation of Israel. This connection seems to 'govern' the type of the international student that is desired at each of the two universities whose social media campaigns she analyses.

Bamberger also draws our attention to questions about students' agency, in particular how students themselves attempt to create and share their self-constructions using social media. The next chapter, by Wendy Maddison, also focuses on student agency; here Maddison considers critical self-constructions of transnational students studying in an Irish university in the Kingdom of Bahrain, in light of the new transnational model for nurse education in Bahrain. The stories told in this chapter reveal that this transnational nurse education model, and its graduates, are initially regarded by locally educated nurses as lacking conformity to local cultural norms, both in terms of identity and practice; a construction that later on, as the chapter reveals changes, as the nurses become agents of change. This initial construction is however captured under what Maddison refers to in her chapter as 'The Look', a gaze that questions how the transnationally educated nurses are presenting themselves socially and physically. Maddison's chapter thus helps us appreciate how 'the phenomena of transnational education (TNE) may shape the lifeworlds of specific groups of local students situated in different geographical and socio-cultural contexts around the globe'. She deconstructs the impact of TNE experiences on a local learner's sense of self and persona is a dimension of TNE which, at least initially, leads to the lack of social and professional legitimacy. The transnationally educated nurses were aware of these constructions but interestingly, rather than trying to avoid them, they actively and strategically negotiated them.

Students' agentic negotiations of self and understanding of others are also mentioned in the chapter by Natalie I. Cruz, Jobila W. Sy, Cassandra Shukla and Alisha Tysor. In this chapter, agency is contrasted with ways in which international students are represented by the domestic students and the institution where they were studying. The insights from the survey conducted by Cruz and colleagues provide a window into assumptions made about (inter-)national students in a federal university in the United Arab Emirates (UAE). A lot of these assumptions are driven by, what we have referred to above, as the characteristics of the 'territory'. Cruz and colleagues show how these characteristics legitimise how international students are 'thought about', particularly within a complex nexus of, on the one hand, a desire to experience and honour cultural diversity, and on the other, support nationalisation strategies. The chapter is interesting in that it does not see these two influences as mutually exclusive, something that is attributed to the philosophical and political aspects of (the Arab Gulf) regionalism. These also have an impact on problematising the label of 'international student', with Cruz and colleagues chapter providing an empirical analysis of the problematisations of this label presented in the conceptual chapters in Part I by Lane and Farrugia and Marchesini and Johnstone.

The issues raised by Cruz and colleagues additionally point to the same constructions of international students as discussed in international literature elsewhere – that is, 'although HEI administrators readily recruit and welcome "international students" to their campus, appropriate levels and structures of support have not always been a priority' and that 'an inherent contradiction is that services may be provided (or not provided) for international students based on what it is *assumed* that they need'. Specifically, the assumptions made by Emirati students about international students seemed to impact their rationale and willingness to engage with their international peers. Similarly, the unique nature and assumptions about what needs international students have seemed to impact the services that were offered.

The question of 'needs' is perhaps most powerfully expressed in the chapter by Ranwa Korsheed, Susan Deeb and Rasha al-Dahhan who discuss ways in which the Syrian crisis and international sanctions imposed on Syria have 'crushed, deferred or put to sleep' dreams of international mobility for many Syrian students. Building on the earlier chapter by Sulaiman Mouselli, Korsheed's chapter problematises several aspects of attempts to regulate and oversee Syrian 'mobility', mainly via the English language testing that Syrians need to access in order to be mobile (either physically or virtually by undertaking an online degree abroad). The roles of Syrian and US governments, NGOs, professionals, experts and technologies are all critically reviewed from the point of view of the students interviewed and surveyed as well as by the authors themselves. We wanted to give enough space in this book to Syrian voices, in order to raise awareness of the ways that war and crisis can lead to the politicisation of higher education, especially in terms of access to international student mobility. Reading Korsheed et al's chapter in the light of the earlier chapter by Sulaiman Mouselli prompted a deeper exploration of how the various aspects of governmentality on the part of such agencies are used to govern the lives of students caught in places and times of conflict. Here while student agency is manifested in strategies such as undertaking online degrees abroad, as this is the closest the Syrians can get to 'the dream of travelling to study abroad', the governmental ways in which the crisis is dealt with are revealed to be actually prohibitive for them, limiting even online options.

So, What Is the Significance of the Contributions to This Volume?

Together, the chapters contributed to this volume have uncovered a number of habitual silences around internationalisation and student mobility, drawing on examples cased in international branch campuses, online mobility, the mobility of international students to state universities, and conflict-ridden higher education. By problematising the geo-political scope and agential nature of supposed 'international mobility', the book has drawn attention to the ways that both of these constructs are dependent on local and national agendas around economic growth and inter-state, intra-regional competition. The chapters in the second part of the book have then explored the impacts of such issues on scope, identity, assumptions and the habitual silences around them in terms of how they impact the students participating in 'international mobility' to, from and within the Middle East.

Our focus here on the Middle East and Arab Gulf thus provides a unique regional context, arguably giving weight to turn-of-the-millennium projections about regionalism, regionality, as the way forward for higher education policy (Corbett, 2005; Robertson, 2008). But in also revealing the lack of 'teeth' in 'policy' per se, the Middle Eastern lens additionally showcases ways in which such 'regionalism' is perhaps best seen in terms of shared cultural heritage, pressures and networks rather than actionable 'policy'. At the same time, our specific geopolitical, regional focus can also be seen as just one, regional, instance of broader issues. The fact that agency issues are habitually silenced through conceptualisations of international mobility lodged within the macro and micro-level contexts of policies and politics, agencies, institutions and individual people described in this volume means that international mobility is not considered comprehensively. Ignoring student agency means limiting top-level discussions about internationalisation to political rationales and reputational or economic self-interests, ignoring critical questions about ethics, care and the social functions of universities towards international students. These habitual silences matter however because they shape the ways in which (inter-)national or mobile students become 'internationalised' and how they are consequently labelled and thought about. This then dictates what indeed should be 'done about them' and how they should be 'managed'. The silences prohibit certain conversations and actions while rationalising others.

Habitual silences should, therefore, not be ignored but rather critically interrogated to enable us to 'say something new' about international students, something that may disrupt the seemingly successful politically focused actions and strategies behind so-called 'internationalisation'. After all, when the focus is on economic benefits it is easy to ignore difficult questions around care and ethics. If the official discourse around internationalisation is about bringing 'business' to the country, that's where the responsibility of the government and any other agencies will be seen to lie. The result is the widespread reporting of incidents to do with international students' social, economic and legal insecurity as well as their discrimination as epistemic equals (e.g., Forbes-Mewett & Nyland, 2008; Hayes & Cheng, 2020; Ramia et al., 2013). As well as clear social justice questions, these silences also question universities' commitment to widely touted rhetorical positions around, for instance, the 'decolonisation' of higher education.

We hope you will read the chapters in this book with the 'regional-agentic' framework in mind to focus your reading on the ways that the chapters interrogate and explode habitual geopolitical, ethical and cultural silences. And that they will give you pause to think about their significance for critical debates about internationalisation, regionalism and regionality as well as help you define 'movement'.

References

Corbett, A. (2005). *Universities and the Europe of knowledge: Ideas, Institutions and policy entrepreneurship in European union higher education policy, 1955–2005*. Springer.

Findlow, S., & Hayes, A. (2016). Transnational academic capitalism in the Arab gulf: Balancing global and local, and public and private, capitals. *British Journal of Sociology of Education*, *37*(1), 110–128. https://doi.org/10.1080/01425692.2015.1100531

Forbes-Mewett, H., & Nyland, C. (2008). Cultural diversity, relocation, and the security of international students at an internationalised university. *Journal of Studies in international Education*, *12*(2), 181–203. https://doi.org/10.1177/1028315307308136

Hayes, A. (2017). Why international students have been “TEF-ed out”? *Educational Review*, *69*(2), 218–231. https://doi.org/10.1080/00131911.2016.1197183

Hayes, A., & Cheng, J. (2020). Datafication of epistemic equality: Advancing understandings of teaching excellence beyond benchmarked performativity. *Teaching in Higher Education*, *25*(4), 493–509. https://doi.org/10.1080/13562517.2019.1689387

Hayes, A., & Findlow, S. (2020). The role of time in policymaking: A Bahraini model of higher education competition. *Critical Studies in Education*, *61*(2), 180–194. https://doi.org/10.1080/17508487.2017.1358756

Hayes, A., & Al’Abri, K. M. (2019). Regional solidarity undermined? Higher education developments in the Arabian gulf, economy and time. *Comparative Education*, *55*(2), 157–174. https://doi.org/10.1080/03050068.2018.1504884

Hayes, A., McGhee, D., Garland, N., & Lally, B. (2019). Could refugee education in Lebanon provide a model for all? *University World News*. https://www.universityworldnews.com/post.php?story=20190827121636840

Hawawini, G. (2011) The internationalization of higher education Institutions: A critical review and a radical proposal. *INSEAD Working Paper*.2011/112/FIN.

Holden, C. (2018). Adapting Tinto’s framework: A model of success and failure in a Middle Eastern transnational setting. *Studies in Higher Education*, *43*(6), 1002–1019. https://doi.org/10.1080/03075079.2016.1212004

Lomer, S. (2014). Economic objects: How policy discourse in the United Kingdom represents international students. *Policy Futures in Education*, *12*(2), 273–285. https://doi.org/10.2304/pfie.2014.12.2.273

Marginson, S. (2012). Equals or others? Mobile Students in a nationally bordered world. In S. Sovic, & M. Blythman (Eds.). *International students negotiating higher education* (pp. 18–36). Routledge.

Mignolo, W. (2011). *The darker side of western modernity: Global futures, decolonial options*. Duke University Press. https://doi.org/10.2307/j.ctv125jqbw

Ramia, G., Marginson, S., & Sawir, E. (2013). *Regulating international students’ wellbeing*. Policy Press.

Robertson, S. (2008). Europe/Asia’ regionalism, higher education and the production of world order. *Policy Futures in Education*, *6*(6), 718–729. https://doi.org/10.2304/pfie.2008.6.6.718

Tran, L. T., & Pham, L. (2016). International students in transnational mobility: Intercultural connectedness with domestic and international peers, institutions and the wider community. *Compare: A Journal of Comparative and International Education*, *46*(4), 560–581. https://doi.org/10.1080/03057925.2015.1057479.

Wiers-Jenssen, J. (2019). Paradoxical attraction? Why an increasing number of international students choose Norway. *Journal of Studies in International Education*, *23*(2), 281–298. https://doi.org/10.1177/1028315318786449

Yu, Y., & Moskal, M. (2019). Why do Christian churches, and not universities, facilitate intercultural engagement for Chinese international students? *International Journal of Intercultural Relations*, 68, 1–12. https://doi.org/10.1016/j.ijintrel.2018.10.006

Part I

Theorising "Internationalised" Students

Points of Departure for Macro-Level Analyses

Chapter 1

Which Students Are "International" at an International Branch Campus? Problematising "International" When Universities and Students Cross Borders

Jason Lane and Christine Farrugia

Introduction

More than five million tertiary students annually move to another country to pursue their studies, at least before the global pandemic in 2020 (Organisation for Economic Cooperation and Development, 2020). These 'international students' are typically defined as individuals who leave their home country to pursue an education in a different country (Lane & Bhandari, 2014). In the most traditional sense, and for a vast majority of international students, they attend an educational institution that largely serves students from the country where the institution is located.

This traditional conception of the international student tends to be used in wide variety of institutional contexts, from data collection to student services, in nearly all parts of the world. Indeed, it underpins much of the relevant writing on this subject as scholars and practitioners look to examine the 'international student experience' (Brown & Jones, 2011; Hellstén & Prescott, 2004; Montgomery, 2010). As such, tertiary policy makers and leaders tend to see international students through the lens of their being a small group of individuals (relative to the overall size of the student body) coming from afar and typically with limited experience in the educational system in which they are now participating. Prior to the pandemic, international students made up 5.5% of tertiary enrolment in the United States and between 20% and 28% of enrolment in the United Kingdom, Canada and Australia (Project Atlas, 2019).

Some scholars have begun to question the standard definitions of international students. In 2017, Jones explored this issue within the context of what one might consider the traditional university setting:

> Although the term "international student" is used for someone who moves to another country specifically to study, in some cases they will be familiar with the social and academic culture of the host country,

DOI: 10.4324/9781003138457-3

> and may be expert in, or even a native speaker of, the language of study. For example, they may have already studied there at high school level. Furthermore, we should recognize that some who are classified as domestic students may have similar needs to students identified as international by passport or visa status and so the traditional divide may be of limited value today. Domestic students may be recent migrants, speak another language at home or be unfamiliar with the academic tradition or the education system of the country.
>
> (p. 934)

This passage summarises some of the key issues missed with the current broad definition of international students, although Jones's critique is still based on the assumption that students, not higher education institutions (HEIs), are mobile. So, how do we consider the nature of the 'international student' when it is the HEI that moves across borders?

Over the last 20 years, we have seen a significant increase in the number of transnational education activities (TNE) and enrollments (Lane et al., 2015). TNE activities include dual degree programmes, franchising arrangements, teaching partnerships and more. In fact, these activities have become so plentiful that universities in the United Kingdom, for example, now serve more students from foreign countries in their TNE activities outside the United Kingdom than the total number of international students who come to the United Kingdom to study (Universities UK, 2019).

One of the most extreme forms of transnational education is the international branch campus (IBC). These institutions have been defined as:

> An entity that is owned, at least in part, by a foreign higher education provider; operated in the name of the foreign education provider; and provides an entire academic program, substantially on site, leading to a degree awarded by the foreign education provider.
>
> (Lane, 2011a, p. 5)

IBCs have been criticised for providing low-quality educational opportunities on the IBCs relative to their home institution campus (see e.g., Altbach, 2013; Altbach & De Wit, 2020), but they have also been described as academic embassies that deliver a different type and quality of education than may otherwise be available in the country and expand access to students who cannot leave their home country (Lane, 2011b). According to the Cross-Border Education Research Team (C-BERT, 2021), more than 300 international campuses were operating worldwide as of 2020 and Waters & Leung (2013) have noted that the 'space and place' of these institutions complicate how students are labelled and interacted with.

As we explore in this chapter, this movement of HEIs across borders further problematises traditional definitions of international students. No longer are the campuses stationary and the students' mobile; now there are various combinations of both institutional and student mobility with which to contend. This issue of the intersectionality of student and institution mobility is particularly poignant in some countries in the Middle East and the Arabian Gulf, such as Bahrain, Kuwait, Qatar and the United Arab Emirates (UAE), where there has been significant importing of IBCs. Each country has taken its own approach to develop these institutions, but the results are similar in terms of expansion of their higher education sector to offer curriculum and degrees from foreign HEIs. Across the board, the IBCs serve a combination of students native to the host country and from afar.

For the purposes of this chapter, we use a case study of the UAE, one of the largest importers of IBCs, to examine the various types of student/institutional relationships that might exist and to explore the various modalities of international students as related to IBCs in the Middle East and across the globe.[1] We first seek to unpack the current reality of some more non-traditional types of international students and then provide an overview of IBCs and the UAE context. We then present a 2 × 2 table, based on students attending an IBC, as a step toward problematising the changing nature of international mobility and why we need a more nuanced understanding of the relationship between a student's permanent domicile and the educational provider they attend, disrupting the more traditional definition of 'international student'.

Problematising International Student Definitions in the Middle East and beyond

The prevailing definition of international students used by UNESCO (2020) refers to students who cross an international boundary for the purpose of academic study. This form of international academic mobility is well known and has been widely adopted by organisations and government agencies that study international education and the flows of students between countries (Farrugia et al., 2017). While UNESCO's definition captures the mobility of students who travel across borders to enroll in an HEI outside their home country, it can overlook students who engage in other forms of cross-border higher education.

In this section, we examine situations where the traditional definition of international students does not apply fully. This discussion raises questions about the limitations of the dominant definition of international students and how well it captures the full range of students who are engaged in an internationally mobile educational experience.

Residency Status

Despite the general consensus around UNESCO's definition of international students, countries differ in how they count international students according to citizenship or residency status. For instance, in the United

States, international students are defined as those who travel to the country on temporary, non-immigrant visas that allow for academic study (Farrugia et al., 2017; US Department of State, n.d.). Students with residency status are excluded from international student counts because the primary purpose of their presence in the United States is to be a resident of the United States, compared to international students who travel to the country for the purpose of enrolling in tertiary education. In contrast to the US approach, Germany includes legal residents without citizenship in its counts of international students (Farrugia et al., 2017; Trines, 2019). Germany's approach casts a wider net than the United States' method by considering any non-citizen an international student, regardless of whether they have been residing in Germany prior to enrolling in tertiary education in Germany or have travelled to the country expressly to enroll in tertiary education.

Displaced and Undocumented Students

Displaced and undocumented students are variably considered as international or domestic students depending on the country and the nature of a student's circumstances. Numbers of refugee and displaced students have surged since 2015 because of economic conditions and political conflict in countries such as Syria, Iraq and Yemen (Bhandari et al., 2018). Refugees and asylees in the United States have visas that grant them residency status, so they are counted as domestic students. However, this designation is not the case everywhere. Consider the case of Syrians who have been displaced from their home country by war. Large numbers of displaced Syrians migrated to the nearby countries of Turkey, Lebanon and Jordan; but they often faced challenges in enrolling in tertiary education in their host countries due to policies that, in effect, restricted their access to tertiary education (Farrugia & Bhandari, 2016; Watenpaugh & Fricke, 2013; Watenpaugh et al., 2014). In light of the challenges that displaced students face, some countries have established supports to facilitate refugee students' access to higher education and integration into the host country (Bhandari et al., 2018). Germany is one example where the government provides German language classes and pathway colleges for displaced populations living in Germany (Streitwieser & Morris-Lange, 2016).

The United States presents an example of undocumented students who are defined variably as international or domestic, depending on who is doing the counting. An estimated 450,000 undocumented students are enrolled in tertiary education in the United States (Feldblum et al., 2020). Most of these students have come from Latin America, arriving in the country as children when their parents settled in the United States without legal documentation. Despite being raised in the United States and attending primary and secondary schools, they are not legal residents of the United

States, which can present barriers to enrolling in tertiary education and accessing financial aid to pay for their studies. At the national level, undocumented students in the United States are not considered international students because they have not travelled to the country for the purposes of academic study. However, at the state level, undocumented students may be considered out-of-state or in-state depending on state policies, and at the institution level, they may be considered domestic or international (Golash-Boza & Merlin, 2016).

Dual Citizens

Dual citizenship is now widely accepted by governments around the world. In 2017, 70% of countries held a tolerant position toward dual citizenship, with near-complete acceptance in the Americas (including North, Central and South America) and Oceania and about 70% acceptance in Europe (Vink et al., 2019). While tolerance of dual citizenship is somewhat lower in Asia and Africa (around 65%), since 1960 all regions have grown substantially in their acceptance of dual citizens (Vink et al., 2019). The existence of dual citizens poses a unique challenge in measuring the mobility of students across international borders, and the expansion of opportunities to obtain dual citizenship makes this a significant issue for capturing mobility patterns.

Since dual citizens can rightfully be considered domestic students in both countries where they hold citizenship, the case of dual citizens can generate anomalies in counts of international students. For example, in the United States, international students are defined by their country of citizenship, regardless of their prior place of residence. Thus, when US dual citizens travel from abroad to study in the United States, they are not categorised as international students even if they have not resided in the United States since they were young or never at all. However, while such students would not be considered international students, they often have similar support needs as international students, such as English language assistance or guidance on adapting to a new academic and cultural environment.

Programme Modality and Structure

Student characteristics such as residency and citizenship status pertain to students themselves and, in both cases, apply to all individuals regardless of the duration, form, or structure of their international study activities. However, student-level characteristics are not the only factors that matter in defining and counting international students. Organisational and academic characteristics also present student enrolment scenarios that do not easily fit the standard definition of an international student. For example, online programmes provide the opportunity for students to enroll in an institution in another country without crossing a border. Although these students engage in a cross-national educational experience, they are not counted as international under the UNESCO definition because they do not physically cross a border to enroll in a tertiary education institution. Duration of studies is another factor that influences whether international students are counted as such. Students engaged in short-term exchanges, vs. students who pursue a full degree or credential in another country, are excluded from UNESCO's international student count, which encompasses only students who study abroad for one year or longer. In line with these examples, the presence of IBCs is likewise problematic when determining whether students are international or domestic. When it is campuses that cross borders, rather than students, multiple possibilities emerge for defining their student populations.

International Branch Campuses: A Global Phenomenon

As with many aspects of cross-border higher education, standard definitions of well-accepted concepts become problematised. For example, previous studies have identified how a private institution in the United States could have an international campus that is perceived as public when operating abroad or vice versa (Lane & Kinser, 2011). Such an example would be in Qatar, where the Qatari government, through the Qatar Foundation, has significantly subsidised the presence of international campuses. These campuses operate as extensions of private US institutions to pursue goals that are traditionally more aligned with public institutions – expanding access for local students and supporting development of the local economy.

In a different example, Lane and associates (2018) explored the complexity of cross-border quality assurance for international campuses. In their work, which provides a foundation for this analysis, they employed a 2 × 2 design to illustrate the different configurations of regulations that affect an IBC based on whether the home and/or host country engages in regulation of the IBC. Their analysis illustrated how some IBCs must navigate dual, and sometimes competing, forms of oversight when the host and home countries engage in regulation of the IBC. In other situations, the IBC may fall between the regulatory cracks if neither the home nor host country engages in oversight of these entities.

IBCs have existed for around a century, although their prevalence has greatly increased in the last 20 years. The basic idea is that IBCs allow for students to pursue a comparable educational experience to the home campus and to earn a degree awarded in the name of the home campus without having to visit the home country of the campus.

The extent to which the educational experience is comparable likely varies markedly among the institutions and is often the focus of debate (Altbach, 2013; Wilkins et al., 2012). Engendering such a debate is not the purpose of this chapter, though it often focuses on such issues as perceived level of teaching quality, student success, value of the diploma, comparability of the experience and so forth. Of course, the mere fact that the IBC exists in a different physical environment than the home campus does mean that IBC students will have different experiences from their peers at the home campus, and how that experience is realised will vary based on the origin, academic readiness, and other individual factors of the student (Healy, 2018; Yang et al., 2020).

While some might dismiss this discussion out of hand, believing the issue is not widespread, the reality is that a growing number of institutions, students and countries are involved with IBCs. As of the end of 2020, the Cross-Border Education Research Team (C-BERT) (2020) had identified 83 countries that are exporting more than 300 IBCs that are operating in 37 countries (not including numerous such institutions that closed earlier). Seventeen of these countries are both importers and exporters. The United States is by far the largest exporter of IBCs, with 86 campuses around the world – double that of the next largest exporter. Rounding out the top five exporters are the United Kingdom (43), France (38), Russia (29) and Australia (20). Iran also exports IBCs to Lebanon and the UAE. The top five importers include China (42), the UAE (33), Singapore (16), Malaysia (15) and Qatar (11). Other countries in the Middle East that host IBCs include Bahrain, Egypt, Kuwait, Lebanon, Oman and Yemen.

According to a 2017 report, the number of students attending IBCs worldwide exceeded 180,000 (Garrett et al., 2016). The interplay of student and institutional mobility is no more apparent than in the Middle East, particularly in Arabian Gulf countries.

While on the small side compared to the total number of tertiary students in the world, this number is not inconsequential.[2] More importantly, in some countries, such as the UAE and Qatar, the number of students enrolled in IBCs represents a substantial proportion of overall tertiary enrolment. For example, in Qatar, there are 2 public and 17 private tertiary institutions. In terms of enrollments, about one-third of the country's 34,000 tertiary students are enrolled in private education, primarily comprised of IBCs and about 40% of all tertiary students were non-Qatari students, again mostly enrolled in IBCs (Ministry of Development Planning & Statistics, 2017; Planning and Statistics Authority, 2019).

Many of these countries, including the UAE, have sought to diversify their economies by becoming multinational business hubs. Developing multinational education hubs, in turn, complements their business aspirations (Knight, 2013). These IBCs serve a wide range of students, from locals who may not be able to attend the home campus for family, financial, or political reasons, to students looking for an entirely new educational adventure and having no affiliation to either the home or host nations. The rich diversity of institution and student relationships created in this part of the world are hardly represented by the insufficient dichotomy between the labels domestic and international, particularly when limited to the perspective of the home campus.

The UAE Context

As we are using the UAE as a case study to better understand the complexities of labelling or identifying types of students in IBCs, it is relevant to provide a brief summary of the nation's educational evolution. As a country, the UAE is relatively young, establishing its independence from the United Kingdom in 1971. The country is comprised of seven semi-autonomous states or emirates. What started as a rural economy with a small population has grown into one of the world's major economic destinations.

The country's oldest university, UAE University, was founded in 1976 in the emirate of Abu Dhabi and served as the country's only tertiary institution for many years. The public sector would eventually expand to include Zayed University and the Higher Colleges of Technology, spread across the UAE. The public sector is only open to UAE citizens. Since the 1980s, however, private tertiary education institutions have developed to serve both UAE nationals and the rapidly growing expatriate population (Donn & Al Manthri, 2010; Kinser et al., 2010).

The first emirate to host an IBC was Dubai, where the University of Wollongong from Australia established a campus in 1993. The growth of IBCs in the country took off in the 2000s and at least four other emirates have also hosted IBCs. There are IBCs from 12 different countries operating in the UAE, with most campuses coming from the United States, United Kingdom and India (see Table 1.1). Abu Dhabi, the nation's capital, sought to offer high subsidies to attract IBCs of elite institutions such as New York University and the Sorbonne. In contrast, Dubai, which hosts the largest number of IBCs, took a more capitalistic approach by setting up economic free zones to both create education hubs and exempt institutions from many of the local rules and regulations that affect domestic campuses (Lane, 2010, 2014). Among the primary drivers for the UAE to allow and attract these foreign institutions is to provide tertiary education options for the expatriate population, to allow Emirati students to pursue a 'foreign' education without leaving the country, and to attract students from other countries to study in the UAE (Lane, 2011b; Schoepp, 2009).

Table 1.1 Home Countries of UAE-Based IBCs[3]

Home Country	*United States*	*United Kingdom*	*India*	*Australia*	*France*	*Other*
# of IBCs in the UAE	7	5	5	3	3	7

The UAE is among a small handful of countries where the expatriate population outnumbers the native population (United Nations, 2019). By most estimates, Emiratis comprise roughly only 10% of the nation's population, with citizenship almost exclusively granted to children born to Emiratis, despite some non-national families' presence there for multiple generations (World Bank, 2020). Residents from India comprise approximately 25% of the population – more than double that of the Emirate population (Edarabia, 2020). Work visas are term-limited, albeit renewable and workers are legally regarded as temporary residents even when they live and work in the country for decades. The UAE is also home to the *Bidoon*, a population of stateless people who have resided in the country for generations but do not hold national citizenship. Though they are among the only non-Emiratis allowed to attend public education in the country (Zacharias, 2018).[4]

The UAE lacks a permanent residency status for expatriates, and this structure is reflected in the country's counts of tertiary education students. In Dubai, government statistics distinguish between Emirati nationals and non-Emiratis, a category that encompasses both expatriate students who normally reside in the UAE and international students who travel to the country specifically to enroll in tertiary education (Dubai Statistics Center, 2019; Farrugia et al., 2017). The two sets of students are grouped together and defined as non-Emirati, effectively marking them under the same label as international students.

The UAE, like neighbouring Qatar discussed previously, has among the highest student mobility rates in the world. The country has one of the highest outward mobility rates for nationals, and its inward mobility rate is a staggering 48.6% and 'dwarfs that of all major destinations' (Kamal & Trines, 2018). However, these numbers do not fully capture what is happening in terms of student experiences, which is what we are attempting to unpack in this chapter.

To better serve the educational needs of their large non-national populations and to enhance its ability to serve as a business and academic hub, the UAE has actively imported IBCs from foreign countries (Lane, 2011b). Now students from the UAE and around the world can choose from IBCs from more than a dozen different countries – an international souk of educational offerings, where students from nearly any nationality can pursue a degree of their choosing. As such, this chapter uses the UAE as a backdrop to problematise the increasing complexities of classifying students as *domestic* or *international*.

Developing an Initial Typology of Students at International Branch Campuses

The intent of this chapter is to use IBCs as a mechanism to explore the new and evolving relationships between students and institutions, particularly as both now are able to cross borders. The UAE also provides a useful backdrop for our discussion given the complexities both of the composition of the tertiary education institutions and the students who attend those institutions.

How do we begin to think about the various relationships that might exist? For example, does the child of an Indian expat who was born and raised in Dubai and pursues a tertiary degree in Dubai really count as an international student in the same way as a student travelling from Nigeria who has never been to Dubai, for example? Should a student who is *Bidoon* be considered differently than an Emirati student, particularly as both may now come through the same compulsory education system?

For some, the answers to these questions may not seem important. However, the answers can have a range of real-world implications from how students are counted (or not) by the government to the type of access and financial aid available to students to the types of academic supports provided to students by the institution. We are not able to fully discuss all of the potential implications or how those implications may be triggered by different scenarios. For example, one limitation concerns grouping students studying in the UAE from other Arabian Gulf countries with students from Africa, India and other places outside of the Arabian Gulf, even though there are many strong cultural, religious, and educational connections among the citizens of the Gulf States. Rather, our primary intent is to use a simple two-dimensional analysis to problematise more commonly accepted definitions of *domestic* and *international* students. In fact, we continue using these terms for the sake of illustrative and familiarity purposes, even though we note some of their limitations above. However, we seek to illustrate the complexities of the intersectionality of labels when both institutions and students move across international borders.

For this analysis, we use a simplified set of definitions and a simplified dichotomy between domestic and international students. Each axis applies the label from the perspective of the home campus or the IBC campus (Along the vertical axis, we position the home campus perspective; along the horizontal axis are the perspectives of the IBC). For the purposes of this typology, a student is considered domestic if their citizenship is from or they have long-term residency in the country where the campus is located.[5] Let us take the IBC of Wollongong University, an Australian-based institution, in the UAE as an example. A student from Australia would be labelled as domestic from the home campus perspective, but international from the IBC perspective. Whereas an Emirati student would be considered domestic by the IBC and international by the home campus in Australia.

For the purposes of this analysis, a student is also considered international if their citizenship is from any country other than where the campus is located (or do not have long-term residency in the country where the campus is located). Using the Wollongong example again, a student from Nigeria would be considered an international student by both the home

Table 1.2 Typology of International Branch Campus Students

	Domestic student (IBC Perspective)	*International student (IBC perspective)*
Domestic student (Home campus perspective)	***Boundary spanner*** *Individuals with an association with both countries, either through dual citizenship or family expat status such that they could be viewed as 'domestic' by both campuses*	***Passthrough*** *Students pursing an education in a foreign country and doing so in an educational context that is likely to be familiar*
International student (Home campus perspective)	***Staycationer*** *Students from the country where the IBC is located, but without formal association with the IBC's home country; seeking a 'foreign' educational experience without leaving the country*	***Explorer*** *Students without a formal association with either the home or host country; pursuing a foreign educational experience*

campus and the IBC. Table 1.2 presents the typology created by the intersection of these labels.

Table 1.2 provides an opportunity to identify four basic prototypes of students enrolled in the IBC: *Boundary Spanner*, *Staycationer*, *Passthrough* and *Adventurer*. These descriptions, however, do not cover all possible student scenarios, and there are likely to be students who blur the lines between the categories here. That stated, having studied IBCs and their students for more than decade, we believe that a vast majority of students both in the UAE and worldwide fit within these categories. We also believe that each type is comprised of many nuances that we are unable to fully explore in this chapter. Our intention here is to problematise the definitions by merely adding one layer of dimensionality to the international and domestic student labels, which also illustrates how quickly the complexity of the situation develops. Here we discuss each type in more depth.

Boundary spanners are individuals who may be considered as domestic students by both the home campus and IBC. Typically, these students would have an affiliation with both countries, and it may well be that these individuals have lived in both countries and are comfortable moving between the different countries. Alternatively, they may be long-term expats who are living in the UAE, which is a quite common situation in the UAE. For example, these students may have dual citizenship in the United Kingdom and the UAE and are attending a UK IBC located in the UAE. In another example, the student may be the child of a long-term expat resident, who by being born to parents with Indian citizenship also has Indian citizenship, but who has been largely raised in the UAE. In fact, Indian students now comprise roughly 20% of all non-Emirati students in the UAE (UNESCO, 2020). Given the large Indian expat population working in the country, it is likely that a significant number of these students spent significant time in the UAE before enrolling in tertiary education. For example, Amity University and the Birla Institute of Technology & Science, Pilani (BITS-Pilani) are branch campuses in Dubai of universities based in India. Both institutions serve students from India, many of whose parents are expats in Dubai. In this context, the student may be able to span the boundary that exists between the home and host country of IBC and thus have a unique relationship with the IBC that is, itself, bridging between the two nations. Regardless of the situation, the student spans the boundaries of the binational associations of the IBC through their own dual associations. Because of the student's citizenship with the home country of the university, the student could be classified as domestic by the home campus. Because of their long-term affiliation with the host country, even if not a citizen, the student may well be viewed as local (i.e., domestic) by the IBC (even though some governments, including the UAE, may not classify them as such).

Staycationers are students who can be considered domestic by the IBC and international by the home campus. The students may have different domestic situations. For example, they could be citizens of the host country, they could be long-term expatriates, or they could be an undocumented resident member of the *bidoon* (as discussed previously). For New York University (NYU) Abu Dhabi, Emirati students comprised 20% of their incoming class in Fall 2020 (NYU Abu Dhabi, 2020).[6] These Emirati students would be considered by NYU in New York as international, and yet these students grew up largely within commuting distance of the NYU Abu Dhabi campus. The commonality of the *staycationers* is that they are predominantly individuals who have resided, at least for some period of time, in the host country. They have no formal association with the IBC's home country, and it is likely that they are pursuing an education delivered in an academic context and/or pedagogical style different from that available in the host country's public tertiary sector. Thus, these students are taking an educational adventure while staying close to home (staycation). There is an important caveat to this scenario to highlight, however. It is possible, that some students may have pursued a private K-12 education that is similar to that of the IBC, so they may have some familiarity with the educational culture of the IBC. Indeed, around a quarter of Emirati students at the compulsory levels now enroll in private schools that offer 17 different national curricula, with more than half of Emiratis in Dubai enrolled in private schools (Godinho, 2021). That said, the IBC still provides an educational opportunity that differs from what would otherwise be available among public and native private institutions in the host country.

Passthrough students are those who come from their home country to pursue an education at an IBC associated with their home country. In many cases, these students will return to their home country or move on to other destinations – essentially passing through the host country while pursuing their education. For example, the UAE is home to the largest number of migrants from India and the 5th largest receiver of students from India (ICEF Monitor, 2019). Many of these students come to earn a degree at an Indian-based IBC, such as the campuses of Manipal Academy of Higher Education, Amity University Dubai and SP Jain School of Global Management. In fact, of the 35 private tertiary institutions in Dubai, those three institutions are the 4th, 5th and 6th largest institutions, respectively, and serve almost entirely Indian students (KHDA Open Data, 2020). In many cases, there has been an increase in students and expats returning to their home country to reunite with family and pursue employment in what was a rapidly growing economy (Zweig et al., 2021). For some, the motivation may lie in accessing an education not attainable at home either because of high levels of competition for limited spots. These students, who could be short-term study abroad or full degree seekers, spend a finite period of time in the host country pursuing their degrees. They may interact with the local culture and build local relationships, but it is also not unusual for such students to remain largely engaged with each other and the IBC, creating something of a cultural bubble of the home country within the host country's environment.

Explorers are those students who have no association with either the home or host country. They could, for example, be a student from an African country who is pursuing a degree from an IBC of an Australian university in the UAE. In fact, many IBC students in the UAE now fit this category, as the UAE emerges as a global hub for attracting students. In fact, this is true of many locations, including Malaysia, Singapore and Qatar, that are strategically using IBCs to create education hubs designed to attract more students from abroad (Knight, 2013). Indeed, the UAE has one of the highest inbound mobility rates for international degree seekers, the total number of international students in the country growing by more than 50% from 2011 to 2016. Other than India, the largest senders have been Syria, Jordan, Egypt, Oman and Pakistan (Kamal & Trines, 2018). The University of Wollongong in Dubai (UOWD) reports its more than 3,500 students come from 105 countries (UOWD, 2018). These students are exploring a new educational environment in a country with which they have little to no familiarity. In many ways, they are among the most intrepid of IBC students. The core aspect of the experience for these students is entirely new, from the academic and cultural context to the broader community environment.

Discussion

The increase in TNE has led to a vast restructuring of the higher education sector as both students and institutions cross borders. The result is that traditional notions of what constitutes an international and domestic student are outmoded and need to be reconsidered.

This chapter provides a typology to assist scholars, practitioners and policy makers in advancing their understanding of the types of students who may attend IBCs. This typology accounts for the mobility of both students and institutions. We acknowledge that the typology has its own limits in that some types of students may not be easily classified and the classification may overlook or mask important nuances between different groups of students. That said, the conceptualisations presented in the typology problematise the basic usage of the terms *international* and *domestic*, move forward understanding of these dynamics, and are intended to be flexible enough to be used in different countries.

For better or worse, the terms domestic and international, as applied to a student, are intended to represent at the broadest level the relation of a student's country of citizenship to the location of their campus. However, in many countries and institutions, these terms have become linked with financial and policy implications. For example, in around half of the OECD countries, international students enrolled in public universities are often expected to pay higher tuition and fees than domestic students (Sanchez-Serra & Marconi, 2018). Because of their visa status, international students are often subjected to heightened government scrutiny and review and do not have the same legal rights as their domestic peers. Their opportunities for employment in their host country can be non-existent or diminished relative to domestic students. They also often have (and need) different support structures within the university.

The typology presented here is a first step toward unpacking the complicated array of student and institutional relationships now manifesting in the UAE and other countries that are importing both educational institutions and students. There are implications for both governmental policy and institutional practice. In the case of the UAE, for example, these efforts are part of a larger strategic intent to position the nation as a multinational business leader and have resulted in the country's citizens becoming a minority of its population. As a result, the country, and its individual emirates, have adopted policies designed to expand tertiary education, particularly the number of foreign education providers available to the expat population as a means to both upskill and retain the local workforce (Kinser et al., 2010). An ancillary effect is that places like Abu Dhabi and Dubai have emerged as educational hubs that attract foreign students, faculty and staff to those destinations (Lane, 2014).

From a governmental policy perspective, the UAE government lumps all students who are not UAE citizens into the same international student category. In part, this designation has to do with governmental policies, including those under the Emiratisation strategy that prioritises funding and hiring Emirati nationals so to improve their participation in the workforce (Sarker & Rahman, 2020). This broad grouping, however, fails to account for the many important nuances in the composition of the UAE population by grouping, for example, the children of long-term expats with those coming from afar with no specific ties or connections to the country. In this conceptualisation, we have grouped long-term expats with host-country nationals as both have longer-term vested interests in the host country and are familiar with many of its cultural and social norms; however, they do not always have the same rights in terms of accessing higher education – in the UAE only residents (and *Bidoon*) can access public tertiary education. For some policy makers, there may be value in considering how to more accurately differentiate these students. For example, there may be a benefit in actively seeking to retain those non-nationals who have a demonstrated vested interest in the host country based on their or their family's having already worked and lived in the country.

More recently, the UAE government has been considering changes to its visa policies that would allow families of international students who are studying in the UAE to travel with them (Mathew, 2021). Rather than providing educational opportunities for the children of current expats, the government is looking to leverage the expat status of the students to recruit their families in the hope that all will stay in the country beyond the student's completion of a degree. These students, many of whom would have the option to attend either a branch of a home institution (passthrough) or that of a different country (explorer), are seen as an opportunity to strategically expand the UAE population and further spur business development by retaining the students and their families.

We have also gone further in distinguishing other types of students, such as the passthroughs and adventurers, with the first group of students seeking a home country educational experience in the host country and the second group seeing a new educational experience in a new land. The distinctions may be helpful for institutional leaders as they develop their internal policies and practices. Taking again the UAE for context, a local Emirati who attends public school in the UAE may need a different orientation when attending an Indian branch campus than would an Indian student who attended public secondary school in India. In the first case, the student would be local (or domestic) in that they reside in the country where the IBC is located, but the student may not have any familiarity with the educational culture of the branch campus. In the second case, the student coming from India may not have any understanding of life in the UAE, but the student may be quite familiar with the educational culture of the Indian IBC. These distinctions are important as they may impact how faculty or university staff interact and support students, but the distinctions are often overlooked and under-recognised, nuances of labelling that become complicated as both students and institutions cross-border.

This chapter problematises the more traditional conceptions of international students in the context of IBCs. We used the case of the UAE as it is home to many IBCs from different countries, hosts a complex population, and is attracting students from around the world. The 2 × 2 typology provides a way to begin to better understand how student and institutional origins may interact. While we have briefly discussed the implications of the presented typologies, additional research is needed to better understand and further problematise these identities within specific institutional and policy contexts.

Notes

1 We use the data provided by the Cross-Border Education Research Team (C-BERT, 2021), which indicates the UAE imports the second highest number of IBCs of any nation.
2 The 180,000 does not include the hundreds of thousands of students worldwide involved in other forms of transnational education (e.g. twining programs, dual degrees, and franchises).
3 Data for this table from CBERT (2021).
4 In the UAE, the *Bidoon* are culturally Bedouin people who led a nomadic lifestyle prior to the country's founding in the 1970s, and for a variety of political and cultural reasons never received Emirati citizenship, but also had no other homeland to which they belong. There are populations of *Bidoon* throughout the Middle East.
5 It is noted that in the UAE, a student is considered domestic by the government only if they are a citizen. All other students are grouped together as "non-Emirati." For the purposes of this typology, however, we use a more inclusive definition that reflects a similar experience rather than only focusing on legal standing. This categorisation further highlights a particular problematisation of the definition of international students in that it is often based on artificial distinctions that do not reflect the lived experiences of students. For example, in the UAE, both a long-term resident (non-citizen) and a student who visits the country for the first time to attend higher education are labeled the same way.
6 In comparison, as of 2019 Emiratis constituted less than 1% of the student population of the Indian-based Amity University IBC in Dubai (Knowledge and Human Development Authority, 2019).

References

Altbach, P. G. (2013). *The international imperative in higher education*. Sense Publishers. https://doi.org/10.1007/978-94-6209-338-6

Altbach, P. G., & De Wit, H. (2020, February 20). Branch campuses are unlikely to blossom. *Times Higher Education*. https://www.timeshighereducation.com/opinion/branch-campuses-are-unlikely-blossom

Bhandari, R., Robles, C., & Farrugia, C. (2018). *International higher education: Shifting mobilities, policy challenges, and new initiatives* (Background paper for Global Education Monitoring Report 2019). https://unesdoc.unesco.org/ark:/48223/pf0000266078

Brown, L., & Jones, I. (2011). Encounters with racism and the international student experience. *Studies in Higher Education*, *38*(7), 1004–1019. https://doi.org/10.1080/03075079.2011.614940

Cross-Border Education Research Team (C-BERT). (2021, January). *C-BERT international campus listing*. [Data originally collected by Kevin Kinser and Jason E. Lane]. http://cbert.org/resources-data/intl-campus/. Author.

Donn, G., & Al Manthri, Y. (2010). *Globalisation and higher education in the Arab gulf States*. Symposium Books. https://doi.org/10.15730/books.73

Dubai Statistics Center. (2019). *Enrolled students by education type and nationality – Emirate of Dubai (2019/2020-2017/2018)*. [Table]. Dubai Statistics Center. https://www.dsc.gov.ae/en-us/Themes/Pages/Education.aspx?Theme=37#DSC_Tab1

Edarabia. (2020). Population of the UAE (2020). Retrieved December 4, 2020, from https://www.edarabia.com/population-uae/

Farrugia, C., & Bhandari, R. (2016). *Open doors 2016: Report on international educational exchange*. Institute of International Education.

Farrugia, C., Bhandari, R., Baer, J., Andrejko, N., & Robles, C. (2017). *Open doors 2017: Report on international educational exchange*. Institute of International Education.

Feldblum, M., Hubbard, S., Lim, A., Penichet-Paul, C., & Siegel, H. (2020). *Undocumented students in higher education: How many students are in U.S. higher education and who are they?* New American Economy; President's Alliance on Higher Education and Immigration. https://www.presidentsalliance.org/report-undocumented-students-in-higher-education-how-many-students-are-in-u-s-colleges-and-universities-and-who-are-they/

Garrett, R., Kinser, K., Lane, J. E., & Merola, R. (2016). *International branch campuses: Trends and developments, 2016*. Observatory for Borderless Higher Education and Cross-Border Education Research Team.

Godinho, V. (2021, Feb 25). Students enrolled in Dubai private schools reach 286,588. *Gulf Business*. https://gulfbusiness.com/students-enrolled-in-dubai-private-schools-reach-286588/

Golash-Boza, T., & Merlin, B. (2016, November 24). Here's how undocumented students are able to enroll at American universities. *The Conversation*. https://theconversation.com/heres-how-undocumented-students-are-able-to-enroll-at-american-universities-69269

Healy, N. M. (2018). The optimal global integration – Local responsiveness tradeoff for an international branch campus. *Research in Higher Education*, *59*(5), 623–649. https://doi.org/10.1007/s11162-017-9480-0

Hellstén, M., & Prescott, A. (2004). Learning at the university: The international student experience. *International Education Journal*, *5*(3), 344–351 (EJ903859). ERIC. https://files.eric.ed.gov/fulltext/EJ903859.pdf

ICEF Monitor. (2019). *More than 750,000 Indian students abroad in 2018*. Author. https://monitor.icef.com/2019/11/more-than-750000-indian-students-abroad-in-2018/

Kamal, K., & Trines, S. (2018). *Education in the UAE*. World Education News & Review. https://wenr.wes.org/2018/08/education-in-the-united-arab-emirates

KHDA Open Data. (2020). Dubai's Private Higher Education Institutions Open Data. https://www.khda.gov.ae/en/opendata

Kinser, K., Levy, D., Casillas, J. C. S., Bernasconi, A., Slantcheva Durst, S., Otieno, W., Lane, J., Praphamontripong, P., Zumeta, W., & LaSota, R. (2010). *The global growth of private higher education*. Jossey-Bass.

Knight, J. (2013). Education hubs: International, regional and local dimensions of scale and scope. *Comparative Education*, *49*(3), 374–387. 10.1080/03050068.2013.803783

Knowledge and Human Development Authority. (2019). *Academic and statistics information*. Retrieved February 6, 2021, from https://www.khda.gov.ae/en/directory/universities-search-results/university?id=737

Lane, J. E. (2010). *International higher education, free zones, and quality assurance in Dubai* (Policy Brief No. 20). Dubai School of Government. https://www.mbrsg.ae/getattachment/00bfa982-daf2-4971-8260-e1dcf757d2e9/International-Branch-Campuses,-Free-Zones,-and-Qua

Lane, J. E. (2011a). Global expansion of international branch campuses: Managerial and leadership challenges. In J. E. Lane, & K. Kinser (Eds.), Multinational colleges & universities: Leadership, administration, and governance of international branch campuses. *New Directions for Higher Education*, *2011*(155), 3–18. https://doi.org/10.1002/he.440

Lane, J. E. (2011b). Importing private higher education: International branch campuses. *Journal of Comparative Policy Analysis*, *13*(4), 367–381. https://doi.org/10.1080/13876988.2011.583106

Lane, J. E. (2014). The local impact of international branch campuses: Educational, economic, and diplomatic factors. In *The future of higher education in the UAE: Innovation and knowledge production* (pp. 123–152). Emirates Center for Strategic Studies and Research.

Lane, J. E., & Bhandari, R. (2014). Measuring higher education internationalization. In J. E. Lane (Ed.), *Building a smarter university: Data, big data, and analytics* (pp. 239–262). State University of New York Press.

Lane, J. E., & Kinser, K. (Eds.). (2011). Multinational colleges & universities: Leadership, administration, and governance of international branch campuses. *New Directions for Higher Education*, *2011*(155).

Lane, J. E., Kinser, K., & Zhang, L. (2018). Cross-border educational accountability: Navigating accountability expectations when education crosses borders. In E. Hazelkorn, H. Coates, & A. McCormick (Eds.), *Research handbook on quality, performance and accountability in higher education* (pp. 81–93). Edward Elgar Press.

Lane, J. E., Owens, T. L., & Kinser, K. (2015). *Cross border higher education, international trade, and economic competitiveness: A review of policy dynamics when education crosses borders*'. ILEAP, CUTS International Geneva and CARIS.

Mathew, J. (2021, February 1). New visa move seen driving next wave of Indian students to the UAE. *Arabian Business*. https://www.arabianbusiness.com/education/458069-new-visa-move-seen-driving-next-wave-of-indian-students-to-the-uae

Ministry of Development Planning & Statistics. (2017). *Education in Qatar: Statistical profile 2016*. https://www.psa.gov.qa/en/statistics/Statistical%20Releases/Social/Education/2016/Education_Statistical_Pro%EF%AC%81le_2016_En.pdf

Montgomery, C. (2010). *Understanding the international student experience*. Palgrave Macmillan.

NYU Abu Dhabi. (2020, October 20). Nearly 500 Students from Over 80 Countries Join NYUAD as the Class of 2024 [Press release]. https://nyuad.nyu.edu/en/news/latest-news/community-life/2020/october/nearly-500-students-from-over-80-countries-join-nyuad-as-the-cla.html

Organisation for Economic Cooperation and Development. (2020). *Education at a glance 2020*. https://doi.org/10.1787/69096873-en

Planning and Statistics Authority (2019). *Education in Qatar, 2019*. Doha, Qatar.

Project Atlas. (2019). *A quick look at global mobility trends*. Institute of International Education. https://www.iie.org/en/Research-and-Insights/Project-Atlas/Explore-Data/Infographics/2019-Project-Atlas-Infographics

Sanchez-Serra, D., & Marconi, G. (2018). Foreign students' tuition fees are a double-edged sword. *University World News*. https://www.universityworldnews.com/post.php?story=20180220142151532

Sarker, A. E., & Rahman, M. H. (2020). Social engineering and emiratization in the UAE. *Public Administration and Policy: An Asia-Pacific Journal*, *23*(2), 173–186. https://doi.org/10.1108/PAP-02-2020-0009

Schoepp, K. (2009). The UAE and the branch campus gold rush. *International Higher Education*, *56*, 22–23. https://doi.org/10.6017/ihe.2009.56.8435

Streitwieser, B., & Morris-Lange, S. (2016, August 12). Barriers to providing higher education to refugees must be breached. *University World News*. https://www.universityworldnews.com/post.php?story=20160809120339971

Trines, S. (2019, October 22). How Germany became an international study destination of global scale. *World Education News and Reviews*. https://wenr.wes.org/2019/10/how-germany-became-an-international-study-destination-of-global-scale

UNESCO. (2020). International (or internationally mobile) students. *Glossary*. UNESCO Institute for Statistics. http://uis.unesco.org/en/glossary-term/international-or-internationally-mobile-students

University of Wollongong in Dubai. (2018). *Facts and Figures*. https://www.uowdubai.ac.ae/about-uowd/facts-and-figures

United Nations, Department of Economic and Social Affairs, Population Division (2019). *International Migrant Stock 2019*. (United Nations database, POP/DB/MIG/Stock/Rev.2019).

Universities UK. (2019). *International Facts and Figures 2019*. https://www.universitiesuk.ac.uk/International/Documents/2019/International%20facts%20and%20figures%20slides.pdf

US Department of State. (n.d.). *Directory of Visa Categories*. Retrieve February 5, 2021, from https://travel.state.gov/content/travel/en/us-visas/visa-information-resources/all-visa-categories.html

Vink, M., Schakel, A. H., Reichel, D., Luk, N. C., & De Groot, G. R. (2019). The international diffusion of expatriate citizenship. *Migration Studies*, 7(3), 362–383. https://doi.org/10.1093/migration/mnz011

Watenpaugh, K. D., & Fricke, A. L. (2013). *Uncounted and unacknowledged: Syria's refugee university students and academics in Jordan*. Institute of International Education. https://www.iie.org/Research-and-Insights/Publications/Uncounted-And-Unacknowledged-Syrias-Refugee-University-Students-And-Academics-In-Jordan

Watenpaugh, K. D., Fricke, A. L., & King, J. R. (2014). *The war follows them: Syrian university students and scholars in Lebanon*. Institute of International Education. https://www.iie.org/Research-and-Insights/Publications/The-War-Follows-Them-Syrian-University-Students-And-Scholars-In-Lebanon

Waters, J., & Leung, M. (2013). Immobile transnationalisms? Young people and their in-situ experiences of 'international' education in Hong Kong. *Urban Studies*, *50*(3), 606–620.

Wilkins, S., Balakrishnan, M. S., & Huisman, J. (2012). Student satisfaction and student perceptions of quality at international branch campuses in the UAE. *Journal of Higher Education Policy & Management*, *34*(5), 543–556. https://doi.org/10.1080/1360080X.2012.716003

World Bank. (2020). *International migrant stock (% of population) – UAE*. https://data.worldbank.org/indicator/SM.POP.TOTL.ZS

Yang, L., Borrowman, L., Meng, Y., & New, J. Y. (2020). Expectations in transition: Students' and teachers' expectations of university in an international branch campus. *Journal of Studies in International Education*, *24*(3), 352–370. https://doi.org/10.1177/1028315319861348

Zacharias, A. (2018, September 5). Explained: Who are the Bidoon? *The National*. https://www.thenationalnews.com/uae/explained-who-are-the-bidoon-1.767398

Zweig, D., Tsai, K. S., & Singh, A. D. (2021). Reverse entrepreneurial migration in China and India: The role of the state. *World Development*, *38*, https://doi.org/10.1016/j.worlddev.2020.105192

Author biographies

Professor Jason E. Lane is the Dean of the School of Education at the State University of New York at Albany. As the founding co-director of the Cross-Border Education Research Team (C-BERT), he and his team track the development of transnational education globally, including managing the only global database of international branch campuses. As a Fulbright New Century Scholar based in Dubai, he has conducted in depth analysis of the IBC phenomenon in the GCC region. Dr. Lane has published more than 10 books and numerous papers on the changing global dynamics of higher education, garnering several awards including for Significant Research on International Higher Education from the Association for the Study of Higher Education.

Dr Christine Farrugia is Deputy Head of Research at the Institute of International Education (IIE) where she leads Open Doors, a large-scale annual survey of international educational exchange in the United States, as well as other studies on international academic mobility. She works extensively with colleges and universities, higher education associations, and national governments on a range of international education research, including studies on US study abroad, pathways to international mobility, and global mobility trends. She has over 15 years of experience as a university administrator and researcher of higher education and regularly authors research reports and articles on international academic mobility. In 2014, she was awarded the Harold Josephson Award for Professional Promise in International Education by the Association of International Education Administrators (AIEA). She holds a Ph.D. from SUNY-Albany and M.A. and Ed.M. degrees from Teachers College, Columbia University.

Chapter 2

Internationalisation of Higher Education in the Middle East and North Africa

Giulia Marchesini and Holly Johnstone

While international student mobility in the Middle East is the focus of this book, this introductory chapter takes a wider angle, both in conceptual scope and in geographical reach. It addresses internationalisation, a means to make higher education more relevant – which includes student mobility but goes well beyond it – and it focuses on the wider region of the Middle East and North Africa (MENA).

The MENA region is a heterogeneous region, stretching from the Maghreb to the Gulf, and comprising many differing social, political, cultural and economic contexts. As such, tertiary education systems and the status and progress of internationalisation processes, as well as institutions' and governments' motivations to internationalise, vary enormously from country to country. Recognising this reality, this chapter nonetheless draws on data from across MENA, in order to provide a broader introduction to internationalisation processes throughout the region. Two caveats are given: first because data are mostly drawn from UNESCO and the World Bank – which do not have identical definitions of the region[1] – and because data is not always available for all MENA countries, in the chapter, countries are sometimes omitted, added or grouped in slightly different ways according to the analytical focus. Second, in order to capture the specificities found within MENA, countries are sometimes grouped together under different geographical classifications or, for example, according to their domestic and foreign student enrolment rates. While this does make for several overlapping groups, it also allows for a more granular analysis in which significant sub-regional trends and patterns can be clearly highlighted.

Internationalisation comprises a broad set of activities including academic partnerships, branch campuses, internationalisation 'at home' (the ensemble of internationalisation activities implemented domestically), internationalisation of research and student mobility, although the latter is perhaps the most commonly cited. Student mobility is also the element that is most often quantified and for which data is most readily available. The following definition encapsulates this broad sense of internationalisation and is the result of a long debate in the literature: 'the intentional process

DOI: 10.4324/9781003138457-4

of integrating an international, intercultural or global dimension into the purpose, functions and delivery of post-secondary education, in order to enhance the quality of education and research for all students and staff, and to make a meaningful contribution to society' (De Wit et al., 2015).

In providing an overview of internationalisation across MENA, this chapter notes that, despite the very heterogenous experiences of internationalisation, the region as a whole could use internationalisation as a tool to increase the relevance and quality of its tertiary education. Today, both in spite of and partly due to the COVID-19 pandemic, a window of opportunity is open for MENA, which could enable the region to 'catch up' on the internationalisation agenda. While the chapter uses student mobility as a proxy, it proposes that MENA could greatly benefit from internationalisation more generally, and in particular, from the increased focus that COVID-19 has given to those activities implemented in domestic settings – internationalisation 'at home' – in order to add relevance to higher education and respond to today's challenges.

Why Is Internationalisation Relevant for the MENA Region?

The internationalisation of higher education is a phenomenon on the rise around the world, and one which has been shown to have several advantages – for students, for tertiary education institutions, and even for countries – both hosting and sending. While some governments and institutions may tend to see its advantages in terms of the benefits that they reap through recruiting international students, internationalisation's benefits go beyond that. One scholar sums up: 'the ultimate benefit of internationalization for tertiary education institutions is to learn from the world, and not just teach the world what the institution already knows in order to satisfy some educational and economic motives' (Hawawini, 2011).

In the MENA region, however, while internationalisation is taking hold, it is happening unevenly across the region. Regarding international student mobility, as far as total numbers go, countries in MENA are not the biggest players on the global scene. Looking at the countries which welcome the highest numbers of internationally mobile students, and those from which most mobile students originate (as percentages of the total number of mobile students worldwide), no MENA country figures among the top ten destination countries, and only one country, Saudi Arabia, can be found in the top ten origin countries of mobile students (CMI & World Bank, 2020). Although these figures position the MENA region rather low down when taken from a global perspective, this does not, however, mean that student mobility is absent from the region. Indeed, some countries have extremely high inbound and outbound mobility rates, which we analyse below.

But the weak attractiveness of the region (CMI & World Bank, 2020) can also be perceived from another angle, thanks to data collected by a recent survey carried out by the International Association of Universities (IAU). The survey showed MENA to be the region which is the least prioritised, by tertiary education institutions around the world, for developing internationalisation partnerships. Grouping universities by region, the survey showed that not one single other region put institutions from the MENA region as their first priority for partnership development, nor as their second, nor third. Even universities in MENA itself reported giving only *second* priority to developing partnerships with institutions within the region; in other words, preferring first to look elsewhere (Marinoni, 2019). Once again, however, this does not entail that there are no partnerships between institutions in MENA and those around the world; rather, it is to say that the region is far from the most attractive on this front when looked at from a global perspective.

Yet given that internationalisation holds advantages on numerous levels, the MENA region could stand to benefit, should it further increase the internationalisation of its tertiary education institutions. First, internationalisation can have beneficial effects on higher education by contributing to improving its quality. As recognised by the United Nation in its Sustainable Development Goals (SDGs), widening access to tertiary education on its own will not suffice; young people need equal access to 'affordable and *quality* technical, vocational and tertiary education, including university' (United Nations 2030 Agenda for Sustainable Development, SDG 4, Target 4.3, emphasis added). Internationalisation can contribute to improving higher education's quality: international cooperation, exchanges with peers, adapted methods of teaching and innovative solutions, introduction of common standards, mutual learning, cross-cultural understanding and foreign language acquisition, are all likely to increase the quality of higher education. Moreover, the relationship is mutually reinforcing; improved education quality can, conversely, be a driver for student mobility (CMI & World Bank, 2020).

A second advantage of internationalisation is the skills gains it can lead to for students, and the boost this can give to their employability. Internationalised education can enable students' acquisition of '21st-century skills': it can help them build self-confidence, increase their interpersonal skills and intercultural understanding, learn languages and so on. Indeed, students invariably report witnessing gains in such skills when surveyed (see the European Commission's *Erasmus Impact Study*, 2016; the British Council Report on *Student Perspectives on Going International*, 2015). Furthermore, the link between such skills gains and improved employability is well documented. The Erasmus Impact Study, for example, showed that more than 12 months after graduation, the unemployment rate among graduates having taken part in the study abroad programme was 2% compared to 4%

for those who did not take part (European Commission, 2016). Studies have also shown that internationalisation 'at home' led to important skills gains, in particular in the development of students' global, international and intercultural competencies (see Parsons, 2009; Soria & Troisi, 2014).

Third, at the economic level, student mobility in particular is recognised to have such beneficial effects on host countries' economies that it is increasingly being labelled an 'exporting' industry, becoming a component of governments' foreign trade policies. International students contribute to host economies through the fees they pay, as well as through renting accommodation, travel and their day-to-day expenses. In the United States, for example, over the 2018–2019 academic year, international students contributed 41 billion USD to the economy (NAFSA, 2019); in Australia, in 2017, international education contributed over 32 billion Australian dollars (Universities Australia, 2018).

Finally, as a result of internationalisation, countries stand to benefit in terms of diplomacy, and regional or global influence. Many governments have recognised the power that the internationalisation of their tertiary education systems can have in fostering stronger links between countries, building reputation and influence. They, therefore, encourage student and staff exchanges, develop and deliver joint and dual degrees, and suchlike, as part of their diplomacy policy and operations (CMI & World Bank, 2020).

Given such identified advantages, then, the ways in which MENA stands to benefit from internationalisation are many and varied. This becomes more evident when we consider the wider socio-economic context of the region: the region has witnessed a series of challenges over recent decades, from political instability to economic hardship. The MENA region has the highest youth unemployment rate in the world, currently at almost 27% (World Bank data, 2019). Huge numbers of young people are graduating from school and university and finding themselves unable to find gainful employment, adding to the high levels of youth exclusion on social, economic and political levels. In addition, both enrolment rates and quality of education vary enormously across the region. For instance, many MENA countries' education systems fall short with regard to quality, when measured by common international measures of education quality such as the Programme for International Student Assessment (PISA) scale (World Bank, 2018).

Against this backdrop, internationalisation, with its capacity to improve education quality and boost students' employability skills, can be seen as a strategy for building human capital in MENA. The World Bank's Human Capital Index (HCI) shows that while the HCI varies enormously across the region, with some countries (Oman, Qatar, Saudi Arabia and the UAE) in the top or second quartile, most countries in the region fall into the third (Jordan, Lebanon, North African countries) or even bottom quartile

(Iraq, Yemen) (World Bank, 2020). Education being one of the key components of human capital, improving education outcomes is essential for MENA, and internationalisation has the means to contribute. Moreover, given the extra potential benefits in terms of the gains, it can generate in revenue and influence at the country level, internationalisation clearly emerges as something to be prioritised and pursued at tertiary education institutions across the MENA region.

Context of Higher Education in MENA

Despite MENA not being the world's leading region on the internationalisation front today, and the challenges it faces in human capital building and delivery of quality of education, the region has been characterised as the 'cradle of higher education' (Devarajan, 2016) due to its long and rich educational history. Indeed, some of the first tertiary education institutions in the world were founded in the region, such as Al-Karaouine University in Fes, Morocco, founded in 859 AD, and Al-Azhar University in Cairo, Egypt, following in 970 AD. It has also historically been a region of internationalisation, with scholars and students moving around the region for centuries, in the quest for knowledge. Moreover, over recent decades, there has been an explosion of institutions in the region: the number of universities has almost doubled in the last decade, from 395 in 2008 to 762 in 2018 (International Association of Universities, 2018), in addition to the thousands of non-university tertiary education institutions present across MENA today.

Together with the boom in institutions, the MENA region has witnessed a large increase in enrolment in tertiary education: between 1999 and 2016, enrolment jumped by 143%, from around 6 million to more than 14 million (UNESCO data) (see Figure 2.1). This increase can be partly explained by demographic trends, since the tertiary education-age population in the region grew by almost 30% during that period (UN DESA, 2017). It is also partly explained by the expansion of access at upper secondary level, and finally, partly by an increase in number of students who today decide to continue into tertiary education after completing secondary – a rise from 40.4%, in 1999, to 54.3% in 2016 (UNESCO data). It should also be noted that this growth in enrolment is not due solely to domestic students, but also due to a continued increase in the enrolment of international students which, as we detail below, has actually grown faster than domestic enrolment in almost all MENA countries over recent years (CMI & World Bank, 2020).

However, enrolment rates do not allow for a full picture of the context: despite this increase in total enrolment, *access* to higher education remains extremely uneven across MENA. In Saudi Arabia, the gross enrolment ratio for tertiary education reaches just over 70%, whereas in Qatar and

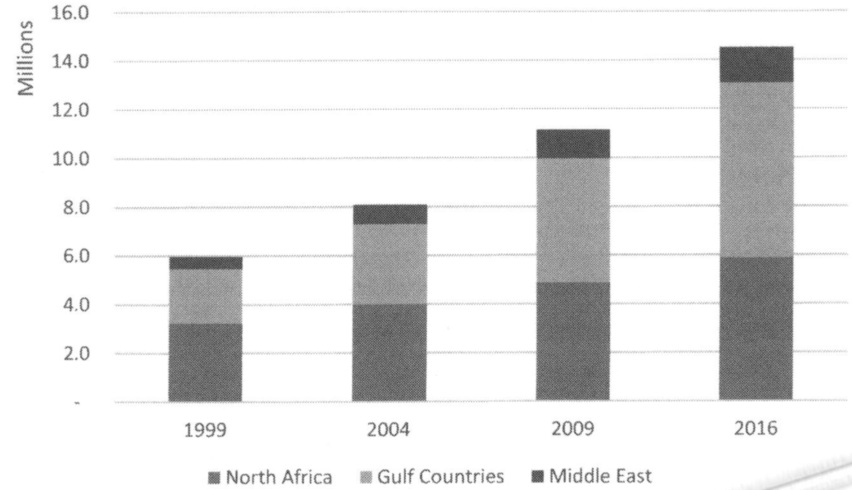

Figure 2.1 Enrolment in Tertiary Education in The Mena Region, Number of Students

Source: Constructed by the CMI using UNESCO data

Note: The countries were clustered in three groups, where, notably, Egypt is classified as North Africa.
North Africa: Algeria, Egypt, Libya, Morocco, and Tunisia; Middle East: Jordan, Lebanon, Palestine, and Syria; Gulf countries: Bahrain, Djibouti, Iran, Iraq, Kuwait, Oman, Qatar, Saudi Arabia, United Arab Emirates, and Yemen.

in Yemen, the rate remains below 20%. In most of the rest of the region, these rates hover around 30%–40% (UNESCO data, 2019, or latest years available: from 2003 (Libya) and 2005 (Iraq) to 2018). Public expenditure on education represents another piece of the region's educational context: in the MENA region, many countries were, for a long time in the decades following independence, investing relatively high shares of their fiscal resources in education. Today, although it varies hugely across the region, on average, the proportion of budget spent by MENA governments on education is similar to the global average.

Nevertheless, despite MENA's rising enrolment rates, increases in numbers of universities, and significant public spending in education, the quality of education across the region is very uneven. While there is no perfect way to measure education quality, several measures can help act as proxies for quality and, taken together, give a rough picture. Students' test scores, compiled by the Programme for International Student Assessment (PISA) and the Trends in International Mathematics and Science Study (TIMSS), can give part of the picture regarding overall education quality, although they refer to secondary education. According to these assessments, the MENA region is falling behind most other regions. For example, Bahrain, the MENA country with the highest math proficiency, remains below Cyprus, the least-well performing EU country. Indeed, on average, MENA 15-year-old students' math proficiency falls behind what 13-year-olds can achieve in all other regions, to the exception of South Asia and sub-Saharan Africa (PISA data, cited in CMI & World Bank, 2020). University rankings, such as the World University rankings compiled by Times Higher Education (THE), constitute another such example, although their shortcomings as measures of quality are recognised. In the 2020 rankings, no MENA university appeared in the top 200 universities in the world, while only two (both Saudi) universities appeared in the top 300 (THE, 2020). While they do not provide a complete picture, these results indeed contribute to highlighting some ways in which the region faces challenges in delivering quality education.

Several factors may be at the root of this education quality issue in some MENA countries (see Figure 2.2). One relates to pedagogical methods: in the region, there is a heavy focus on memorisation, which can be to the detriment of

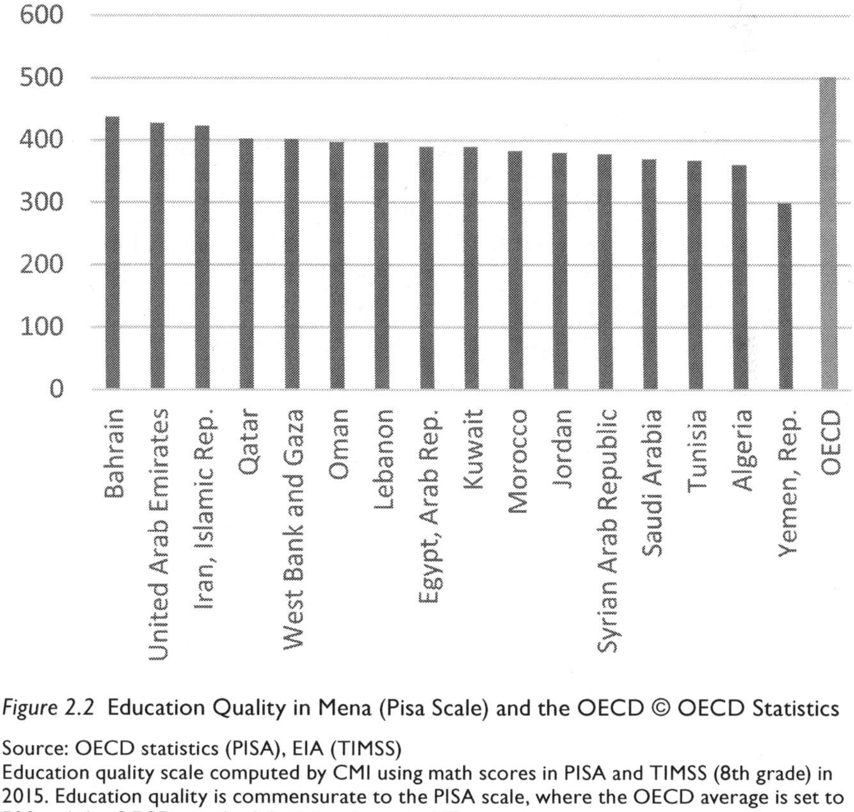

Figure 2.2 Education Quality in Mena (Pisa Scale) and the OECD © OECD Statistics

Source: OECD statistics (PISA), EIA (TIMSS)
Education quality scale computed by CMI using math scores in PISA and TIMSS (8th grade) in 2015. Education quality is commensurate to the PISA scale, where the OECD average is set to 500 and the OECD standard deviation is set to 100.

the development of critical thinking skills. The World Bank's 2018 MENA Education Flagship Report showed the numbers of eighth-grade children in the region having to memorise facts and rules to be almost twice the international average; it also showed the proportion of time dedicated to subjects like religious education to be much higher in MENA when compared to the OECD average, leaving less time for other subjects (World Bank, 2018).

Another factor that may play a role is the extent to which institutions are autonomous. The World Bank has found that greater autonomy over staffing, finances and curriculum matters tends to be correlated with improved performance (World Bank, 2018). Yet, in MENA, although some level of decentralisation has occurred in some countries, this has often been less than successful and has not always translated into greater autonomy at the education and school level (World Bank, 2018). Indeed, school teachers in MENA have been shown to hold less autonomy over curriculum matters than those in the OECD countries (OECD data, cited in World Bank, 2018), and at the tertiary level, benchmarking surveys on governance show most universities in the region to have little autonomy over academic, staffing and financial matters, especially in public universities (CMI & World Bank, 2012; see also World Bank, 2018). Moreover, the question of autonomy – and governance more generally – is also pertinent in the framework of internationalisation. Since weak autonomy – as well as the heavily constrained policy and regulatory environments which still characterise many of the MENA region's education systems – proves not to be conducive to the delivery of quality higher education, it is moreover unlikely to contribute to creating the conditions within which internationalisation can be most effectively implemented. In this regard, improving governance and strengthening autonomy may indeed help tertiary education institutions take full advantage of internationalisation's benefits (CMI & World Bank, 2020).

Current Status of Internationalisation in the MENA Region

One of the most striking things about internationalisation across the MENA region is the variety of degrees to which, or ways in which, it is implemented. Differing socioeconomic contexts have a role to play in this heterogeneity, as do diplomatic, cultural and linguistic ties between MENA countries and those outside the region. In many ways, it is the Gulf countries that are steaming ahead, attracting the highest numbers of international students, and hosting by far the most international branch campuses, although with the tertiary education systems in these countries burgeoning only over recent decades, this is an emerging phenomenon. But countries in the Mashreq, including Egypt, Iraq and Syria, have historically been learning centres throughout the centuries. And countries in the Maghreb region invariably have ties with France, highlighted by the many Franco-Maghrebin partnerships and by the strong presence of North African students in France.

The preceding analysis demonstrated that MENA, as a whole, is not the most attractive region for internationalisation partnerships, nor for internationally mobile students. Yet there are plenty of examples of internationalisation in MENA. Student mobility and international branch campuses are some of the elements with the most readily available data, we detail these below. But aside from those, we find numerous types of cooperation, such as the *Franco-Tunisian University for Africa and the Mediterranean*, situated in Tunis, and the Union for the Mediterranean-labelled *Euro-Mediterranean University of Fes*, in Morocco, and several examples of internationalisation 'at home'; once again, we give further details below.

Refugees, Fragility Contexts and Internationalisation

An important specificity of the MENA region is the extremely high number of refugees hosted there, especially Syrians. Including Turkey, the majority of the more than five million registered Syrian refugees are hosted in neighbouring countries, with Lebanon and Jordan being the second and third biggest host countries after Turkey (UNHCR, 2020). When considering internationalisation in MENA, it is, therefore, useful to reflect on contexts of fragility and consider how refugees might be included in internationalisation processes.

For refugees, access to tertiary education in the region can be very restricted. Globally speaking, only 3% of refugee youth are enrolled in higher education, compared to 37% of youth worldwide (UNHCR, 2019). For Syrians in Jordan, for example, obstacles include the rising costs of living, the common English language requirement, the low enrolment of Syrians in pre-tertiary education, and the insufficient number of scholarships available to them (El-Ghali & Al-Hawamdeh, 2017). Further barriers are presented by the lack of recognition of qualifications gained in home countries: apart from the few bilateral agreements which do exist in MENA, until 2019, no regionwide agreement had been signed since 1978. The 2019 UNESCO Global Convention on the Recognition of Qualifications concerning Higher Education, together with its 'Qualifications Passport' for refugees, aims to remedy this, but its adoption being so recent, it is yet to be seen to what extent this will be effective.

However, refugees should and can have a role to play in internationalised education. In Turkey, universities are being internationalised in a variety of different ways, in what has been coined 'forced internationalisation' (Ergin et al., 2019). Admissions policies have been reformed, by which institutions must accept Syrians whether they can produce proof of qualifications or not, while Arabic taught programmes have been introduced in several universities near the border, and many Syrians have been provided with scholarships, with international student fees being waived. Efforts have also been made to employ more Syrian faculty, notably with the implementation of an online platform collecting CVs (Ergin et al., 2019). Such reforms have led to a huge rise in enrolment of Syrian refugees, from just over 600 in 2011 to over 20,000 in 2018 (Ergin et al., 2019). Naturally, there will be upsides and downsides to these reforms since sudden influxes of refugee students can put high pressure on education systems, but, considering that the benefits of increased inbound student mobility are many, lessons could be drawn from the Turkish case for countries in MENA which host large numbers of refugees.

International Student Mobility to, from and within MENA[2]

International student mobility can be seen from two different angles: 'inbound' mobility or foreign students arriving, and 'outbound' mobility, i.e., students leaving to study abroad.[3] In the MENA region, both inbound and outbound mobility is higher than the global average, yet, when analysed in further detail, the region is shown not to be the most attractive region for mobile students.

Inbound Mobility to MENA

Inbound student mobility to the MENA region as a whole is higher than the world average: latest UNESCO data shows that the 'inbound rate' (the number of foreign students enrolled as a percentage of total students enrolled) for MENA is 3.1%, compared to the world average of 2.5% (UNESCO data, 2018). Moreover, inbound mobility to the region has been steadily growing over recent years, although there was a drop in 2017 (UNESCO data; see Figure 2.3) – and, given the COVID-19 crisis and the impact it is likely to have on student mobility, one may assume that this will decrease further. Nonetheless, over the last decade, foreign enrolment has been continuously growing, with at least two points of interest to mention. First, in 2011 with the eruption of the 'Arab Spring', while growth in domestic enrolment fell to negative, the growth rate of foreign enrolment, although witnessing a decrease, remained positive and significantly higher than that of domestic. Second, in the decade running up to the recent decline, foreign enrolment grew faster than domestic enrolment in all MENA countries where data was available, with the exception of Algeria and Saudi Arabia.

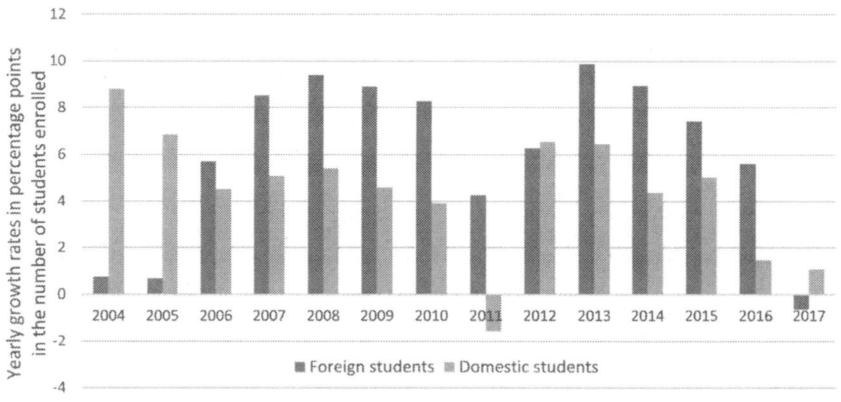

Figure 2.3 Growth of Domestic and Foreign Students Enrolment in Arab States (UNESCO Definition)

Source: Constructed by the Authors using UNESCO data

This overall picture, then, shows the MENA region to be rather successful at attracting foreign students. However, when one takes a closer look at the details, the picture is more nuanced. First, the high inbound rate for the region taken as a whole is in fact, in large part, due to only a handful of countries. The inbound rates for the UAE and Qatar are extremely high: foreign students make up almost half, and more than a third, of their total student populations, respectively (UNESCO data, latest years available: 2016, 2019). Jordan, Bahrain and Lebanon also have much higher-than-average inbound rates, at around 14%, 14% and almost 10%, respectively (UNESCO data, 2018, 2019). This has the effect of pushing up the whole-of-MENA inbound rate, hiding the fact that many other countries have much lower rates. In North Africa, for example, Tunisia and Morocco fall more or less in line with the world average, while Algeria remains all but closed to foreign students, its inbound rate at less than 1% (UNESCO data, 2018, 2019).

Not only are the inbound rates hugely variable across countries but certain *patterns* of domestic and foreign enrolment can also be discerned, allowing for a classification of MENA countries as 'destination countries'. Although there is a generally positive correlation between growth rates in domestic enrolment and in foreign enrolment (see Figure 2.4), we can further distinguish four main groupings.

- 'Mature destinations' refers to the well-established student destinations. Although these countries may not host the highest proportions of foreign students, they have all witnessed moderate growth rates in both domestic and foreign enrolment in recent years. Egypt, Jordan

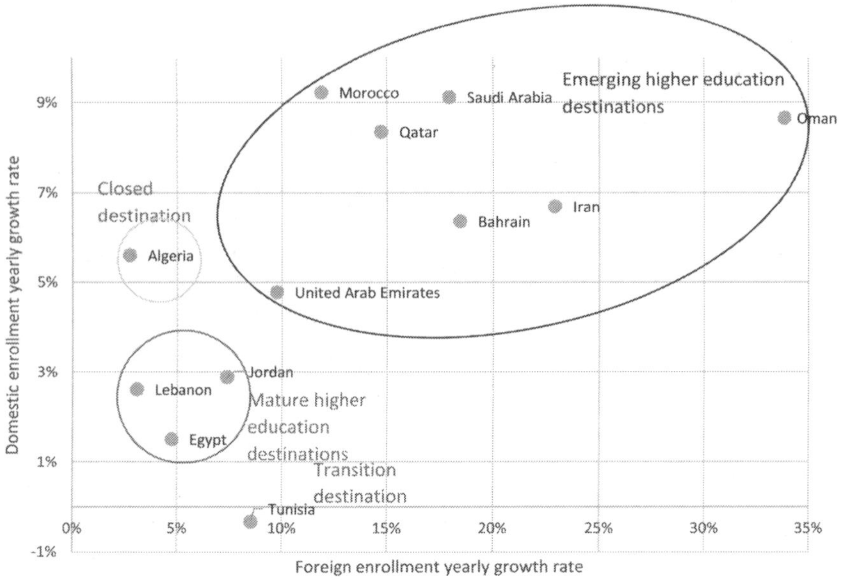

Figure 2.4 Comparison of the Annual Growth Rate of the Domestic and Foreign Student Population over the Period 2005–2016

Source: Authors' construction using UNESCO data

and Lebanon can all be considered mature destinations. There is, nonetheless, a large degree of heterogeneity among the three countries: Egypt, for example, has the largest tertiary education system in the MENA region and has historically been an important actor insofar as it has attracted many foreign students. This may owe to its prestigious universities, its limited tuition fees – especially when compared to Gulf countries – and its scholarship programmes open to foreigners, particularly in religious studies. In Jordan, one specificity is the huge proportion of both Palestinian and Syrian students. One in four students in Jordan is Palestinian, while the number of Syrian students there quadrupled between 2011 and 2016. In Lebanon, the number of foreign students peaked around 2011 and it has since been declining, perhaps due to factors such as the war in neighbouring Syria, Lebanon's macroeconomic difficulties and so on.

- 'Emerging destinations' refers to those countries which may not already have the highest international status as student destinations, but which have been on the rise since the 2000s. These emerging destinations have generally experienced moderate growth in their domestic enrolment over recent years, but more dramatic growth in the enrolment of foreign students. The group includes mostly Gulf countries, and also Morocco. Considering absolute numbers, Saudi Arabia is the largest provider of higher education for foreigners, having overtaken the UAE, while the UAE and Qatar remain those countries with the highest *proportion* of foreign students – the highest inbound rates (see Figure 2.5). Indeed, the Gulf countries, in general, have been those pushing forward the most on many fronts in their internationalisation strategies, including hosting huge numbers of international branch campuses. Morocco has also emerged as a significant player: despite its relatively low inbound rate, it has witnessed significant growth in foreign enrolment. In terms of geographical reach, most of its inbound students come from sub-Saharan Africa.

- Two North African countries can be categorised as a 'transition destination' and as a 'closed destination'. In Tunisia, the only MENA country in which the domestic student population has declined while the foreign population has grown over recent years, its tertiary education system is going through a *transition period*, whereby it is pivoting towards the international, perhaps seeking to compensate for the domestic decline. In Algeria, higher education has seen domestic enrolment growing steadily, while foreign enrolment only grew very slowly, reflecting the fact that the country is opening only timidly to the outside.

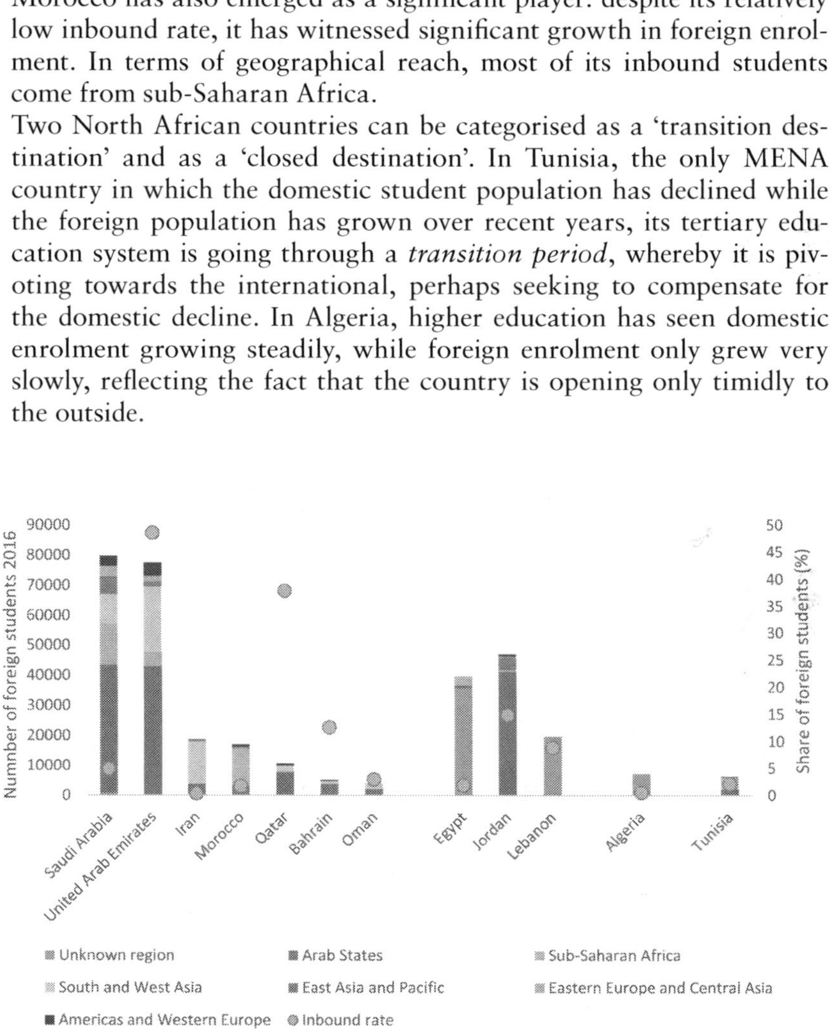

Figure 2.5 Number of Foreign Students by Region of Origin, 2016

Source: Authors' calculation using UNESCO data

In terms of the origins of MENA's foreign students, more than half of the inbound students come from the region itself: 45% from the Middle East and 10% from North Africa (UNESCO data, 2016). Significant proportions come from sub-Saharan Africa, from South and from South East Asia (these three together make up more than a third of MENA's inbound students), while the region hardly attracts any students from countries in Europe, the Americas or other parts of Asia (see Figure 2.6). This geographical reach can be explained by a variety of factors, including diplomatic and cultural ties, linguistic proximity, economic factors and so on; in some cases, the differences owe to deliberately targeted policies. The majority of Morocco's inbound students coming from (mainly francophone) sub-Saharan African countries may reflect linguistic proximity, as well as Morocco's broad outreach strategy to sub-Saharan Africa; the UAE, which attracts mostly South Asian students, also brings in students from OECD countries, which may highlight its ambition to become a more influential global player (CMI & World Bank, 2020).

Finally, tertiary education institutions in the MENA region are less likely to attract students from well-performing education systems than those of other regions may. Again, there is no perfect indicator of education quality, but using the PISA and TIMSS systems, we see that the average foreign student (globally) comes from a place where the education quality corresponds to two years of schooling below the OECD average. However, the average foreign student studying in a MENA country comes from a place where the education quality is two years below that of our average

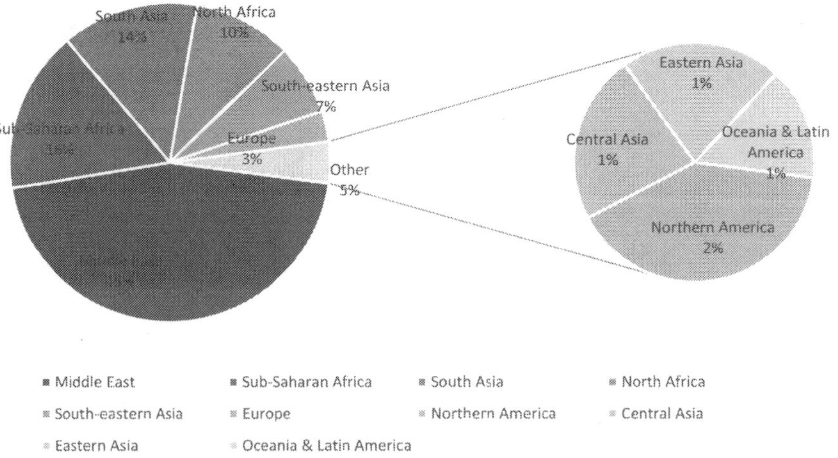

Figure 2.6 Distribution of Foreign Students Studying in Mena by Region of Origin, 2016

Source: Authors' calculation using UNESCO data

global student, meaning four years below that of the OECD average (CMI & World Bank, 2020). Yet this too varies within the region, highlighting disparities that arise from MENA countries' different geographical reach in student recruitment. The mostly sub-Saharan African inbound students to Morocco and Tunisia generally come from less well-performing education systems, whereas in the Gulf countries, private institutions charging high fees are attracting higher-skilled students. In Jordan, Palestinian students, who are some of the most proficient in the region, make up around 25% of its inbound students (CMI & World Bank, 2020).

Outbound Mobility from MENA

Outbound mobility from the MENA region is also above average: latest UNESCO data shows that the outbound rate for the region is around 4.6%, compared to the global average of 2.5% (UNESCO data, 2018). But once again, a closer look allows for a more nuanced understanding. First, this whole-of-MENA rate, when broken down, shows the Middle East and Gulf to be pushing up the average: high outbound rates are found in many of those countries, while in North Africa the outbound rates are mostly closer to the world average.

In addition, outbound mobility can be perceived in different ways: some countries may push for more of their students to go to study abroad in the hope that, with their new skills and knowledge, upon their return, they will contribute to building human capital in their home countries. Moreover, if students complete their studies abroad, boosting both their hard and soft skills, when they return home and join the labour force, create businesses and so on, they may contribute to the phenomenon labelled 'brain gain' or 'brain circulation', playing a part in the mechanisms supposed to mitigate the negative effects of flight of talent, 'brain drain'. In the MENA region, Saudi Arabia is big on this argument and provides state scholarships for hundreds of thousands of its outbound students (see, for example, the King Abdullah Scholarship Programme).

But high numbers of outbound students leaving to study elsewhere may also raise the worry that they find the education system at home wanting. Indeed, in the case of MENA, its attractiveness as a region, for its own students, is rather weak: today, considering all of MENA's outbound students, a much higher proportion choose to study in a country *outside* of the MENA region than those who choose to study in a country *within* the MENA region. Moreover, this proportion is on the rise. A comparison between the evolution of inter-regional and intra-regional outbound mobility from MENA shows that in 2016, more than two-thirds chose to leave the region, whereas in 1999 that proportion was not much over half (UNESCO data) (see Figure 2.7). This highlights that although outbound mobility from MENA may be higher than average, the region struggles to retain its own students.

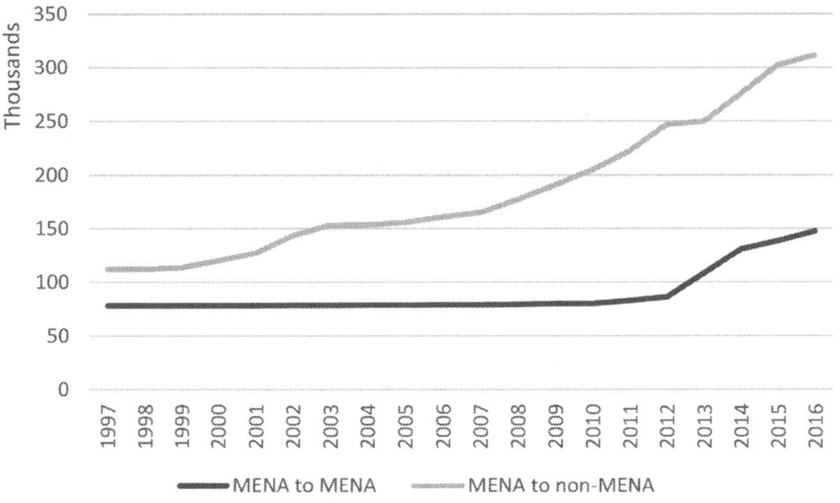

Figure 2.7 Evolution of Inter-Regional and Intra-Regional Students Leaving Their Country in the Mena Region © UNESCO Data

Source: UNESCO data

Lastly, with MENA's outbound mobility as with its inbound, language, cultural and diplomatic ties have high importance when it comes to the choice of destination country (see Figures 2.8 and 2.9). For example, while the vast majority of mobile North African students go to study in France, those from the Middle East go mostly to the United Kingdom and the United States (Gulf students in particular), and to other countries within the MENA region.

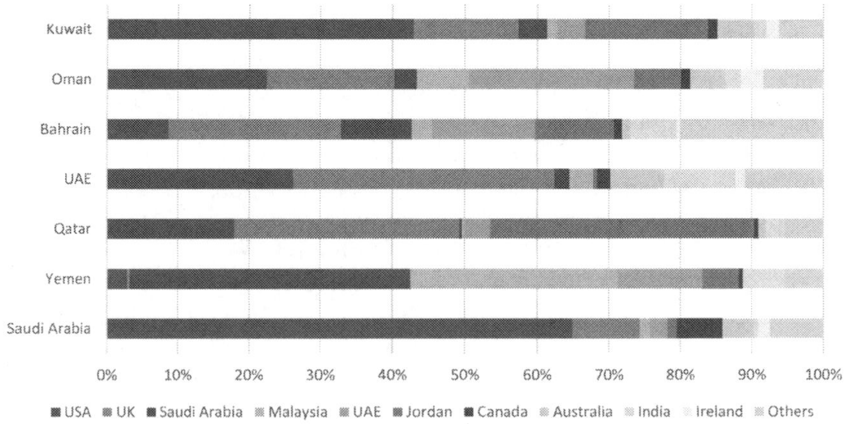

Figure 2.8 Shares of Outbound Students from Gulf Countries by Destination: Top 10, 2018

Source: Authors' calculation using UNESCO data

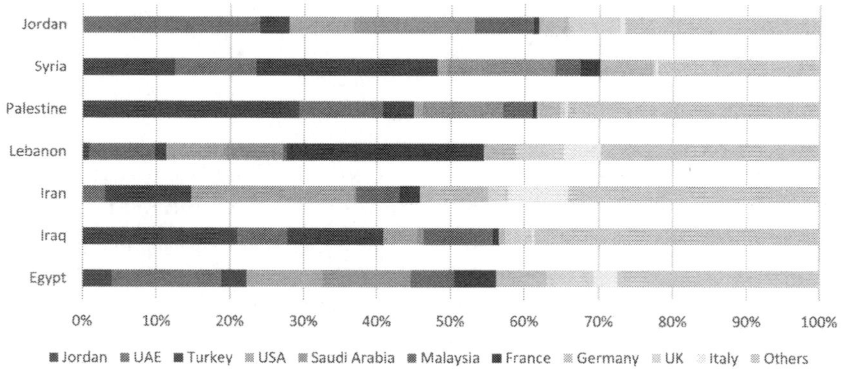

Figure 2.9 Shares of Outbound Students from Mashreq Countries by Destination: Top 10, 2018

Source: Authors' calculation using UNESCO data

Branch Campuses and Education Hubs

Aside from mobility, another rather visible – and countable – element of internationalisation is the establishment of international branch campuses (IBCs). An emergent phenomenon in the region, most of the IBCs in MENA were set up in the 2000s, with a rapid expansion from 2005 onwards. Branch campuses are, however, unevenly distributed across the region, with the bulk of them located in the Gulf countries. Indeed, Qatar and the UAE figure in the top four host countries of IBCs worldwide (see Figure 2.10).

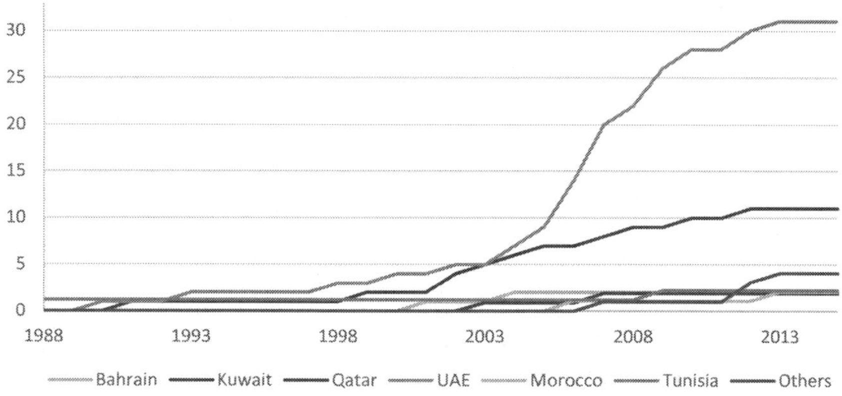

Figure 2.10 Evolution of the Number of Branch Campuses in Mena © C-BERT's Branch Campus Listings

Source: C-BERT's Branch Campus Listing

Set up by home institutions on the territories of host countries, several motivations for establishing IBCs can be discerned for both home and host. For the home institutions, exporting IBCs presents opportunities for student recruitment and, through the strategic setting up of IBCs in countries that provide significant research funding (such as Qatar), revenue generation. Moreover, establishing IBCs provides concrete evidence of an institution's internationalisation efforts, which can contribute to enhancing institutions' reputations (World Education Services, 2019). Importing countries, for their part, may see IBCs as an opportunity to satisfy local demand for higher education, or to upgrade a workforce for the transition towards a knowledge-based economy (a key motivation for the UAE); they may also identify education and the establishment of IBCs as a revenue-creating economic sector (Leibniz Institute for Research on Society and Space, 2020). In the MENA context, researchers have also argued that a benefit of IBCs can be their less restrictive social environments; in the case of the Gulf, in particular, for women (Al Mutawa, 2017).

However, IBCs can also pose difficulties, from the potentially high-costs and high-levels of risk involved for exporters to the array of worries regarding academic freedoms, quality assurance and institutions' reputations, cultural domination and so on (Kinser & Lane, 2013, 2016). Indeed, despite the mushrooming of IBCs over recent decades, at least 40 have also closed worldwide (C-BERT listing, 2017).

While there are noticeable differences in the approaches of the UAE and Qatar towards the establishment of IBCs – from a centralised and strategic approach from the Qatari government to Dubai's free-market, laissez-faire approach (Kinser & Lane, 2016) – both countries have created physical infrastructure and regulatory frameworks to integrate IBCs into their tertiary education systems. This has contributed to the recognition of both states as international education 'hubs', there being only six countries generally recognised as such, globally. In the UAE, schools and IBCs are grouped together in areas such as the Knowledge Village and the Dubai International Academic City, whereas the Qatari education hub is centred around its Education City, which today hosts eight IBCs and is the most comprehensive education hub at the global scale.

Internationalisation 'At Home'

Internationalisation 'at home' can be defined as 'the purposeful integration of international and intercultural dimensions into the formal and informal curriculum for all students within domestic learning environments' (Beelen & Jones, 2015). It covers a wide range of activities and has the comparative advantage of the capacity to reach all domestic students as well as those who study abroad. Internationalisation 'at home' moreover aims to serve the same purposes as other elements of internationalisation

– including boosting students' intercultural awareness and their wider skill-sets, increasing mutual understanding and so on – without necessitating that students or staff travel abroad. However, when compared to student mobility flows and the presence of branch campuses, where one may simply count the numbers of mobile students or the numbers of campuses, the wide variety of activities grouped under 'internationalisation 'at home' are less easily measured. Accordingly, we do not aim to present comprehensive data on the status of internationalisation 'at home' across all MENA countries; rather, we highlight some concrete examples.

The internationalisation of the curriculum is a key aspect of internationalisation 'at home' and can include the addition of 'international' subjects, a focus on foreign language acquisition and so on. In Egypt, for instance, we find several clear examples where departments and institutions at several institutions, including Cairo University, Zagazig University and Fayoum University, have made headway in the internationalisation of their curriculum by adding a focus on international and regional affairs.

Another important element, enabled by ICT, is the group of activities labelled 'virtual exchange', 'virtual mobility', 'COIL' (Collaborative Online International Learning) and so on. Such activities use 'virtual classrooms' to enable students to collaborate across borders and engage in student-centred, collaborative and experiential learning. Virtual exchange or COIL-enhanced modules aim to more deeply connect people and cultures, leveraging students' own local knowledge and have been reported to develop students' skills and employability (Guth & Helm, 2017; Rubin, 2019), especially for a world of work in which people are increasingly working remotely and in 'virtual teams' (Rubin, 2019).

Several examples of such programmes have been implemented in the MENA region. The Steven's Initiative is a US-based project which, through its grant system, connects US universities with those across the MENA region. In one such programme, the State University of New York COIL centre partnered with institutions in Egypt, Lebanon and Morocco to run a COIL programme, and students reported effectively learning from other people, gaining authentic perspectives and developing their 21st-century skills (Guth & Helm, 2017). Another example is the Erasmus+ Virtual Exchange programme, which aimed to engage young people in intercultural learning and dialogue, and which was available to all young people (18–30 years) in both Europe and the Southern Mediterranean. Again, the Erasmus+ programme connected young people in MENA with those in other regions, using technology and learner-led pedagogical methods. Yet another example is the *JOVITAL* project: the Jordan opportunity for virtual innovative teaching and learning, which supports institutions in Jordan in adopting and implementing ICT-based internationalisation 'at home' activities, aiming to integrate Jordanian institutions in global networks of virtual mobility.

As is evident in the previous three examples, a significant part of internationalisation 'at home' relies on ICT to some extent. In the MENA region, online learning is being adopted slowly, but obstacles remain, such as uneven Internet access, issues around accreditation and so on. However, today many countries are rolling out online learning. In the UAE, tertiary education institutions are developing links with online and blended universities around the world; in Egypt and Jordan, online modules are becoming increasingly accredited (The Open University, 2018). Online learning platforms are proliferating, such as the Jordanian 'Edraak', with Arabic-language MOOCs (Massive Open Online Courses) increasingly dispensed through them. While online learning alone may not entail internationalisation, MENA countries upping their game on this front shows a vast potential opening for increasing internationalisation 'at home' activities such as virtual exchange, whether intra-regional or in partnership with institutions around the world.

Reflections on the Way Forward for the Region

The above analysis has shown that there are lots of examples of internationalisation in MENA countries, with some countries already champions internationalisation. However, at the regional level, MENA suffers from weak attractiveness, both as a destination for foreign students (and the region's own students) and as a potential partner for internationalisation partnerships with institutions around the world. Moreover, much of MENA's internationalisation is concentrated in just a few countries.

Going forward, in order for the region to take fuller advantage of its benefits, internationalisation needs to become a higher priority for institutions and countries throughout the region. Efforts must be made to stimulate policy dialogue and debate, as well as general awareness raising around internationalisation and its benefits. MENA countries could also benefit from working together at the regional level. A first step could be to focus on regional cooperation.

Socioeconomic contexts vary enormously across the region, so there is not likely to be one internationalisation strategy for all MENA countries: strategies need to be tailored accordingly. This includes specific strategies for countries hosting many refugees. In those contexts, governments should work towards improving refugees' access to primary and secondary education, as a means to ensuring their improved access to higher education, and also provide the legal framework necessary for refugees to have their competencies recognised. Institutions, in parallel, could provide scholarships specifically for refugees, and offer preparatory programmes at university to facilitate widened access.

More generally, today, internationalisation 'at home' is what emerges as instrumental for the MENA region. Institutions internationalising 'at home' means that *all* students can benefit, and not only those who are able to travel abroad to study – only a minority of students. When compared to study abroad, it also holds the advantage of being less costly, as well as easier to implement, relatively speaking.

Moreover, in the current context of the COVID-19 pandemic, internationalisation 'at home' appears as even more pertinent. We are witnessing massively reduced physical mobility, which is likely to last, due to both travel restrictions and economic recessions, so internationalisation 'at home' activities emerge as more feasible internationalisation strategies. In these circumstances, the MENA region could seize the opportunity to advance on this front, thereby putting itself in a better position to 'catch up' with other regions of the world on internationalisation of its tertiary education systems.

Already, since the spreading of the pandemic and the lockdowns put in place to stem it, tertiary education institutions around the world – including in MENA – have had to make an almost overnight change to online learning and adapt quickly. This provides evidence of a certain capacity to move rapidly towards new methods and models and could allow for increased virtual exchange, a key element of internationalisation 'at home' going forward. Indeed, even well before the pandemic, the strategy of 'blended mobility', a mixture of physical and virtual mobility, was taking hold around the world. Such strategies, together with increased internationalisation of the curriculum and other 'at home' activities, could be further explored by the MENA region while its institutions adapt to the 'new normal'. In this way, MENA could seriously invest in and increase the internationalisation of its higher education, as well as reaping the many benefits.

Notes

1 We generally follow the World Bank's definition of MENA, which includes Algeria, Bahrain, Djibouti, Arab Republic of Egypt, Islamic Republic of Iran, Iraq, Israel, Jordan, Kuwait, Lebanon, Libya, Malta, Morocco, Oman, Qatar, Saudi Arabia, Syrian Arab Republic, Tunisia, United Arab Emirates, West Bank and Gaza, and Republic of Yemen; however, we mostly omit Malta and Israel. When using UNESCO data, this usually follows its 'Arab States' classification, which omits Iran and Israel, and adds Mauritania, Somalia, and Sudan.

2 The COVID-19 pandemic has had, and continues to have, a significant impact on student mobility. Yet due to data availability, what follows is based on pre-pandemic trends in mobility in the region.

3 We consider 'internationally mobile students' as those who move from their native country to another country to study, where they count as foreign nationals. In line with UNESCO and the World Bank, from whom we source our data, we employ this ''national' vs. 'foreign national' distinction when talking of 'mobile', 'foreign', 'domestic', 'inbound', and 'outbound' students. This distinction is notwithstanding any further differentiation which may be made in national contexts. It also implies that in countries with large expat populations, such as in the GCC, 'outbound' mobility captures only that of their nationals.

References

Al Mutawa, R. (2017). Women and restrictive campus environments: A comparative analysis between public universities and international branch campuses in the UAE. In *Higher education in the Gulf states: Present & future*. Oxford University Publication.

Beelen, J., & Jones, E. (2015). Redefining internationalization at home. In A. Curaj, L. Matei, R. Pricopie, J. Salmi, & P. Scott (Eds.), *The European higher education area*. Springer.

British Council and the UK HE International Unit. (2015). Student Perspectives on Going International. https://www.britishcouncil.org/education/ihe/knowledge-centre/student-mobility/report-student-perspectives-going-international

Center for Mediterranean Integration (CMI) and World Bank. (2012). Universities through the Looking Glass: Benchmarking University Governance to Enable Higher Education Modernization in MENA.

Center for Mediterranean Integration (CMI) and World Bank. (2020). Internationalization of Tertiary Education in the Middle East and North Africa.

Cross-Border Education Research Team. (2017). C-BERT International Campus Listing.

Devarajan, S. (2016). The Paradox of Higher Education in MENA. Brookings Future Development Blog. https://www.brookings.edu/blog/future-development/2016/06/27/the-paradox-of-higher-education-in-mena/

De Wit, H., Hunter, F., Howard, L., & Egron-Polak, E. (2015). Internationalisation of higher education. European Parliament Directorate Generale for Internal Policies Policy Dept B: Structural and Cohesion Policies, Culture and Education.

El-Ghali & Al-Hawamdeh, (2017). *Higher education and Syrian refugee students: The case of Jordan*. Issam Fares Institute for Public Policy and International Affairs.

Ergin, H., De Wit, H., & Leask, B. (2019). Forced internationalization of higher education: An emerging phenomenon. *International Higher Education*, *97*, 9–10.

European Commission. (2016). *The Erasmus impact study regional analysis: a comparative analysis of the effects of Erasmus on the personality, skills and career of students of European regions and selected countries*. European Union.

Guth, S., & Helm, F. (2017). *SUNY COIL Stevens initiative assessment: Final report*. The State University of New York.

Hawawini, G. (2011). The Internationalization of Higher Education Institutions: A Critical Review and a Radical Proposal. INSEAD Working Paper 2011/112/FIN.

International Association of Universities (IAU). (2018). Worldwide Database of Higher Education Institutions, Systems and Credentials.

Kinser, K., & Lane, J. (2013). The problems with cross-border quality assurance. *International Higher Education*, *73*, 18–19.

Kinser, K., & Lane, J. (2016). International branch campuses: EVOLUTION of a phenomenon. *International Higher Education*, *85*, 3–5.

Leibniz Institute for Research on Society and Space. (2020). Global Geographies of Offshore Campuses.

Marinoni, G. (2019). *Internationalization of higher education: An evolving landscape, locally and globally*. International Association of Universities (IAU), 5th Global Survey.

NAFSA: Association of International Educators. (2019). International Student Economic Value Tool. https://www.nafsa.org/policy-and-advocacy/policy-resources/nafsa-international-student-economic-value-tool-v2

The Open University. (2018). Online Learning in Tertiary Education in the Middle East and North Africa.

Parsons, R. L. (2009). The effects of an internationalized university experience on domestic students in the United States and Australia. *Journal of Studies in International Education*, *14*(4), 313–334.

Rubin, J. (2019). Collaborative online international learning (COIL): Now preparing students for international virtual work. In R. Coelen, & C. Gribble (Eds.), *Internationalization and employability in higher education*. Routledge.

Times Higher Education (THE). (2020). World University Rankings. https://www.timeshighereducation.com/world-university-rankings/2020/world-ranking#!/page/0/length/25/sort_by/rank/sort_order/asc/cols/stats

Soria, K. M., & Troisi, J. (2014). Internationalization at home alternatives to study abroad: Implications for students' development of global, international, and intercultural competencies. *Journal of Studies in International Education*, *18*(3), 261–80.

UN DESA. (2017). World Population Prospects: The 2017 Revision.

UNESCO Institute for Statistics (UIS). (2016, 2018, 2019). *Education statistics*. http://data.uis.unesco.org/

UNHCR. (2019). Stepping up: Refugee education in crisis.

UNHCR. (2020). Syria Regional Refugee Response. https://data2.unhcr.org/en/situations/syria.

Universities Australia. (2018). Quality Central to Australia's International Education Success Story. https://www.universitiesaustralia.edu.au/media-item/quality-central-to-australias-international-education-success-story/

World Education Services. (2019). Transnational Education and Globalization: A Look into the Complex Environment of International Branch Campuses. https://wenr.wes.org/2019/05/the-complex-environment-of-international-branch-campuses

World Bank. (2018). *MENA education flagship report: Expectations and aspirations: A new framework for education in the Middle East and North Africa*. World Bank Group.

World Bank. (2019). World Development Indicators. https://databank.worldbank.org/source/world-development-indicators

World Bank. (2020). Human Capital Project: The HCI 2020 Visualization. https://www.worldbank.org/en/publication/human-capital

Author biographies

Giulia Marchesini is Human Capital Senior Programme Manager at the Center for Mediterranean Integration (UNOPS), which she joined in 2014. Giulia leads the human capital agenda, including education, migration, forced displacement, and mobility components. In the field of higher education, she recently led the authoring and production of the CMI-World Bank report 'Internationalization of Tertiary Education in the Middle East and North Africa'. Before joining the CMI,

Giulia worked for the French Development Agency (AFD), and from 2012 to 2013, she was advisor to the French Ministry for Development, where she was notably in charge of dialogue with the MENA region. Her experience in the MENA region also includes coordinating MENA economic and commercial issues for the French Ministry of Economy and Finances (2007–2009). Giulia holds master's degrees in Public Administration from Ecole Nationale d'Administration in France, and in International Affairs and Diplomacy from the University of Bologna in Italy.

Holly Johnstone is Programme Officer on Human Capital at the Center for Mediterranean Integration (UNOPS), which she joined in 2018. Her main work and research areas are education, migration, and mobility, with a focus on higher education; she contributed significantly to the production of the CMI-World Bank (2020) report 'Internationalization of Tertiary Education in the Middle East and North Africa'. Prior to joining the CMI, Holly gained experience as an educator in Morocco and the United Kingdom, and worked for several organisations in the field of migration and refugees and in international development. Holly holds a European Joint Master's Degree in Intercultural Mediation and Migration in the Mediterranean and a bachelor's degree in Philosophy from the University of Bristol.

Chapter 3

Gulf Cooperation Council Academic Mobility

What Works, for Whom and Why?

Clare Walsh

Introduction

This chapter focuses on the identification of mechanisms and contexts framing the intra-regional mobility of students 'in and of' the Gulf Cooperation Council (GCC) (Mazawi, 2009). In 2017, 29% of mobile students from the Arab states stayed within the region (UIS, 2020) compared to 12% in 1999 (Bridgestock, 2015) and mostly in one of three countries: UAE (29.8% or 42,263), Jordan (28.15% or 39874) and Saudi Arabia (27% or 38,336). The number of students from the Arab states studying outside their home country has increased from 231,133 (3.1%) in 2007 to 486,752 (4.3%) in 2017 from a total of over ten million students enrolled in tertiary education in the 22 Arab League states. In comparison, the GCC 2017 figures (UIS, 2020) indicate that less than 1% (0.8%) of the almost two million students enrolled in GCC tertiary education were studying in another GCC state and less than 1% (0.6%) in another Arab State. This means that of the 145,133 students who left a GCC state to study, 15,246 went to study in another GCC state, predominantly UAE (9,532) and 11,005 in another Arab state, predominantly Jordan (10,185). This raises questions about which factors are influencing the low level of GCC student intra-regional mobility. In the same timeframe, regions such as Central Asia have seen significant increase in student mobility (4.3–13%) while Latin America & Caribbean has seen little change (1.1–1.2%). Of the 220 million students enrolled in higher education globally as of 2017 (UIS, 2020), 5.3 million are considered mobile (2.4%), an increase from 3 million (1.9%) in 2007.

Academic mobility is not a new phenomenon; scholars and knowledge have been traversing the world for centuries (Knight & Woldegiorgis, 2017). Academic mobilities (Jöns, 2018) can be understood in the widest possible sense as spatial movements linked to universities, involving people and organisms, technologies and material things, knowledge and practices, imaginations and representations, communications and virtual information. Academic mobility includes mobility of students, academics, educational programmes and higher education institutions (Bouhlal & Wells,

DOI: 10.4324/9781003138457-5

2019; Knight & Woldegiorgis, 2017). Student mobility can be explained as involving students that cross borders and stay in another country to undertake programmes of study; mobility can be international, within a region–intra-regional or among countries across different regions inter-regional (Teichler, 2009). The UNESCO Institute of Statistics (UIS) data is utilised in this chapter; UIS define student mobility as 'individuals who have physically crossed an international border between two countries with the objective to participate in educational activities in the country of destination, where the country of destination of a given student is different from their country of origin' (UOE, 2020, p. 32).

Student mobility occurs as a result of the intersection of a variety of measures including political stability, availability of quality higher education infrastructure, availability of credit transfer systems and instruments of qualifications recognition, flexible entry mechanisms, supportive visa procedures, and harmonised or comparable higher education systems (Teichler, 2009; 2011). Regional mobility initiatives are part of the process; examples include the Erasmus+ programme in the European Union (EU, 2015), Mwalimu Nyerere mobility scheme in the African Union (Woldegiorgis & Doevenspeck, 2015), and the ASEAN International Mobility for Students (AIMS) in ASEAN region. While there are bilateral agreements between universities in the GCC, there are no region wide student mobility programmes. At a higher level, academic mobility, regional and intra-regional networks, quality assurance, qualification frameworks, recognition of qualifications, curriculum and skills competencies, as well as the financing and governance of higher education are mechanisms utilised in the regionalisation of higher education (Knight & Woldegiorgis, 2017). It has been suggested the increased trend for GCC student mobility to UAE could be as a result of the increased number of international branch campuses; large number of Arab expatriates living in UAE who influence their children to stay and study; and the high degree of social, cultural and religious similarity (Jafar & Knight, 2020). As outlined above, a range of measures has been identified as important for student mobility and regionalisation. The chapter attempts to explain the complex interactions of quality assurance networks – as one measure in the stable of measures necessary for student mobility and regionalisation – and to understand how and under what conditions they contribute to the construction of student mobility within the GCC. By investigating intraregional development and collaborative activities, using Pawson and Tilley's (1997) realist evaluation contexts, mechanisms and outcomes (CMOs), the intention is to identify and explain how quality assurance networks work, how outcomes are produced, among whom, and in what circumstances. The intention is to fill the gap in Arab state and GCC national higher education in terms of the paucity of analysis, research and scholarly work related to higher education in the GCC and the Arab states.

Intra-Regional Mobility Mechanisms

The current literature on intra-regional mobility is narrow (Chao, 2020; Macrander, 2017), and the research has yet to examine mobility patterns within the Arab region and the GCC. Noted developments include the relatively recent growth of intra-regional student mobility and the creation of regional education networks such as quality assurance networks (e.g. Arab Network for Quality Assurance in Higher Education, ANQAHE) (Macrander, 2017; Zapp & Ramirez, 2019). Outside the GCC, other regions such as the Association of Southeast Asian Nations (ASEAN) and Latin America and Caribbean also have low intra-regional mobility (Chao, 2020; UNESCO-IESALC, 2019). The benefit of intra-regional mobility of students, as well as faculty, researchers and professionals is argued as contributing to economic development, construction of regional identity and moulding of future citizens, entrepreneurs and leaders (Chao, 2020).

While student decision-making relating to participation in intra-regional mobility is not explored here, it has been in other studies of inter-regional student mobility. Findlay et al. (2017) identified features of international student mobility linked to globalisation (e.g. desired international career path), internal student mobility shaped by local specificities (e.g. available degree programmes) and an interest to be close to home as key findings. In the case of the GCC, a small-scale study noted that reasons for choosing an intra-regional GCC destination included: a growing higher education system, university accreditation, increased prospects following graduation, and the availability of international branch campuses as well as the availability and practice of various sects of Islam (e.g. Sunni/Shia) (David et al., 2017). Measures identified in relation to intra-regional mobility in the case of Latin America and the Caribbean include perceived quality differential, individual financial capacity to assume the cost of education, and cultural and linguistic similarities (UNESCO-IESALC 2019). These findings identify inter and intra-regional mobility as a profoundly distinct phenomenon (Jöns, 2018), requiring further research.

The development and implementation of mechanisms to enhance the mobility of students between institutions in and across national borders has been on the wider Arab regional agenda since 1945 and the GCC Supreme Council agenda for the last 30 years. These mechanisms include regional conventions on the recognition of qualifications and for-profit and non-for-profit networks as two examples. The UNESCO Regional Convention on Recognition of Qualifications in Higher Education in the Arab States has been in place since 1978. It is one of six regional recognition conventions created to establish legal frameworks allowing recognition of higher education qualifications between State Parties at a regional level in the 1970s and 1980s (UNESCO, 2016). A new generation of conventions has been instigated, including the 2019 Global Convention on the Recognition of Qualifications. Europe, Asia Pacific and Africa regions have recent updates, with the Arab states' regional convention in the process of revision. These revised conventions and the long-awaited global convention promote the right of individuals to have their higher education qualifications evaluated through fair, transparent and non-discriminatory mechanisms (UNESCO, 2020).

Since the establishment and launch of the Arab Network for Quality Assurance in Higher Education (ANQAHE) in 2007, multiple networks have emerged, driven by both profit and non-profit organisations.[1] ANQAHE was established because of the recognised need to enhance the quality of higher education in the Arab region following the publication of the 1998 Beirut Declaration of the Arab Regional Conference on Higher Education (Tarawneh, 2011). ANQAHE is preceded by regional organisations such as the Association of Arab Universities, Arab Bureau for the Gulf States (ABEGS) and the Arab League Educational, Cultural and Scientific Organisation (ALESCO) among others. Since ABEGs inception in 1970, it has been tasked with facilitating GCC-wide student and faculty exchange through regional cooperation in the form of joint universities. This has yet to be brought to fruition (Findlow & Hayes, 2016).

Even where national and regional quality assurance initiatives related to quality assurance policies and processes exist, many have not been implemented in practice and often exist on paper only. One important example can be seen in relation to the UNESCO Regional Convention on Recognition of Qualifications in Higher Education in the Arab States. The convention remains unrevised since its publication in 1978, unlike Europe, Asia Pacific and Africa regions. It is important to note, that while the Arab states convention remains unrevised; the non-ratification of the 2011 UNESCO Asia and Pacific Recognition Convention, and the slow implementation of various regional frameworks supporting the establishment of an ASEAN Higher Education Area have limited the potential contribution of mobility and mutual recognition to the ASEAN Community building project (Chao, 2020). The resolution concerning equal treatment of GCC students in terms of admissions and treatment in higher education institutions of the GCC states took 27 years to progress from a resolution at the Supreme Council 8th session (December 1987) to an agreed proposal at the meeting of the Ministers of Higher Education and Scientific Research in February 2014 (GCC Secretariat General, 2014, 'GCC The Process and Achievements'). While a range of measures are in place, including a 30-year GCC regional intention for student mobility, a range of challenges exist (nationalism, competition, etc.,) detracting from the ability for students to move intra-regionally.

Integration

Two major trends identified over the last two decades in higher education include the process of internationalisation (Knight, 2014), and the concept of isomorphism (Meyer & Frank, 2007). Both concepts have been explored comprehensively elsewhere in the literature (de Croucher & Woelert, 2016; Fay & Zavattaro, 2016; OECD 1999; Teichler, 2004; 2009; Wit & Altbach, 2021; Zapp & Ramirez, 2019). In the broadest sense, internationalisation involves increasingly mobile students, staff, programmes and campuses; while isomorphism refers to increasing cross-national similarity in higher education discourses, policies, structures and curricula. The literature more recently identifies a third trend – the process of global higher education integration – where integration describes the process by which 'a set of novel, supranationally constructed, authoritative discourses, norms and rules increasingly complements and influences national higher education governance' (Zapp & Ramirez, 2019, p. 474). The concept of integration is expressed in the form of global discourses; international, regional and national networks; quality assurance frameworks and accreditation; as well as the cross-national standardisation and recognition of qualifications. In the case of the GCC, the concept of integration is expressed through a range of initiatives that have been achieved through the development and implementation of national education reform policies. Political and economic reforms – identified in all six GCC states in their respective 2030 Vision's – have a common goal to reduce dependence on oil and diversify their economies. These economic and political reforms across the GCC states have been the impetus for education reform, particularly in the move towards knowledge economies and human capital being identified as the new oil wealth. This is demonstrated in the decision by authorities to create new structures and measures through education reform policies (Badry & Willoughby, 2015). Evidence of this move can be seen in the policy shift in the region including promoting western-orientated educational reforms; emergence of new academic centres; efforts to gain positions in the global rankings space and therefore be comparable regionally and globally; the elite branch campus phenomenon, evident in particular in Qatar and UAE; as well as a move towards common language, curricula and academics which can be seen as a move towards joint degree programmes, global network branch campuses and Western accreditation as well as the implementation of national and regional qualifications frameworks (Badry & Willoughby, 2015). In the case of the Latin America and Caribbean region, mechanisms including regional integration policies and frameworks and institutional incentives such as scholarships or financial support are identified (UNESCO-IESALC 2019). Although scholarship programmes are in place, only 6% offer full scholarship and in many cases the plans for scholarship are not implemented or there is no resourcing available for promotion and sustainability.

While almost one-third of mobile students from the Arab states stayed within the region in 2017, no statistics are available to demonstrate the intra-regional mobility trends of academics. It has been suggested that political instability as well as the preference of Western university branch campus to hire academics with Western credentials preclude this form of academic mobility (Jafar & Knight, 2020). GCC higher education institutes are 'territorialised' spaces in terms that GCC citizens are more likely to be employed within their own country's universities and less likely in other GCC higher education institutes. This activity of employing citizens of the state is re-enforced with state-level policies which seek to recruit faculty and academics from among citizens (Mazawi, 2008). Programme and provider mobility are also limited within the region. Over 70 Western and international universities have been established in the GCC in recent years, i.e. Dubai International Academic City is home to at least 32 branch campuses, delivering more than 400 undergraduate and postgraduate programmes. However, in contrast, only three universities from other Arab states have established branch campuses – of which two are under development – within the GCC. This includes Lebanon's Saint Joseph University in Dubai and pending developments of Lebanon's University of Balamand in Dubai and Egypt's Al-Azhar University in Abu Dhabi (Cross-Border Education Research Team, 2017). Finally, research collaboration, as a component of regionalisation, is low among universities within the Arab states (Almansour, 2006), with greater number of publications co-authored inter-regionally than those co-authored by research-active scholars in the Arab states (Jafar & Knight, 2020).

Regionalism and Regionalisation

Regionalism is a term used interchangeably referring to region, regional co-operation, and regional integration among others and is considered as a general term covering a broad range of different developments and processes (Hurrell, 2008). Five distinct processes including regionalisation; regional awareness and identity; interstate cooperation; state-led integration and regional consolidation have been identified (Hurrell, 2008, p. 242). Regionalism 'is best viewed as an unstable and indeterminate process of multiple and competing logics with no overriding teleology' (Hurrell, 2008, p. 243). As well as a range of distinct processes, several approaches have been used in regionalism studies: EU studies, open regionalism and regulatory regionalism.

Applied to the Arab region, regionalism studies tend to be from neorealist and dependency perspectives, where the focus lies on the power asymmetries between global actors and the pursuit of their interests and that of the states of the region (Legrenzi & Harders, 2008, p. 1). Constructivist, institutionalist and liberal approaches lean more towards regional and national autonomy instead of dependency. However, regardless of the theoretical approach to studies of the Arab region, there is a general agreement that despite the high degree of social, cultural and religious similarity, the spatial proximity and interaction from a political, economic and military perspective, there is a 'low degree of institutional cooperation and integration' (Legrenzi & Harders, 2008, p. 2). Specifically, cooperation and collaboration in Arab region higher education have been described as moving towards a 'state of isolation' or 'balkanization', with Hafaiedh (2010, p. 102) suggesting that Arab cooperation can be considered a 'bouquet of noble projects, suffering from lack of resources, opportunities, and means of implementation'. El Hassan (2013) notes that while efforts have been made to address the regional quality of education challenges (curricula, student assessment, governmental roles and faculty), few tangible results are identifiable. The outcome of which is that challenges related to regional quality of education remain ongoing with improvements to a purely paper-based reality.

Regionalisation refers to the 'outcome of integration processes involving the coalition of social forces: (i) markets, private trade and investment flows; (ii) policies and decisions of companies or organisations; and (iii) state-led initiatives' (Robertson, 2008, p. 720, citing Hurrell, 1995). In work on regionalisation of higher education in the GCC, it has been noted that higher education initiatives tend to remain located within national spaces with an absence of initiatives with regional characteristics (Aljafari, 2016). As a regional arena, 'very little is institutionalised and embedded at the regional scale' primarily as a result of historic tensions and competition between the GCC member states (Aljafari, 2016, p. 291). In further support of this argument, it has been noted that while organisations may try to work on a regional basis, 'a concerted and pro-active regional policy on higher education governance remains largely lacking' (Mazawi, 2005, p. 178), and that trying to achieve a GCC academic region is multifaceted in terms of the linkage between institutions at a 'local, regional, Arab and global level' (Mazawi, 2008, Chapter 3, para. 17), while regional agencies in the field of education do not have a binding role (Mazawi, 2008; Findlow & Hayes, 2016). The multi-faceted relationship between national and regional institutions, confounded by various political, economic and socio-cultural tensions and competition, plays an important role in the drive to regionalise and create a GCC common higher education area.

As a region, UNESCO identifies 22 Arab states within the Arab League as a regional organisation that are tied together economically, politically and linguistically.[2] As a subregion, the GCC states include Bahrain, Kuwait, Oman, Qatar, United Arab Emirates and Saudi Arabia. Education in the Arab region can be viewed as a complicated plethora of human and political influences that have multifaceted spatial articulations, be it analysis of educational processes within the borders of a nation-state, or wider spatial contexts such as the regional-geopolitical, civilisational and transnational (Mazawi & Sultana, 2010). From a spatial perspective, the Arab region is not a homogenous and harmonious ethnic, national or linguistic geographic space (Mazawi & Sultana, 2010), which is no less the case for higher education across the region. However, despite an abundance of diversity and apparent differences, several common characteristics such as majority Islamic religion, shared Arabic language, political systems, and common history, as well as the presence of various pan-Arab political, economic and civil organisations, support a comprehendible analysis of the Arab region (Herrera, 2007, p. 409).

To summarise the above, less than 1% of GCC students engage in intra-regional mobility, with most GCC mobile students traveling to UAE to study. The literature identifies that the intersection of political systems, availability of higher education infrastructures, credit transfer systems, quality assurance, education networks, accreditation, tools for qualification recognition, flexible entry and harmonious education systems are important mechanisms, in which the complex interactions of these mechanisms contribute to regionalisation and student mobility. The GCC states have engaged in political and economic reform which has been the impetus for education reform and a shift in policy, the consequences of which include growth in branch campuses, engagement with the global rankings space, development and implementation of national and regional qualification frameworks; increases in quality assurance networks among other interventions. But in the decade that has passed since the implementation of these measures, why does GCC intra-regional mobility remain so low, particularly as regional mobility has been on the GCC Supreme Council agenda since 1987.

In an attempt to understand the complexity of these interactions, a realist evaluation of how quality assurance networks contribute to a GCC higher education area was undertaken by the author in 2019. The interactions identified demonstrate the complexity of mechanisms and contexts such as competition, nationalism, political patronage, governance and government regulation, political will, intergovernmentalism and Arab culture as intertwining in intricate ways (Walsh, 2019). At the state level, the desire to promote student mobility was thereby called into question.

Realist Evaluation of Quality Assurance Networks

Realist evaluation is a theory-driven approach to understanding 'what works, for whom, under what circumstances and how' for programmes, services, interventions and policies. Realist evaluations ask not, 'What works?' or, 'Does this programme work?' but asks instead, 'What works for whom in what circumstances and in what respects, and how?' (Pawson & Tilley, 2004, p. 2). Pawson and Tilley's (1997) realist evaluation contexts, mechanisms and outcomes (CMOs) identify and explain how a programme, service, intervention or policy works, how outcomes are produced, among whom, and in what circumstances. In essence, realist evaluation is a valuable approach in that it allows for the problematising of a programme, intervention or policy beyond the surface by identifying and explaining particular sets of contexts and mechanisms and their subsequent intended and unintended consequences. In Pawson and Tilley's (1997) realist approach, mechanisms are considered as 'usually hidden, sensitive to variations in context and generate outcomes' (Dalkin et al., 2015, p. 3). Mechanisms, when applied, describe what it is about a programme (intervention) that brings about any effects. Sometimes, mechanisms are hidden; while you may be able to see the outcome, you may not be able to see the workings. In using a realist evaluation approach, the purpose is not just looking at whether the intervention(s) works, but it also gives evidence of how they work, how they produce outcomes, among whom, and in what circumstances. Realist evaluation contexts, mechanisms and outcomes (CMO) configuration is used as a means to consider both enabling and constraining mechanisms as well as the contexts that allow for the mechanisms to be activated and the outcomes of such interactions (Pawson & Tilley, 2004). Realist evaluation is used across many sectors including health (Salter & Kothari, 2014), social service (Dalkin et al., 2019), education (Wong et al., 2012), crime prevention (Tilley, 2009), social policy (Westhorp, 2018), international development (Mukova-Moses, 2017) and environmental studies (Crabbe & Leroy, 2008) and form part of the family of theory driven evaluation. It allows us to consider why is it an intervention works in some instances and not others, for some people and not others.

Beginning with the development of a series of realist questions, the Critical Cultural, Political Economy of Education (CCPEE) (Robertson & Dale, 2015) was used to develop a conceptual framework. The CCPEE was an abstracting device to conceptualise the cultural, political and economic and makes use of prior theories. The conceptual framework was developed from the literature where the focus was on the underlying structures and mechanisms. Abstraction (Sayer, 2000, 1998, 1992) and reintroduction (Danermark et al., 2002; Olsen, 2010) were used to synthesise how the political, economic and cultural elements of the conceptual framework work in combination. Interviews were utilised as they are recognised as the most common method of data collection in realist studies (Manzano, 2016; Pawson & Tilley, 2004), while document analysis (Pawson & Tilley, 2004) was used as it is considered important to theory building. Pawson and Tilley's (1997) CMOs was used to identify contexts (C), mechanisms (M) and outcomes (O) in order to respond to the research aims.

Results of Realist Evaluation of Quality Assurance Networks

This evaluation found that the GCC region lacks a regional approach to higher education in general and quality assurance in particular. The role of the quality assurance networks in contributing to the regionalisation of quality assurance across the GCC is compounded by a range of mechanisms.

Firstly, the blurring of boundaries between the networks (as non-governmental organisations (NGOs) and state quality assurance agencies as an outcome, occurs through a range of mechanisms and contexts. The 'multi-layered network governance structure' as a mechanism affords the quality assurance agencies the ability to undertake administrative roles within the networks (e.g. BQA and ANQAHE and AQAAIW) meaning that the visibility, identity and role of the networks is blurred by the fact that the networks are viewed not as independent organisations, but as organisations whose identity is linked to that of the quality assurance agency. This occurs as a result of the state agency executives holding governance roles in the networks. The impact of this close association between agency and network is one that leads to a lack of independence and networks that are viewed as extended state apparatus.

The evaluation also found that NGOs and civil organisations have difficulty in acting independently of the state due to the 'status' mechanism. Government entities require civil society organisations be granted 'status' without which organisations have challenges in being able to operate in terms of renting premises, opening a bank account, holding public meetings and employing staff. The 'status' mechanism is a result of the state regulatory environment that requires networks to be recognised as social organisations which are identified in the 'government as regulator' context. The outcome of the acquisition of regulatory 'status' grants the network's legitimacy to operate. Subsequently, NGOs cannot form and act independently of state power.

The third finding of this evaluation was that formal and informal political patronage as a mechanism leads to political insulation. It is this very political patronage that ensures the sustainability of the quality assurance networks, whereby the close relationships between the networks and quality assurance agencies give them a power of their own, even if the boundaries are blurred. It is this close relationship, such as that identified between Bahrain BQA and ANQAHE that enables the network to contribute to the regional agenda, but only through the actions of the executives of the state quality assurance body. The role of quality assurance networks acting as a conduit between the state agencies in the competitive context detracts from bilateral approaches extending beyond political and economic relationships.

The evaluation argued that quality assurance networks have little formal role in contributing to the regional agenda. It is instead, the state quality assurance agencies driving the agenda, but through a bilateral and not regional basis as an outcome. In the context of political will and the absence of regional higher education regulations and policy, there appears little desire within the community of quality assurance agencies and networks to engage in a regional approach, with bilateral arrangements through the quality assurance agencies identified as a preferred route. The state quality assurance agencies, as GCC actors, are notable by their absence in the GCC quality assurance arrangements. They do not play any role in delegation of tasks by the multitudinous GCC Supreme Council committees. That responsibility is left, at the national level, to Ministries of Education. In the context of Bahrain for example, the Higher Education Council – under the chairmanship of the Minister of Education – has responsibility for improving, monitoring, evaluating and regulating the higher education sector. The dual responsibility for quality assurance within the context of a state, in two very different conceptual ways, creates tensions for institutes of higher education, such as the Bahrain HEC American credit system and the BQA European credit system.

In relation to understanding under what conditions the regionalisation approach to quality assurance in the GCC higher education space happens, it was found in this evaluation that intergovernmentalism as an outcome lends itself to a competitive, nationalist view of quality assurance. The driving forces of national sovereignty, territorial survival, political and economic interests, geo-strategic environment are key features of the GCC. Arab culture is identified as an obstacle as alliances and allegiances change on the basis of economic and political influences. Nationalism and national pride create competition in relation to how education is viewed. Positioning of regional educational institutions on global and regional rankings becomes important. Each state is vying for the best possible position on the global rankings, with a view to being best in the region and ultimately being positioned within the same categories of achievement as leading international educational institutions. This is furthered by the political will of governments to support the national pride which is combined with powerless institutions. Nationalism and rivalry disable the ability to engage in a regional approach to quality assurance. Comity and cooperation are embedded throughout GCC governance, detracting from the ability to get things done in terms of implementation of GCC Supreme Council resolutions. The absence of a regional policy further restricts the regional approach to quality assurance across the GCC. Therefore, as an outcome, the intergovernmental nature of the GCC, bound in comity and cooperation of committees as a form of governance, detracts from a regional approach to quality assurance in the GCC higher education space.

So, are the quality assurance networks contributing to a regional approach to higher education quality assurance in the GCC? It was noted on the previous page that the networks act as conduit between the state quality assurance agencies, with the very notable exception of the ONQHE. The ONQHE is focused solely on quality assurance within the state of Oman and deals exclusively with the institutions of higher education as direct stakeholders. ANQAHE as a network connects state agencies across the wider Arab region, where the sharing of ideas and mutual recognition of one state agency to another occurs. The relationship between executives within the networks and those within the state quality assurance agencies is intertwining with BQA senior executives acting as the driving force of ANQAHE, as an example. It is this relationship that sees a focus on a preference for bilateral arrangements between the quality assurance agencies. The networks act as means to connect the state agencies, while the state agencies drive their own agendas through the network. If quality assurance bilateral coordination occurs between two states, through the development and implementation of qualification frameworks and credit frameworks as an example, this may facilitate a regulatory process supporting recognition of qualifications and enhancement of student mobility. However, competitiveness and nationalism compound the political will to focus on such things. At the state level, the desire to promote student mobility is called into question. The GCC documents – GCC Process and Achievements, the Charter of the Council and the Economic Agreement – all indicate student mobility as an objective. Student mobility has been on the wider regional agenda since 1945 and the GCC agenda since its inception. Perhaps, as indicated by one interview participant, 'it is not a priority for government to exchange students'. The underlying reality is one that is driven by political and economic alliances. The political in the sense that rulers maintain power through political and economic liberalisation in the form of a top-down approach instead of implementing actual reforms that challenge the patriarchal power structure. The survival of ruling elites is interlinked, and therefore the power relations between states ensure that the quality assurance networks can at best achieve bilateral or multilateral participation in quality assurance matters.

In the context of the above discussions, quality assurance which is seen as important harmonisation tool in the European Higher Education Area and more recently in the ASEAN region, is absent in this form within GCC higher education, although there is a noted desire for a regional approach at the GCC Supreme Council level. The development and implementation of a GCC network for quality assurance, while on the regional agenda, has yet to come to fruition. The consequences of these findings ultimately place restrictive boundaries on issues such as student mobility. The mechanisms and contexts in the construction of a GCC higher education area are bound in complex cultural, political and economic relationships. These contexts and mechanisms mediate the ability of quality assurance as a harmonisation tool to contribute to the construction of a GCC higher education area.

Notes

1 Association of Quality Assurance Agencies of the Islamic World (AQAAIW); Arab Observatory for Education; Arab Network for Open and Distance Education (ANODE); Arab Network for Quality Assurance in Higher Education (ANQAHE); Arab Network for Literacy and Adult Education (ANLAE); Arab Regional Agenda for Improving Education Quality (ARAIEQ); Arab

Organisation for Quality Assurance in Education (AROQA); Islamic Educational, Scientific and Cultural Organisation (ISESCO). Oman Quality Network in Higher Education (OQNHE). This list is not exhaustive, there are other less well-known organisations.

2 The 22 Arab countries are Algeria, Bahrain, Comoros, Djibouti, Egypt, Iraq, Jordan, Kuwait, Lebanon, Libya, Mauritania, Morocco, Somalia, Sudan, Oman, Palestine, Qatar, Saudi Arabia, Syria, Tunisia, United Arab Emirates, Yemen.

References

Aljafari, T. (2016). Regionalisation, higher education and the Gulf Cooperation Council. In S. L. Robertson, K. Olds, R. Dale, & Q. A. Dang (Eds.), *Global regionalisms and higher education – projects, processes, politics* (pp. 289–304). Edward Elgar Publishing.

Almansour, A. H. (2006). Comprehensive development of education in the gulf cooperation council countries – A study of the directives stated in the supreme council Resolution. The twenty third session (Doha, December 2002) on education. The Cooperation Council for the Arab States of the Gulf Secretariat General.

Badry, F., & Willoughby, J. (2016). *Higher education revolutions in the gulf globalization and institutional viability*. Routledge.

Bouhlal, A., & Wells, P. J. (2019). UNESCO conventions on the recognition of higher education qualifications. In A. Badran. E. Baydoun & J.R. Hillman (Eds.) *Major challenges facing higher education in the Arab world: Quality assurance and relevance* (pp. 225–236). Springer. https://doi.org/10.1007/978-3-030-03774-1_1

Bridgestock, L. (2015). Middle Eastern students abroad: In numbers. https://www.topuniversities.com/blog/middle-eastern-students-abroad-numbers

Chao, R. Y. (2020). Intra-ASEAN student mobility: Overview, challenges and opportunities. *Journal of Applied Research in Higher Education*. https://doi.org/10.1108/JARHE-07-2019-0178

Crabbe, A., & Leroy, P. (2008). *The handbook of environmental policy evaluation*. Earthscan.

Cross-Border Education Research Team. (2017). C-BERT Branch Campus Listing. [Data originally collected by Kevin Kinser and Jason E. Lane]. http://cbert.org/branchcampuses.php

Croucher, G., & Woelert, P. (2016). Institutional isomorphism and the creation of the unified national system of higher education in Australia: An empirical analysis. *Higher Education*, *71*(4), 439–453. https://doi.org/10.1007/s10734-015-9914-6

Dalkin, S. M., Forster, N., Hodgson, P., Lhussier, M., Philipson, P., & Carr, S. M. (2019). Exposing the impact of intensive advice services on health: A realist evaluation. *Health & Social Care in the Community*, *27*(3), 767–776. https://doi.org/10.1111/hsc.12695

Dalkin, S. M., Greenhalgh, J., Jones, D., Cunningham, B., & Lhussier, M. (2015). What's in a mechanism? Development of a key concept in realist evaluation. *Implementation Science*, *10*(1), 49. https://doi.org/10.1186/s13012-015-0237-x

Danermark, B., Ekstrom, M., Jakobsen, L., & Karlsson, J. C. (2002). *Explaining society: Critical realism in the social sciences*. Routledge.

David, S. A., Taleb, H., Scatolini, S. S., Al-Qallaf, A., Al-Shammari, H. S., & George, M. A. (2017). An exploration into student learning mobility in higher education among the Arabian gulf cooperation council countries. *International Journal of Educational Development*, *55*, 41–48. https://doi.org/10.1016/j.ijedudev.2017.05.001

El Hassan, K. (2013). Quality assurance in higher education in 20 MENA economies. *Higher Education Management & Policy*, *24*(2), 73–84.

European Union. (2015). *ECTS user's guide*. https://ec.europa.eu/assets/eac/education/ects/users-guide/docs/ects-users-guide_en.pdf

Fay, D. L., & Zavattaro, S. M. (2016). Branding and isomorphism: The case of higher education. *Public Administration Review*, *76*(5), 805–815.

Findlay, A., Packwood, H., McCollum, D., Nightingale, G., & Tindal, S. (2017). Fees, flows and imaginaries: Exploring the destination choices arising from intra-national student mobility. *Globalisation, Societies and Education*, *16*(2), 162–175. https://doi.org/10.1080/14767724.2017.1412822

Findlow, S., & Hayes, A. (2016). Transnational academic capitalism in the Arab gulf: Balancing global and local, and public and private, capitals. *British Journal of Sociology of Education*, *37*(1), 110–128.

GCC Secretariat General. (2014). *GCC the processes and achievements*. https://www.gcc-sg.org/en-us/CognitiveSources/DigitalLibrary/Lists/DigitalLibrary/The%20GCC%20Process%20and%20Achievement/7161117306380.pdf

Hafaiedh, A. (2010). On building an academic space for the Arab region – the possible, the probable and the hoped for. In B. Lamine (Ed.), *Towards and Arab higher education space – International challenges and societal responsibilities—Proceedings of the Arab regional conference on higher education 2009* (pp. 93–109). UNESCO.

Herrera, L. (2007). Higher education in the Arab world. In J. Forest, & P. Altbach (Eds.), *International handbook of higher education* (pp. 409–421). Springer.

Hurrell, A. (2008). *On global order: Power, values and the constitution of international society*. Oxford University Press.

Jafar, H., & Knight, J. (2020). Higher education in the Arab states: The realities and challenges of regionalization. *Comparative and International Education*, *48*(2). https://doi.org/10.5206/cie-eci.v48i2.10788

Jöns, H. (2018). Boundary-crossing academic mobilities in global knowledge economies: New research agendas based on triadic thought. *Globalisation, Societies and Education*, *16*(2), 151–161. https://doi.org/10.1080/14767724.2017.1413977

Knight, J. (2014). Three generations of cross-border higher education: New developments, issues and challenges. In B. T. Streitwieser (Ed.), *Internationalisation of higher education and global mobility* (pp. 43–58). Symposium Books.

Knight, J., & Woldegiorgis, E. T. (2017). *Regionalization of African higher education: Progress and prospects*. Sense Publishers.

Legrenzi, M., & Harders, C. (2008). Introduction—beyond regionalism? Regional cooperation, regionalism and regionalization in the Middle East. In C. Harders, & M. Legrenzi (Eds.), *Beyond regionalism? Regional cooperation, regionalism and regionalization in the middle East* (pp. 1–12). Ashgate.

Macrander, A. (2017). Fractal inequality: A social network analysis of global and regional international student mobility. *Research in Comparative & International Education*, *12*(2), 243–268. https://doi.org/10.1177%2F1745499917712616

Manzano, A. (2016). The craft of interviewing in realist evaluation. *Evaluation*, *22*(3), 342–360. https://doi.org/10.1177%2F1356389016638615

Mazawi, A. E. (2005). Contrasting perspectives on higher education governance in the Arab states. In J.C. Smart (Ed.), *Higher education handbook of theory and research* (Vol. XX, pp. 133–189), Springer.

Mazawi, A. E. (2008). Policy politics of higher education in the gulf cooperation member states: Intersections of globality, regionalism and locality. In C. Davidson & P. Mackenzie-Smith (Eds.), *Higher education in the Gulf states: Shaping economies, politics and culture* ([Kindle] Ch. 3). SAQI Books.

Mazawi, A. E. (2009). Naming the imaginary: "Building an Arab knowledge society" and the contested terrain of educational reform for development. In O. Abi-Mershed (Ed.), *Trajectories of education in the Arab world—Legacies and challenges* (pp. 201–225). Routledge.

Mazawi, A., & Sultana, R. (2010). Editorial introduction: Situating the 'Worlds' of Arab education: Critical engagements. In A. Mazawi & R. Sultana (Eds.), *World yearbook of education 2010: Education and the Arab 'World': Political projects, struggles, and geometries of power*. Routledge.

Meyer, J. W., & Frank, D. J. (2007). University expansion and the knowledge society. *Theory and Society*, 36, 287–311. https://doi.org/10.1007/s11186-007-9035-z

Mukova-Moses, M. (2017). A case for the advancement of utilisation of realist evaluation in international development: An Oxfam focused illustration. *Evaluation Journal of Australasia*, *17*(2), 37–41. https://doi.org/10.1177/1035719X1701700206

OECD. (1999). *Quality and internationalisation in higher education*. OECD Publishing. https://doi.org/10.1787/9789264173361-en

Olsen, W. (2010). Editor's introduction: Realist methodology—a review. In W. Olsen (Ed.), *Realist methodology* (pp. xix–xivi). SAGE.

Pawson, R., & Tilley, N. (1997). *Realistic evaluation*. Sage Publications.

Pawson, R., & Tilley, N. (2004). *Realist evaluation*. Sage Publications. http://www.communitymatters.com.au/gpage1.html

Robertson, S. L. (2008). 'Europe/Asia' regionalism, higher education and the production of world order. *Policy Futures in Education*, *6*(6), 718–729. https://doi.org/10.2304%2Fpfie.2008.6.6.718

Robertson, S. L., & Dale, R. (2015). Towards a 'critical cultural political economy' account of the globalising of education. *Globalisation, Societies and Education*, *13*(1), 149–179.

Salter, K. L., & Kothari, A. (2014). Using realist evaluation to open the black box of knowledge translation: A state-of-the-art review. *Implementation Science*, *9*, 115. https://doi.org/10.1186/s13012-014-0115-y

Sayer, A. (1992). *Method in social science: A realist approach* (2nd ed.). Routledge.

Sayer, A. (1998). Abstraction: A realist interpretation. In M. Archer, R. Bhaskar, A. Collier, T. Lawson, & A. Norrie (Eds.), *Critical realism: Essential readings* (pp. 120–43). Routledge.

Sayer, A. (2000). *Realism and social science*. SAGE.

Tarawneh, E. (2011). Assessing and understanding quality in the Arab region. In T. Townsend, & J. MacBeath (Eds.), *International handbook of leadership for learning* (pp. 1107–1124). Springer.

Teichler, U. (2004). The changing debate on internationalisation of higher education. *Higher Education*, *48*, 5–26. https://doi.org/10.1023/B:HIGH.0000033771.69078.41

Teichler, U. (2009). Internationalization of higher education: European Experiences. *Asia Pacific Education Review*, *10*(9), 93–106. http://dx.doi.org/10.1007/s12564-009-9002-7

Teichler, U. (2011). Bologna—Motor or stumbling block for the mobility and employability of graduates? In H. Schomburg, & U. Teichler (Eds.), *Employability and mobility of bachelor graduates in Europe* (pp. 3–41). Sense Publishers.

Tilley, N. (2009). *Crime prevention*. Willan Publishing.

UIS. (2020). Data for the sustainable development goals. http://uis.unesco.org/ data extracted 04 May.

UOE. (2020). *Data Collection on formal education—Manual on concepts, definitions and classifications*, UNESCO-UIS/OECD/EUROSTAT. http://uis.unesco.org/sites/default/files/documents/uoe-data-collection-manual-2020-en.pdf

UNESCO. (2016). *Evaluation of UNESCO's regional conventions in the recognition of qualifications in higher education*. Internal Oversight Service, IOS/EVS/PI/149. https://www.hrk-nexus.de/fileadmin/redaktion/hrk-nexus/07-Downloads/07-08-RT_Anerkennung/Evaluation_of_UNESCO_s_Regional_Conventions_on_the_recognition_of_foreign_qualifications_in_Higher_Education_Juni_2016.pdf

UNESCO. (2020). *Global convention on the recognition of qualifications concerning higher education*. UNESCO. https://en.unesco.org/themes/higher-education/recognition-qualifications/global-convention#:~:text=The%20Convention%20is%20designed%20to,transparent%20and%20non%2Ddiscriminatory%20mechanisms

UNESCO-IESALC. (2019). *Mobility in higher education in Latin America and the Caribbean: Challenges and opportunities of a renewed convention for the recognition of studies, degrees and diplomas*, IESALC. https://www.iesalc.unesco.org/en/2019/09/25/unesco-iesalc-reveals-that-only-38-of-mobility-from-latin-america-and-the-caribbean-is-to-the-same-region/

Walsh, C. (2019). *Mechanisms and contexts of quality assurance in the construction of a Gulf Cooperation Council higher education area*. [Doctoral Dissertation]. https://research-information.bris.ac.uk/en/studentTheses/mechanisms-and-contexts-of-quality-assurance-in-the-construction-

Westhorp, G. (2018). Understanding mechanisms in realist evaluation and research. In N. Emmel, J. Greenhalgh, A. Manzano, M. Monaghan, & S. Dalkin (Eds.), *Doing realist research* (pp. 41–58). SAGE.

Wit, H., & Altbach, P. G. (2021). Internationalization in higher education: Global trends and recommendations for its future. *Policy Reviews in Higher Education*, *5*(1), 28–46. https://doi.org/10.1080/23322969.2020.1820898

Woldegiorgis, E. T., & Doevenspeck, M. (2015). Current trends, challenges and prospects of student mobility in the African higher education landscape. *International Journal of Higher Education*, *4*(2), 105–115. https://doi.org/10.5430/ijhe.v4n2p105

Wong, G., Greenhalgh, T., Westhorp, G., & Pawson, R. (2012). Realist methods in medical education research: What are they and What can they contribute? *Medical Education*, *46*, 89–96. https://doi.org/10.1111/j.1365-2923.2011.04045.x

Zapp, M., & Ramirez, O. (2019). Beyond internationalisation and isomorphism—The construction of a global higher education regime. *Comparative Education*, *55*(4), 473–493. https://doi.org/10.1080/03050068.2019.1638103

Author biography

Dr Clare Walsh (EdD, MBA, MBS, MA, BSc, PgCT T&L) is a Senior Lecturer & Programme Director at the RCSI Graduate School of Healthcare Management. She has been based in Bahrain for over a decade. Her research interests include political economy of education, civilisation analysis, realist evaluation, management and leadership education and quality assurance. Clare has published widely in areas of Arab higher education, including high impact journal articles such as in International Journal of Diplomacy and Economy and in proceedings of key regional conferences such as Proceedings of the Third International Conference on Emerging Research Paradigms in Business and Social Science, Dubai, UAE and Proceedings of the Fifth Annual Gulf Comparative Education Society Symposium, Dubai, UAE. She is currently working on five projects: 'Realist evaluation of FinTech and higher education: What works, for whom and why?' 'Changing constructions of public legitimacy as reflected in GCC higher education spaces', 'A BEME scoping review of educational interventions to develop cultural competence in health professionals', 'Decolonising the curricula: A realist evaluation of Global North bias' and 'Research ethics and the use of social media'.

Chapter 4

The Representation of International Students

Student Mobility from the Middle East to Turkey

Omer Caliskan and Hilal Buyukgoze

Introduction

International student mobility (ISM), referring to the mobility of 'students who have crossed borders expressly with the intention to study' (Organisation for Economic Co-Operation and Development [OECD], 2009, p. 311), has become a global phenomenon in the last decades (Barnett & Wu, 1995; de Wit et al., 2013). Hence, the scale of ISM has accelerated across the world, from 2 million international students in 2000 to over 5.3 million as of 2017 (United Nations Educational Scientific and Cultural Organization [UNESCO], 2019). While traditional destinations of study-abroad (e.g. the United States, the United Kingdom, Canada and Australia) host half of the international student population, various regional hubs across the globe have also emerged as alternative study-abroad destinations for international students (Altbach & Engberg, 2014). Assumed as a regional hub for its nearby territories (Jon et al., 2014; Kondakci et al., 2016), Turkey owns some unique geographical, socio-political, historical and educational characteristics influential in attracting international students from its periphery including the Middle East, the Balkans and the Turkic region from central Asia. In addition to these inherent attributes, Turkey has recently enacted some affirmative policies (e.g. scholarships, increasing student capacity, easing entry exams) to expand its potential in attracting students (Çetinsaya, 2014). As a result of these efforts, the number of in-bound students at tertiary level in Turkey increased from 72,000 in 2014 to 178,000 in 2019 (Council of Higher Education [CoHE], 2020) (see Figure 4.1). Almost one-third of those students are coming from nearby Middle Eastern countries (a total of 54,710 students) including Syria, Iran, Iraq and Afghanistan, making Turkey a leading international student-hosting country in the Middle East.

It is acknowledged that global higher education has turned into a trading environment (Marginson, 2007), which compels countries to compete with each other in attracting more intellectual capital through their universities

DOI: 10.4324/9781003138457-6

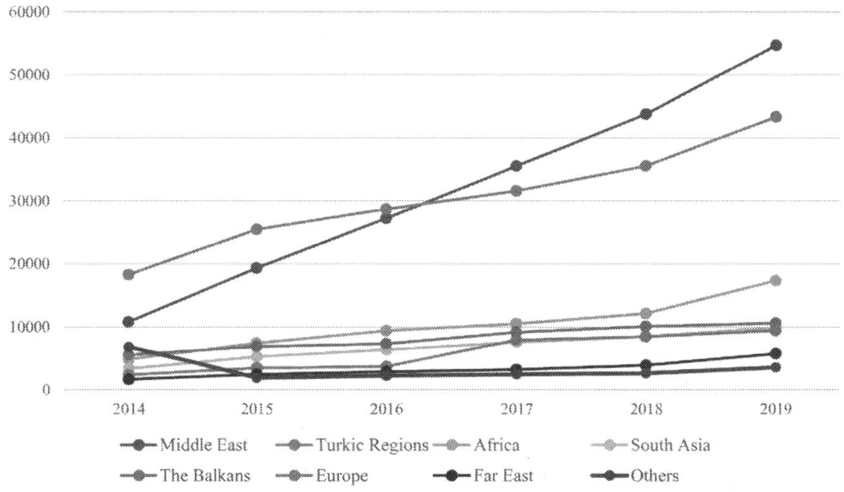

Figure 4.1 Regional Distribution of In-Bound Students in Turkey

(Krücken, 2021). Accordingly, in the literature, much has been said about international students in terms of in-bound student numbers, nation state's ability in attracting them, and contribution of ISM to knowledge economy (Guruz, 2011; She & Wotherspoon, 2013). However, one missing but important issue is the question of how certain dynamics, assumptions, ideologies and interrelationships can shape the issue of internationalisation and the construction of 'international students' in a given context. In relation to this, it is stressed that universities' close relationship with nation state and its dominant ideology may create a dilemma in a way that tension emerges between nationalism and cosmopolitanism (Hayes, 2017; Rizvi, 2009). Based on this perspective, Turkey's peculiar characteristic making it a regional hub for the Middle East may shed some light on how international students are represented in policy documents, political discourse and public perception. Employing a critical perspective, uncovering the established representations may reveal marginalisation, injustices and stigmatisation that international students encounter during their stay in the host country because several research indicates that international students are, either explicitly or implicitly, exposed to marginalisation perpetrated by nation states understandings of international student (Hayes, 2018; Marginson, 2013; Vural-Yılmaz, 2018). Drawing on this perspective, this chapter focuses on three main issues.

1 In what ways do Turkey and Middle East relationships shape the constructions of international students coming from Middle East countries?

2 In what ways do Turkey and Europe/EU relationships shape the constructions of international students coming from Middle East countries?
3 What kinds of local challenges exist shaping the construction of international students?

The Turkish Higher Education Context

Prior to talking about the construction of international students in Turkish Higher Education Institutions (HEIs), it would be helpful to understand the context of Turkish HEIs. The history of modern Turkish higher education dates back to 1863, the times of large-scale European-oriented reform movements in educational, social and political life (Dölen, 2009), but the actual expansion of higher education institutions across the country was initiated after the 1950s. In the contemporary history of Turkey, especially with the establishment of the Republic of Turkey in 1923, education has played a significant role in advancing the nation. Building an education system of comparable quality and scope to those in industrialised Western countries has since become a policy agenda (Eğilmez, 2018), yet the reform initiatives have been affected by the socio-political tensions and conflicts, leading the national government to adopt a more centralised system of governance that is subject to international criticisms because of the limited autonomy of Turkish universities (Çelik & Gür, 2014; Doğramacı, 2007).

Today, the current higher education system consists of 209 universities, 131 of which are state universities, and 78 of which are non-profit foundation universities (CoHE, 2020). Two-thirds of all universities were founded after 2006 with the motivation of opening a state-funded university in each city (Cin et al., 2021) to meet the ever-growing public demand for higher education (Özoğlu et al., 2016). The rapid expansion has contributed to the access and participation of students in higher education from various geographical areas with diverse socio-economic backgrounds (Mizikaci, 2003; Özoğlu et al., 2016). However, the higher education policy of the ruling political party has been criticised to utilise higher education institutions as a venue for neoliberal, market-oriented political transformations (Aslan, 2014; Günel, 2009). Allocation of public resources to rural transformation projects such as opening new universities in 'economically less vibrant' regions of Turkey (Cin et al., 2021) has been perceived as populist public investments (Erensü & Madra, 2020) to contribute to the economic development of those areas by creating demand for housing, dining, health services and socialisation facilities such as cinemas, theatres, restaurants, cafes, game houses and shopping centres. Local people in these rural regions of Turkey have benefitted from the newly established universities and expansion in the numbers of incoming students in terms of business ownership, enterprises and employment, but the other side of the coin is that universities have encountered a number of foundational, political and contextual problems including lack of

Table 4.1 Enrolments in Tertiary Education by Leading Emerging Economies (2000–2018)

	Number of enrolled students		
Country	*2000*	*2018*	*Growth rate*
China (Mainland)	7,364,111	44,935,169	510%
Turkey	1,594,462	7,560,371	374%
India	9,404,460	34,337,594	265%
Brazil	2,781,328	8,741,996	214%
Indonesia	3,126,307	8,037,218	157%
World	100,159,144	225,070,099	125%

Source: The table was developed by the authors based on the data from UNESCO database (2020).

quality academic staff, insufficient learning facilities provided at campuses, infrastructure and buildings, high student quotas, dominant political atmosphere and also the attitudes of local people (Meşe, 2019; Özoğlu et al., 2016).

In spite of these challenges, the demand for higher education in Turkey has always been high because of the public perception that higher education facilitates economic prosperity and upward social mobility (Mizikaci, 2003). One source of this demand has been population increase over the years, which leaves universities having to address enrolment capacity (Özcan, 2011). Therefore, with the establishment of new universities, the tertiary enrolment rate has increased by almost 370 percent, from 2000 (1.6 million) to 2018 (7.5 million), making Turkey one of the leading countries for student enrolment growth in tertiary education among its counterparts, leading emerging economies (see Table 4.1, UNESCO, 2020). In relation to the growth of universities across the country, Erdoğan has summarised the process with the following statement:

> Access to higher education has been one of the crucial challenges that Turkey has faced over the decades. In order to decrease the gap between supply and demand, new universities have been established and extended enrolment capacity for programmes has been applied. These increased the enrolment rate, equal opportunity in access to some extent, enlargement and diversity of higher education institutions. With these developments, higher education has been massified in Turkey from 2000 onwards.
>
> (Erdoğan, 2015, p. 745)

In Turkey, a few state universities adopt English (e.g. Boğaziçi University, Middle East Technical University and Izmir Institute of Technology) or other languages such as French (e.g. Galatasaray University) as a compulsory medium of instruction. Among others, though the language of instruction is Turkish, some undergraduate programmes are offered either in English, French, German (especially in mechanical engineering programmes) or in other languages and/or some universities apply a '30% English rule' as the medium of instruction (e.g. Hacettepe University, Istanbul Technical University, Yıldız Technical University and Dokuz Eylül University). A number of foundation universities are also English medium universities such as Bahçeşehir (except for the Law Faculty), Bilkent, Koç, MEF and Sabancı Universities. International students are accepted to all degree programmes and they study either in Turkish or English, after taking one-year language preparation class. Local students do not generally pay tuition fees at state universities, but foundation universities charge varying levels of fees. For international students pursuing undergraduate and graduate programmes, both state and foundation universities charge fees relatively lower than those of countries in Europe and the United States. State universities depend on funding from the government which is allocated to specific budgetary categories, leaving little room for institutionalised decision making. In relation to the administration of internationalisation processes in higher education, the CoHE as the upper governing body for all universities function as a rule-maker and coordinator for Turkish universities. However; universities are, to some extent, left to enact their own policies in accordance with the CoHE's main legislations in areas of determining curriculum content, student capacity and recruitment of staff (Çelik & Gür, 2014).

International Student Mobility in Turkey

Attracting international students has become a policy agenda for Turkey since the 1990s, especially with the collapse of the Soviet Union (Kavak & Baskan, 2001). Not being a traditional study-abroad destination for international students, Turkey has principally sought to attract international students from its nearby territories such as the Balkans, the Turkic region and Middle East countries (Gök & Gümüş, 2018). The main characteristics of these regions are that they own mutual historical, cultural, racial and political proximities with Turkey. Being aware of such a potential, Turkey has primarily focused on these regions to attract more international students through governmental tools and various non-governmental organisations (NGOs) (Özoğlu et al., 2012). As a result of these efforts, over the years, the number of international students coming from these regions has dramatically increased (see Figure 4.2).

It should also be noted that Turkey is not a leading and single study-abroad destination in the region. For instance, Russia is an important and primary study-abroad destination for students from the Turkic region. In the same way, regionally, EU countries are more attractive destinations for the students from the Balkan countries. For the Middle East region, international branch universities of the Gulf region – though they have been

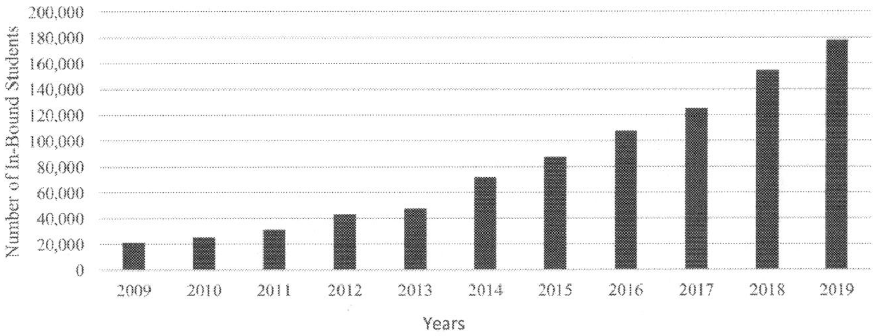

Figure 4.2 Number of International Students

questioned for their contribution to the continuation of colonial relations in higher education and the reproduction of 'world-class' ideology (Siltaoja et al., 2019) – are prominent destinations in Qatar, the United Arab Emirates and the Kingdom of Saudi Arabia (Madichie, 2015). It is also evident that students coming from Gulf countries (19,092 students – CoHE, 2020) are less than half of those coming from the Middle East countries like Syria, Yemen and Palestine (44,767 – CoHE, 2020), which could be interpreted that students from wealthy countries prefer the EU countries or the United States for international mobility. In that sense, Turkey's current position as an emerging regional hub in the Middle East is open to some challenges associated with the competitive policies enacted by its counterparts, especially the Gulf countries.

The Turkey-Middle East Relationship and Its Consequences on International Student Construction

The relationship between Turkey and the Middle East countries has a number of distinctive attributes in diverse aspects, shaping the representation of international students from those regions. To comprehend this relationship, a set of interlinked historical, political and economical dynamics need to be appreciated.

First, Turkey's geographical proximity with the countries which were formerly a part of the late Ottoman Empire is assumed to make it a pioneering heavyweight country within the region surrounding (Akgün & Senyücel-Gündoğar, 2013; Bechev & Hiltermann, 2017). Centuries of living together within the same borders enabled the formation of strong historical, socio-political, religious and ethnic ties among the people of Middle Eastern countries. These strong and historic ties have created a widespread assumption that Turkey is a regional soft power and receives the appreciation of the communities living there (Bilgin, 2011; Kalın, 2011). Therefore, a common discourse much perpetuated among the public and politicians is that this region was conflict-free for long years during the sovereignty of the Ottoman (Alkan, 2016; Turan, 2017). Fromkin reminds us that in this period, 'Most of the Middle East still rested, as it had for centuries, under the drowsy and negligent sway of the Ottoman Empire, a relatively tranquil domain in which history, like everything else, moved slowly' (Fromkin, 2009, p. 25).

Nevertheless, the assumption of Turkey's being a regional soft power in the Middle East is more of a political discourse fuelled by the current Turkish administration especially after the 2000s, with the arrival of the current administration in power, because of the recent conflicts experienced with Syria, Egypt, Saudi Arabia and the United Arab Emirates, Turkey has been deeply isolated from the region (Ekşi & Erol, 2018; Tür, 2019).

In spite of ups and downs in Turkey's interaction with the region, the cemented relationship between Turkey and the Middle East is quite old (Hoffmann, 2019), yet Turkey had preferred to be an outsider in relation to the region since the establishment of modern Republic in 1923 (Elhusseini, 2018). This was especially because the collapse of the Ottoman Empire following years of lost territories and the rising idea of nation-statehood in the region and across the world led the new Turkish state to deny its Ottoman past and connections with Middle East, and thereby to turn its face to the West/Europe to adopt the secular and 'modern' standards of civilised world (Öniş, 2004). One other important factor in this radical change was to bring about the nation-state idea of 'Turkishness' in the newly established Republic of Turkey (Bayar, 2016).

As a turning point, with the arrival of the JDP (Justice and Development Party) to power in 2002, Turkey's attitude towards the region changed in a noticeably positive manner as it adopted broader economic, diplomatic and political objectives in international affairs (Bilgin, 2011; Elhusseini, 2018; Kalın, 2011). The JDP is identified as a movement of 'Muslim brotherhood-inspired ideology with participatory politics and free market economics' (Bechev & Hiltermann, 2017, p. 50). In line with these principles and ideology, to benefit from the potential ties in educational, economic, industrial and political means, Turkey has attempted to make important investments in the region such as opening new consulates, holding conference meetings, sending humanitarian aids and military assistance, opening some NGOs active in the region, signing bilateral agreements in education and providing a range of scholarships.

Turkey's recent policies on encouraging international mobility from the Middle East countries point to its expectations of benefitting politically from internationalisation (Aydinli & Mathews, 2020). To this end, the current Turkish administration is signally attempting to restore Ottoman glory with an inclusive manner and interventionist agenda across the Mediterranean Sea neighbourhood (Hoffmann, 2019; Oğuzlu, 2008;

Özpek & Tanriverdi-Yaşar, 2018). As a reflection of Turkey's perspectives towards the region, former Prime Minister Ahmet Davutoğlu has stated as follows:

> The other states say to us, 'do not engage in adventures in foreign policy, and do not follow an active politics.' And we keep saying 'Turkey has always been a subject, can never be objectified. We have always been a subject, and no one can make this nation an object. Today, could anyone, particularly Palestine, oppose anything in the Middle East without the presence of Turkey? We should do what our history necessitates. This nation has always been a subject of history and will continue to be so.
>
> (Saraçoğlu & Demirkol, 2015, p. 315)

The increasing international student population from Middle Eastern countries contributes to Turkey's desired image in the context of international politics, affirming and expanding its power in the international arena. Likewise, in the 2010s, before the Syrian Civil War, Turkish government opened the borders (almost like EU borders) with Syria and envisioned that the nearby countries would cooperate with each other like EU member countries. Yet, after the war, Turkey has sustained its continuing support (Keyman, 2016), and granted temporary protection to almost 4 million Syrian refugees (United Nations High Commissioner for Refugees [UNCHR], 2020), with an emergent expansion in the numbers of refugee-background students at higher education level. Here, large numbers of Syrian undergraduate and graduate students have also spotlighted Turkey's role as the 'region's rule setter' (Bechev & Hiltermann, 2017), allowing its soft power to reach and influence both in the war-affected region and in international diplomacy. However, it should also be noted that Turkey and EU have been criticised because of abusing these vulnerable people as a political leverage in negotiations, especially in issues of immigrant influx to Europe and funding of refugees within Turkish borders (Kaytaz, 2021; Oztig, 2020).

These efforts and regulations, though intensified during the past 20 years by the government, symbolise Turkey's long interest in the Middle East region, motivated by particular economic and political intentions (Keyman, 2016). As Marginson suggests, political actors interpret globalisation within the context of 'economic bargains' (Marginson, 2013, p. 13), and therefore organise and treat international mobility as a capacity for cross-border trade and investment. Turkey assesses Middle Eastern international students as economic subjects, by whom the continuity of mutual financial benefits is maintained, attained and strengthened among neighbouring countries within the region. In other words, Middle Eastern students serve as a means of regional marketplace and economic expansion within the region.

To increase its influential and strategically important role, Turkey offers a growing number of scholarship programmes which have been designed for each level of education in Turkish HEIs and various forms of support for incoming international students (Aras & Mohammed, 2018). These include full-time programmes such as undergraduate, postgraduate and arts scholarship programmes, short-term programmes such as one-year success scholarships and three to twelve months' research scholarships, Turkish language and culture programmes like KATIP (Turkish language programme for public officials and academicians) offering eight to ten months of stipend. They also include partnered programmes customised to serve specific target groups and tailored on the basis of cooperation provided by international organisations and governmental institutions: the Syrian students scholarship programme, a Yemeni pioneers scholarship programme, the WIPO (World Intellectual Property Organisation) scholarship and EU scholarships in partnership of European Union and UNHCR (United Nations High Commissioner for Refugees) (Yurtdışı Türkler ve Akraba Topluluklar Başkanlığı [YTB], 2020). The Scientific and Technological Research Council of Turkey (TUBITAK) also supports students' and academics' mobility from the countries of the region within diverse scientific projects and cooperation agreements (TUBITAK, 2020). As Turkey sees incoming international students and academics as its 'culture ambassadors' in their homelands (Ercan, 2012), who help deepen appreciation for Turkey, it tends to increase the number of projects, opportunities and student quotas to offer experience in the country (Aydinli & Mathews, 2020), and then represent it to the greater Middle Eastern community.

In the last two decades, Turkey has paid greater attention to the Middle Eastern countries to stimulate dialog, strengthen friendship and revive already existing bonds. To unlock this internationalisation potential and to reach its intended 200,000 international students by the year 2023 (YTB, 2020), Turkey has made a series of regulations including legal frameworks, policy and strategy statements, principles and general directions supported by a wide variety of government departments, agencies and diplomatic services such as the Yunus Emre Institute (similar to the British Council or the Goethe Institute), Presidency for Turks Abroad and Related Communities, Turkish Cooperation and Coordination Agency, Cultural Diplomacy Academy. These public, private and joint initiatives have chiefly originated from the JDP's Muslim-brotherhood-infused ideology (Bechev & Hiltermann, 2017). With a neo-Ottomanist motivation (Hoffmann, 2019), Turkey apparently plans to gain greater popularity and networks by attracting Middle Eastern publics (Murinson, 2006; Saraçoğlu & Demirkol, 2015). In that respect, international students coming from Islamist traditions and principles are expected to serve Turkey's Islamic 'brotherhood' objective and support its recently assumed 'leader of the Islamic umma' role as agents towards religious and political goals (Bechev & Hiltermann, 2017).

Overall, Turkey's apparently rising interest in the Middle East region is not a temporary strategy. Rather, affairs between the two regions have a long-established continuum and tradition. As a regionally prominent country, Turkey is adopting and developing dynamic, diverse, inclusive and solid steps to recruit international students from its periphery, both corresponding to the particular needs and expectations of the young people from the region, and enlarging the sphere of influence at global scale (Aras & Mohammed, 2018; Vural-Yılmaz, 2018). In so doing, the essence of Turkey's motivation lies in emerging neo-Ottomanism, Muslim-brotherhood-infused ideology, international diplomacy and soft power, and cross-border trade and investment. These moves result in representations of Middle Eastern international students as cultural ambassadors, agents towards supporting regional political and/or economic objectives, and economic subjects (e.g. Ercan, 2012).

Turkey-Europe/EU Relationships and Its Consequences on International Student Construction

Being a natural bridge between the East and the West, the geopolitical position of Turkey is acknowledged as an advantage both in culture and experience. Located at the intersection of Asia and Europe, Turkey is mostly seen as a gateway for neighbours seeking access to industrialised European countries and sustainable economies (Kahraman, 2011). Holding unique geographical importance, setting close neighbourly relations and having a high ability of regional cooperation, Turkey attracts international students from its periphery that are interested in getting quality education aligned with the values of European type of higher education, research and science (Kondakci, 2011). Yet, assessing Turkey as a gateway has particular connotations both for the host country and the incoming international students. It is clear that Turkey is not a desired final destination for those hoping to get tertiary and/or graduate education in European countries (Ercan, 2012). This also suggests that incoming Middle Eastern students are constructed as 'supplicants' within the system (Marginson, 2013) because Turkey has what they do not have in their home nation – a 'European-like' higher education.

Universities in Turkey have been part of the Bologna Process since 2001. The Bologna Process is a unique intergovernmental collaboration undertaking a set of commitments by 'structural reforms and shared tools' (European Higher Education Area [EHEA], 2020). Through the process, Turkey has transformed its universities into more Anglo-Saxon type institutions (Furuzan, 2012), accepting the credits, degrees and learning periods of students that are completed at other universities of the EHEA, providing diploma supplement and performing an effective system of quality assurance (Çetinsaya, 2014). The Bologna Process has also supported and enhanced mobility and cooperation in higher education among member countries by Erasmus+ partnerships, traineeship opportunities, student and staff mobility, mutual recognition of academic qualifications and diplomas (Erdoğan, 2015). In line with the key priorities of the process, the HEIs in Turkey warrant that their diplomas are of quality assurance standards of the European Association of Quality Assurance in Higher Education (ENQA), as part of their membership of the Higher Education Quality Council (HEQC) of Turkey in 2020 (ENQA, 2020). That is, aligned with European qualification frameworks, Turkish higher education system offers EHEA-recognised degrees, course credits and tertiary education experience, specifically for those aiming to transfer to a European university, although some programmes (e.g. Dentistry, Medicine and Law) in European and/or Northern American universities may still require extra certificates or qualifications to recognise these degrees.

This discrepancy points to a deficit in the Middle Eastern higher education, signifying a 'superior' aspect to the Turkish system over those of incoming students' home nations. Such a 'superiority' inevitably represents international students from Middle East countries in Turkey as 'beneficiaries of the (Turkish) system'. The notion of 'student as a beneficiary' belongs only to international students coming from the neighbourhood countries to Turkey, further creating a hierarchy between local and international students ([illegible] & [illegible], 2013).

Mobility and cross-border cooperation policies have also been designed to boost internationalisation and intercultural relations within the Bologna Process (Çetinsaya, 2014). The advantages of these mobility and exchange opportunities are well-recognised, and widely benefited from by the member HEIs in Turkey, as well. Students with mobility experience abroad develop intercultural competencies, perspectives and openness, gain transferrable skills, improve their foreign language and communication skills, and strengthen their employability (European Commission, 2019). Turkey's large access to mobility opportunities in higher education is therefore well suited to act as a springboard for participation of the Middle Eastern students in international higher education, both fitting their needs and expectations considerably.

Having a relatively rooted and more modern university system compared to the surrounding region, offering English medium of instruction in some public and non-profit foundation universities located in big cities, and providing joint and/or international dual diploma programmes with some of the European Union and the United States for their students, the HEIs in Turkey have become increasingly attractive destinations for prospective international students (Özoğlu et al., 2012). It must be highlighted, however, that because of the previous colonial rulers' impact on diverse parts of the Middle East countries, programmes in higher education are widely conducted in Arabic, English and French across these countries, therefore, the HEIs and programmes providing English medium of instruction in Turkey are one of the pull factors in enhancing ISM, especially from the Middle East region.

Returning to the joint and dual diploma programmes and international mobility, the careers of the participants and/or graduates of these international programmes are considered to develop quicker than non-mobile students like finding their first job and starting their own business based on the skills they adopted during their experience education abroad (European Commission, 2019). These kinds of opportunities may be more appealing particularly for students from neighbourhood countries with lower GDPs, deteriorating job market conditions and high rates of unemployment. War-torn countries like Syria, Yemen, Iraq and Libya especially have significant negative trends in poverty, unemployment and income inequality. Therefore, Turkey is a reasonable option for international students coming from these countries both for getting quality education, having a Europe-study experience during their stay in Turkey, and investing in their future careers.

Though United States and European HEIs require higher levels of tuition fees from students of other nationalities, they provide less financial support to them (Sovic & Blythman, 2013). Besides, the cost of living and accompanying expenditure in the United States and Europe are remarkably higher than that of Turkey. Given the comparably low tuition fees, rather low cost of living, housing and transportation, and final goods, Turkish HEIs become noticeably favoured destinations for international students coming from lower-income countries of neighbourhood seeking to experience affordable living in a peaceful and dynamic country in a Western lifestyle (Özoğlu et al., 2012; Vural-Yılmaz, 2018). Though a non-EU member country, Turkey provides a free and sophisticated environment with a friendly and open culture.

Last, in spite of the democratic backsliding of Turkey in recent years (Economist Intelligence Unit, 2019; European Commission, 2019), with its Western type of parliamentary, secular democracy and public administration (Keyman, 2016), Turkey is considered as a relatively stable (Kondakci et al., 2016) and free country by the current standards of the region. Further, Turkey is perceived as a model in the Middle Eastern region due to its economic system, democratic regime, secular policies, Muslim identity and strategic importance (Akgün & Senyücel-Gündoğar, 2013; Kalın, 2011). The democratic traditions of governance and public policy of Turkey, therefore, set it apart from its neighbouring territory, and make it an independent, secure and preferred venue, especially for those coming from autocratic and theocratic political systems and regimes like Iran. Operating as a 'safe' land also serves as a tool of nation-branding, promoting the country's image and highlighting its regional activism and dominance further contributing to the creation of 'inferior' status for those international students, suggesting that they have lower standards in their home country.

In accordance with the objective of internationalisation in higher education, and by virtue of recent improvements at national and institutional levels in recruiting international students, Turkey has recently sharpened its efforts and expanded its relations with the European and the EU member countries (Çetinsaya, 2014). Being a transcontinental country, Turkey has created its own unique position by taking advantage of these multilateral relations with Europe and elevating attraction in the context of ISM, and using internationalisation as a means of establishing and furthering relationships with the Middle East. Accordingly, offering access to Europe, employment and income opportunities, benefits of the Bologna Process, European type of higher education and low cost of living have been main moves of Turkey in attracting international students from the Middle East countries (e.g. Aras & Mohammed, 2018; Özer, 2012). Nevertheless, these are additional ways in which supply-demand factors within the internationalisation project lead to specific constructions of international students as 'supplicants', 'inferiors', 'people with education deficit' and 'beneficiaries of the system' in the host country, Turkey, representing it as a 'superior' system.

Challenges to ISM and Its Influence on Student Constructions in Turkey

It is evident that Turkey aspires to expand its international student capacity from its nearby regions including the Middle East countries. Even more, Turkey's current policy vision relative to international students is to increase enrolments, up to 200,000 students by 2023 (YTB, 2020). This suggests that Turkey's primary understanding of 'development' in the ISM area is currently related to the number of students from the region. However, a number of concerns are shared by scholars in response to the rapidly increased numbers of international students while disregarding the current problems of Turkish higher education system (Gözler, 2019), because accepting much more international students in short time without strengthening current HEIs is not sustainable and may negatively affect both international students and home students. For example, a two-thirds majority of Turkish universities have been opened since 2006, and almost all universities suffer from academic, structural and functional difficulties (Acar, 2012; Doğan, 2013; Habibi, 2017). In line with considerable previous research about rapid expansion of higher education institutions (e.g. Bloom & Rosovsky, 2007; Levin & Xu, 2005; Trow, 2007), this unprecedented expansion in Turkish higher education has inevitably created problems with staffing, teaching and learning, funding and infrastructure (Çetinsaya, 2014; Özoğlu et al., 2016).

With regard to staffing, the already fragile number of academic staff in universities has been unable to meet the excessive demand due to the rapid growth in the first place (Çetinsaya, 2014). At the same time, continuing conditions have led to dramatic increases in student-faculty ratio and in faculty workload likewise (Doğan, 2013; Habibi, 2017). Along with other challenges, the lack of academic staff has invariably resulted in adjunct teaching staff being recruited for short terms from other HEIs outside the university (Bloom & Rosovsky, 2007). Accordingly, the quality of instruction and research has decreased with the sharp growth in tertiary enrolment (Habibi, 2017; Yavuz, 2010). The respective drop in teaching quality may well stem from the difficulty in hiring qualified faculty (Doğan, 2013), whereas the decline in research quality is closely associated with inadequate funding resources due to the transition to mass higher education over a fairly short period (Acar, 2012). These developments have been accompanied by issues in particular functional areas related to institutional infrastructure needs (Altınsoy, 2011). There has been a general shift to more crowded classes, a lack of sufficient maintenance in classrooms and across university campuses, and limited quality educational materials and research facilities including laboratories, libraries, research centres, required hardware and software, creating a disadvantaged learning environment and campus life for home students.

These issues and concerns, which are also closely linked to the quality of education and training offered to international students, may prove that HEIs are not able to operate, establish and maintain quality without accompanying expansion in resources (Altbach, 2011; Bloom & Rosovsky, 2007), creating a dilemma for Turkey to invest in quantity or quality. Given that the government provides scholarships to almost half of the international students coming to Turkey (Özoğlu et al., 2016; Radmard, 2017), this leads to arguments that the quantity of students is much more primed than the quality of education (Gözler, 2019).

Currently, the student flow from the Middle East is shared as an important progress by the officials of CoHE and related authorities. However, the internationalisation of higher education through student mobility cannot be limited to just student capacities because it is not ethical to just identify this group of students with quantities or numbers. Like home students, maybe more than them, international students experience several challenges, mostly resulting from the fact that the current HE system and universities are not ready enough to respond adequately to the needs of international students. As for the international students from Middle East countries, most of them come from quite low GDP countries where social, political and economic stabilities are quite weak, or from war and conflict zones in countries like Syria, Yemen, Palestine and Iraq. Therefore, incoming students are often financially in need of support. Some of them are supported with scholarships, but they express their financial struggles and they have work-permit limitations (Arar et al., 2020; Ercan, 2012). Due to its recent economic instability (Esen & Gumuscu, 2020), Turkey is not in a position to provide a wide range of employment opportunities for international students.

These issues shape perceptions of public and home students in a way that students of this region are stigmatised as ones who are in need of help, beneficiaries of education system and students in educational deficit. In addition to this prevailing perception, the refugee flow from Syrian war zones in recent years has changed the student profile at universities, making the Syrian student population higher than those from other Middle East countries. The refugee crisis and related conflict between Syria and Turkey also negatively affects public perception, leading to the marginalisation of these displaced international students. Syrian refugee students have to register at Turkish universities during their compulsory stay, but since their numbers have increased they are considered to be the ones using the scarce sources of the host country, especially by home students (Arar et al., 2020). Turkey's own economic challenges, more apparent in recent years, affect the well-being of home students. This ultimately feeds the idea among home students that the government is helping the people of those poor Middle East countries at their expense (Arar et al., 2020).

International students have to take one-year compulsory Turkish language preparation class, but this one-year education is criticised because of being far away from preparing these students for subsequent education, and international students are still reported to experience critical language difficulties during their education in Turkey (Gebru & Yuksel-Kaptanoglu, 2020), which constitutes a further barrier for the incoming Middle Eastern students.

One other issue is drop-outs among international students: only one-third of students graduate from universities (Özoğlu et al., 2012). In the past, few Turkish HEIs accepted international students, and these universities were organisationally more capable of responding to the needs of international students. Currently, almost all universities accept international students though newly established universities suffer from lack of resources.

To sum up, Turkey wants to accept much more international students from all regions including the Middle East. However, it seems that naïve government policies not protecting international students, universities' organisational inability to respond to the needs of international students, and the lack of local cosmopolitan perspective about diverse groups of international students challenge the lives of international students, leading to the creation of stereotypes and stigmatisation. In the media and scholarly papers, it is apparent that Turkey's primary understanding of 'development' in ISM area is currently related to the increase of number of students from the region, but neglects policies protecting rights of international students.

Conclusion

This chapter has presented a detailed contemporary overview of ISM from the Middle East region to Turkey through elaborating on two issues; how Turkey's distinctive relationships with the Middle East and Europe shapes the representations of international students coming from Middle East countries, and in what ways the current challenges of Turkish HEIs have an impact on the particular construction of international students.

Regarding the acknowledged ties between Turkey and the Middle East, Turkey positions itself as a country having strong and historic connections with the people of the Middle East (Keyman, 2016). This understanding leads to a particular perspective on incoming international students from the region, which is distinct from that of the international students from other regions like the Americas or East Asia. As evident from media speeches and policy documents identifying Turkey's stance towards the region, some of which are shared in previous sections, international students of the region are considered as the ones who need the support of their 'brothers' or 'relatives' (Vural-Yılmaz, 2018). This approach can be associated with Turkey's Neo-Ottomanist politics, which has become more apparent in the last decades (Hoffmann, 2019), though this imperial sense is rejected by Turkish authorities and instead, they define this policy with the words of 'common history and cultural depth' with the region (Wastnidge, 2019). This perspective implies that international students are primarily constructed as the agents of national policy rather than global intellectual skills. The current higher education policy, greater expansion of HEIs and attracting more international students from the region is an aim of the current administration, but the sustainability of this strategy may be weak because the assumed 'powerful and strong' relations with the region are subject to a number of threats, such as bilateral disagreements with the countries of the region.

Regarding Turkey's close relationship with the European Union, Turkey is perceived as a model country in the Middle East with its open market economy, more democratic regime, secular policies, Muslim identity and European type of higher education (Akgün & Senyücel-Gündoğar, 2013). This positive perception contributes to the flow of international students from the region, and Turkey sells these values to attract international students, most of whom cannot find opportunities to go to European countries and North America.

Depending on this advantage, Turkey aspires to take many more international students (YTB, 2020), by capitalising on its strong connections with the Middle East and selling itself as a model country for the countries of the Middle East. This strategy seems to be partly working, considering the increasing number of international students in recent years. Yet, given the current challenges of Turkish higher education, taking many more students is not sustainable for Turkish HEIs (Aydinli & Mathews, 2020). The issue of international students must be handled with a cosmopolitan approach rather than nation-state aspirations and a hegemonic perspective, which regard international students as the vectors of economic gains, political agenda and ideological tools.

Though the current study maps out the trends, rationales and dynamics guiding ISM from the ME countries to Turkey, further research and discussion are favourably needed to investigate the course of this mobility in the long term. Future researchers into learning mobility in higher education between these countries may consider contributing to the methodology of available literature by conducting qualitative studies and mixed methods research to better understand the dynamics and reasons implicit in choosing destinations for studying abroad. One more possible line for future investigation would be focusing on the academic and non-academic rationales of incoming students studying in Turkey and exploring Turkish higher education leaders' perspective on the phenomenon.

References

Acar, M. (2012). Üniversitelerde yeniden yapılanmanın aciliyeti ve yeni üniversitelerin sorunları [The urgency of restructuring in universities and the problems of the newly-founded universities]. *Journal of Education Overview*, *8*(23), 21–27.

Akgün, M., & Senyücel-Gündoğar, S. (2013). Ortadoğu'da türkiye algısı 2013 [The middle East's perception to Turkey]. *Turkish economic and social studies foundation [TESEV], foreign policy programme*. İmak.

Alkan, M. (2016). Osmanlı devletinin "İslam birliği" siyaseti: Ortadoğu'nun osmanlılaşması ["Islamic unity" policy of the Ottoman empire: Ottomanization of the middle East]. *Gazi Akademik Bakış*, *9*(18), 17–32.

Altbach, P. G. (2011). Reforming higher education in the Middle East – and elsewhere. *International Higher Education*, *64*, 2–3.

Altbach, P. G., & Engberg, D. (2014). Global student mobility: The changing landscape. *International Higher Education*, *77*, 11–13. 10.6017/ihe.2014.77.5676

Altınsoy, S. (2011). Yeni devlet üniversitelerinin gelişimi: Sorunlar ve politika önerileri [Development of new public universities: Problems and policy recommendations]. *Journal of Higher Education and Science*, *1*(2), 98–104. 10.5961/jhes.2011.015

Arar, K., Kondakci, Y., Kasikci, S. K., & Erberk, E. (2020). Higher education policy for displaced people: Implications of Turkey's higher education policy for Syrian migrants. *Higher Education Policy*, *33*, 65–285.

Aras, B., & Mohammed, Z. (2018). The Turkish government scholarship program as a soft power tool. *Turkish Studies*. 10.1080/14683849.2018.1502042

Aslan, G. (2014). Neo-liberal transformation in Turkish higher education system: A new story of a turning point: Draft proposition on the higher education law. *Journal of Critical Education Policy Studies*, *12*, 255–283.

Aydinli, E., & Mathews, J. (2020). Searching for larger status in global politics: Internationalization of higher education in Turkey. *Journal of Studies in International Education*, 1–19. 10.1177/1028315320932325

Barnett, G. A., & Wu, R. Y. (1995). The international student exchange network: 1970 & 1989. *Higher Education*, *30*, 353–368.

Bayar, Y. (2016). *Formation of the Turkish nation-state, 1920–1938*. Springer.

Bechev, D., & Hiltermann, J. (2017). Turkey's forays into the middle East. *Turkish Policy Quarterly*, *16*(3), 49–59.

Bilgin, M. S. (2011). The historical direction of Turkey's foreign policy towards the middle East. *Adam Akademi*, *1*, 61–78.

Bloom, D. E., & Rosovsky, H. (2007). Higher education in developing countries. In J. J. F. Forest, & P. G. Altbach (Eds.), *International handbook of higher education* (pp. 443–459). Springer.
Cin, M., Gümüş, S., & Weiss, F. (2021). Women's empowerment in the period of the rapid expansion of higher education in Turkey: Developments and paradoxes of gender equality in the labour market. *Higher Education*, *81*, 31–50. 10.1007/s10734-020-00587-2
Council of Higher Education (2020). *Higher education data management system*. https://istatistik.yok.gov.tr/
Çelik, Z., & Gür, B. S. (2014). Yükseköğretim sistemlerinin yönetimi ve üniversite özerkliği: Küresel eğilimler ve türkiye örneği [The governance of higher education systems and university autonomy: Global trends and the case of Turkey]. *Journal of Higher Education and Science*, *4*(1), 18–27.
Çetinsaya, G. (2014). *Growth, quality, internationalization: A road map for Turkey higher education*. Publication of Higher Education Council (in Turkish).
De Wit, H., Ferencz, I., & Rumbley, L. E. (2013). International student mobility: European and U.S. perspectives. *Perspectives: Policy and Practice in Higher Education*, *17*(1), 17–23.
Doğan, D. (2013). Yeni kurulan üniversitelerin sorunları ve çözüm önerileri [Problems of newly-founded universities and solution offers]. *Journal of Higher Education and Science*, *3*(2), 108–116. 10.5961/jhes.2013.065
Doğramacı, İ (2007). *Türkiye'de ve dünyada yükseköğretim yönetimi [Higher education governance in Turkey and the world]*. Meteksan.
Dölen, E. (2009). *Osmanlı döneminde Darülfünun [darülfünun during the ottoman period] (1863–1922)*. Bilgi Üniversitesi Yayınları.
Economist Intelligence Unit. (2019). *Democracy index 2018: Me too? Political participation, protest and democracy*. https://www.eiu.com/public/topical_report.aspx?campaignid=Democracy2018.
Eğilmez, M. (2018). *Değişim sürecinde türkiye [Turkey in the process of change]*. Remzi Kitabevi.
Ekşi, M., & Erol, M. S. (2018). The rise and fall of Turkish soft power and public diplomacy. *Gazi Akademik Bakış*, *11*(23), 15–45.
Elhusseini, F. (2018). *The Arab spring effect on Turkey's role, decision-making and foreign policy*. Cambridge Scholars Publishing.
Ercan, M. S. (2012). *Uluslararası öğrencilerin uyum sorunlarının incelenmesi ve bu sorunların çözümüne yönelik beklentilerin araştırılması [examination of cultural adaptation problems of international students and their expectations toward the solutions of these problems]* (uzmanlık tezi). Yurtdışı Türkler ve Akraba Topluluklar Başkanlığı: Ankara.
Erdoğan, A. (2015). Current and future prospects for the Bologna process in the Turkish higher education system. In A. Curaj, L. Matei, R. Pricopie, J. Salmi, & P. Scott (Eds.). *The European higher education area: Between critical reflections and future policies* (pp. 743–762). 10.1007/978-3-319-20877-0
Erensü, S., & Madra, Y. M. (2020). Neoliberal politics in Turkey. *The Oxford Handbook of Turkish Politics*. 10.1093/oxfordhb/9780190064891.013.17
Esen, B., & Gumuscu, S. (2020). Why did Turkish democracy collapse? A political economy account of AKP's authoritarianism? *Party Politics*, 1–17. Advance online publication. 10.1177/1354068820923722

European Association of Quality Assurance in Higher Education. (2020). *Member and affiliate database*. https://www.enqa.eu/membership-database/theqc-turkish-higher-education-quality-council-2/

European Commission. (2019). *Erasmus+ higher education impact study: Final report*. Luxembourg: Publications of the European Union. https://op.europa.eu/en/publication-detail/-/publication/94d97f5c-7ae2-11e9-9f05-01aa75ed71a1/language-en

European Higher Education Area. (2020). *How does the Bologna Process work?* https://ehea.info/page-how-does-the-bologna-process-work

Fromkin, D. (2009). *A peace to end all peace: The fall of the Ottoman empire and the creation of the modern Middle East*. Henry Holt and Company.

Furuzan, V. G. (2012). Adaptation to the Bologna process: The case of Turkey. *Excellence in Higher Education*, *3*, 104–110.

Gebru, M. S., & Yuksel-Kaptanoglu, I. (2020). Adaptation challenges for international students in Turkey. *Open Journal of Social Sciences*, *8*, 262–278.

Gök, E., & Gümüş, S. (2018). International student recruitment of Turkish universities: Rationales and strategies. *Annual review of comparative and international education 2017: International perspectives on education and society* (pp. 231–255). 10.1108/S1479-367920180000034019

Gözler, K. (2019). Problem of number of foreign students in universities. http://www.anayasa.gen.tr/yabanci-ogrenci.htm#_ftn4 (in Turkish).

Guruz, K. (2011). *Higher education and international student mobility in the global knowledge economy: Revised and updated second edition*. Suny Press.

Günel, G. (2009). Producing neoliberal subjects: The case of Koç university. *Berkeley Journal of Sociology*, *53*, 4–25.

Habibi, N. (2017). Higher education policies and overeducation in Turkey. *European Journal of Higher Education*, *7*(4), 440–449. 10.1080/21568235.2017.1308832

Hayes, A. (2017). The teaching excellence framework in the United Kingdom: An opportunity to include international students as "equals"? *Journal of Studies in International Education*, *21*(5), 483–497. 10.1177/1028315317720768

Hayes, A. (2018). Nation boundedness and international students' marginalisation: What's emotion got to do with it? *International Studies in Sociology of Education*, *27*(2–3), 288–306.

Hoffmann, C. (2019). Neo-Ottomanism, Eurasianism or securing the region? A longer view on Turkey's interventionism. *Conflict, Security & Development*, *19*(3), 301–307.

Jon, J. E., Lee, J. J., & Byun, K. (2014). The emergence of a regional hub: Comparing international student choices and experiences in South Korea. *Higher Education*, 67, 691–710. 10.1007/s10734-013-9674-0

Kahraman, S. (2011). Turkey and the European union in the middle East: Reconciling or competing with each other? *Turkish Studies*, *12*(4), 699–716.

Kalın, İ (2011). Soft power and public diplomacy in Turkey. *Perceptions*, *16*(3), 5–23.

Kavak, Y., & Baskan, G. (2001). Educational policies and applications of Turkey towards Turkic republics and communities. *Hacettepe University Faculty of Education Journal*, *20*, 92–103.

Kaytaz, E. S. (2021). Held at the gates of Europe: Barriers to abolishing immigration detention in Turkey. *Citizenship Studies*, *25*(2), 203–223. https://doi.org/10.1080/13621025.2020.1859192

Keyman, E. F. (2016). Turkish foreign policy in the post-Arab spring era: From pro-active to buffer state. *Third World Quarterly*, *37*(12), 2274–2287.

Kondakci, Y. (2011). Student mobility reviewed: Attraction and satisfaction of international students in Turkey. *Higher Education*, *62*(5), 573–592. 10.1007/s10734-011-9406-2

Kondakci, Y., Caliskan, O, Sahin, B. B., Yilik, M. A., & Demir, C. E. (2016). Regional internationalization in higher education between Turkey and the Balkans. *Bilig*, *78*, 287–308.

Krücken, G. (2021). Multiple competitions in higher education: A conceptual approach. *Innovation*, *23*(2), 163–181.

Levin, H. M., & Xu, Z. (2005). Issues in the expansion of higher education in the People's Republic of China. *The China Review*, *5*(1), 33–59.

Madichie, N. O. (2015). An overview of higher education in the Arabian gulf. *International Journal of Business and Emerging Markets*, *7*(4), 326–335.

Marginson, S. (2007). The public/private divide in higher education: A global revision. *Higher Education*, *53*, 307–333.

Marginson, S. (2013). Equals or others? Mobile students in a nationally bordered world. In S. Sovic, & M. Blythman (Eds.), *International students negotiating higher education: Critical perspectives* (pp. 9–27). Routledge.

Meşe, İ (2019). Bir mekan olarak taşra üniversitesi ve sosyolojinin taşrası: Eleştirel bir deneyim analizi *['Taşra' university as a space and 'taşra' of sociology: A critical analysis of experience]*. *Moment Dergi*, *6*(1), 209–226.

Mizikaci, F. (2003). Quality systems and accreditation in higher education: An overview of Turkish higher education. *Quality in Higher Education*, *9*(1), 95–106.

Murinson, A. (2006). The strategic depth doctrine of Turkish foreign policy. *Middle Eastern Studies*, *42*(6), 945–964. 10.1080/00263200600923526

Oğuzlu, T. (2008). Middle easternization of Turkey's foreign policy: Does Turkey dissociate from the West? *Turkish Studies*, *9*(1), 3–20. 10.1080/14683840701813960

Organisation for Economic Co-Operation and Development (2009). Education at a glance 2009: OECD indicators. https://www.oecd.org/education/skills-beyond-school/43636332.pdf

Oztig, L. I. (2020). The Turkish–Greek border crisis and COVID-19. *Borders in Globalization Review*, *2*(1), 78–81.

Öniş, Z. (2004). Turkish modernisation and challenges for the new Europe. *Perceptions: Journal of International Affairs*, *9*(3), 5–28.

Özcan, Y. Z. (2011). Challenges to the Turkish higher education system. In the *22nd International Conference on Higher Education*, Bilkent University, Ankara.

Özer, M. (2012). Türkiye'de uluslararası öğrenciler [international students in Turkey]. *Journal of Higher Education and Science*, *2*(1), 10–13. 10.5961/jhes.2012.027

Özoğlu, M., Gür, B. S., & Coşkun, İ (2012). *Küresel eğilimler ışığında Türkiye'de uluslararası öğrenciler*. SETA Publications.

Özoğlu, M., Gür, B. S., & Gümüş, S. (2016). Rapid expansion of higher education in Turkey: The challenges of recently established public universities (2006–2013). *Higher Education Policy*, *29*, 21–39.

Özpek, B. B., & Tanriverdi-Yaşar, N. (2018). Populism and foreign policy in Turkey under the AKP rule. *Turkish Studies*, *19*(2), 198–216. 10.1080/14683849.2017.1400912

Radmard, S. (2017). Türk üniversitelerindeki uluslararası öğrencilerin yükseköğretim taleplerini etkileyen etkenlerin incelenmesi [exploration of the factors effecting higher education demands of international students in Turkish universities]. *Journal of Higher Education & Science*, *7*(1), 67–77.

Rizvi, F. (2009). Global mobility and the challenges of educational research and policy. *Globalization and the Study of Education*, *108*(2), 268–289.

Saraçoğlu, C., & Demirkol, Ö (2015). Nationalism and foreign policy discourse in Turkey under the AKP rule: Geography, history and national identity. *British Journal of Middle Eastern Studies*, *42*(3), 301–319.

She, Q., & Wotherspoon, T. (2013). International student mobility and highly skilled migration: A comparative study of Canada, the United States, and the United Kingdom. *Springer Plus*, *2*(1), 132.

Siltaoja, M., Juusola, K., & Kivijärvi, M. (2019). World-class fantasies: A neo-colonial analysis of international branch campuses. *Organization*, *26*(1), 75–97.

Sovic, S., & Blythman, M. (Eds.) (2013). *International students negotiating higher education: Critical perspectives*. Routledge.

The Scientific and Technological Research Council of Turkey (2020). *Yabancılara yönelik eğitim bursları*. https://www.tubitak.gov.tr/tr/burslar/yabancilara-yonelik/egitim-burs-programlari

Trow, M. A. (2007). Reflections on the transition from elite to mass to universal access: Forms and phases of higher education in modern societies since WW-II. In J. J. F. Forest, & P. G. Altbach (Eds.), *International handbook of higher education* (pp. 243–280). Springer.

Turan, K. (2017). Sources of conflict in the Middle East: Borders or stratified identities? *The Journal of Defense Sciences*, *16*(1), 85–113.

Tür, Ö (2019). Turkey's role in Middle East and gulf security. *Asian Journal of Middle Eastern and Islamic Studies*, *13*(4), 592–603.

United Nations Educational Scientific and Cultural Organization. (2019). *Outbound internationally mobile students by host region*. http://data.uis.unesco.org/Index.aspx?queryid=172

United Nations Educational Scientific and Cultural Organization. (2020). *Institute for statistics*. https://data.worldbank.org/indicator/SE.TER.ENRR?end=2018&locations=1A&start=1970&view=chart

United Nations High Commissioner for Refugees. (2020). *Refugees and asylum-seekers in Turkey*. https://www.unhcr.org/tr/en/refugees-and-asylum-seekers-in-turkey

Vural-Yılmaz, D. (2018). Studying abroad: Experiences of international students in a Turkish university. *Journal of Higher Education*, *8*(1), 23–32.

Wastnidge, E. (2019). Imperial grandeur and selective memory: Re-assessing neo-Ottomanism in Turkish foreign and domestic politics. *Middle East Critique*, *28*(1), 7–28.

Yavuz, A. (2010). Üniversiteler liseleşiyor, liseler yok oluyor! [Universities become high schools; high schools perish]. *Contemporary Education Journal*, *35*(374), 30–40.

Yurtdışı Türkler ve Akraba Topluluklar Başkanlığı. (2020). *International student mobility*. https://www.ytb.gov.tr/uluslararasi-ogrenciler/uluslararasi-ogrenci-hareketliligi

Author biographies

Dr Omer Caliskan is Associate Professor in the Department of Educational Sciences at Yozgat Bozok University, Turkey. Omer received his Ph.D. in Educational Administration and Planning from Middle East Technical University in 2017. His research interests include higher education, international student mobility, graduate education, education policy, educational leadership, and educational administration.

Dr Hilal Buyukgoze is currently working as a researcher in the Department of Educational Sciences at Hacettepe University, in Ankara – Turkey. Hilal received her Ph.D. in Educational Administration from Hacettepe University in 2021. Her research interests include data-driven school effectiveness and improvement, higher education, education policy, and leadership. Hilal's prior research about higher education focused on the role of soft power on internationalisation, widening policies among the EHEA, identity development of research assistants, and university students' attitudes toward multicultural education and democratic values.

Chapter 5

International Credit Mobilities of Syrians during Conflict

Opportunities and Challenges

Sulaiman Mouselli

Introduction

With over 415,000 students enrolled in the academic year 2019/2020, the Syrian population of higher education students is one of the largest in the region with around 100,000 students entering Higher Education (HE) studies every year according to the Ministry of Higher Education and Scientific Research (MOHESR). The Syrian crisis triggered the largest influx of refugees and displacement in 21st century and increased national student mobilities between Syrian universities. The closure of universities in cities, outside the government control, forced thousands of students to move to universities in safe areas. MOHESR ordered public universities to host those students and let them attend classes, even without documents and admit exams until it is safe to go back to their home universities. In many cases, they were permitted to transfer their registration to the hosting universities upon fulfilling certain conditions.

However, while the Syrian conflict led to greater *national* mobility, it has reduced opportunities for *international* mobility. The international mobilities of Syrian students remain more complex because of limited opportunities, recognition complexities and favouritism. The international community has taken responsibility for reintegrating Syrian refugees into higher education through scholarships from international donors such as the UNESCO and many programmes (e.g., Albert Einstein German Academic Refugee Initiative (DAFI)), and through a number of projects funded by the European Union such as Higher and Further Education Opportunities and Perspectives for Syrians (HOPES), Language and Academic Skills and E-learning Resources Project (LASER), Refugees Education Support in Mena Countries (RESCUE), and Massive Open Online courses eNhancing LInguistic and Transversal skills for social inclusion and Employability (MOONLITE). DAFI for example, is a scholarship programme that offers qualified refugee students the possibility to earn an undergraduate degree in their country of asylum. This programme is supported by the German Government, UNHCR and private donors. An EU-funded project, HOPES,

DOI: 10.4324/9781003138457-7

cooperates with an NGO specialised in providing online education called KIRON, to offer free online courses to Syrian refugees and asylum seekers to enable them re-integrate into higher education. LASER is another EU-funded project that supported Syrians and disadvantaged Jordanian youth in Jordan and Lebanon who could not access, or who had dropped out of formal education, to find new opportunities to continue their higher education. RESCUE is a capacity building project in the field of higher education that aims at structuring specific services supporting refugee students in resuming their academic training path in Syrian neighbouring countries of Lebanon, Jordan, Iraq as well as in Turkey. MOONLITE engages Syrian refugees on online accredited courses and MOOCs. However, the majority of these scholarship opportunities are fully or partially based on providing online education to upscale educational opportunities for refugees, increase educational equity and overcome the problem of restricted capacities in hosting universities (Halkic & Arnold, 2019).

Syrian students from inside Syria, however, have no access to such scholarships. They can only apply for general scholarships such as Deutscher Akademischer Austauschdienst (DAAD) scholarships, the UK government scholarships (Chevening), Karim Rida Said Foundation (KRSF) scholarships along with other international scholarships (e.g., the government of Hungary scholarships (stipendium hungaricum) and the government of Turkey scholarships (Turkiye Burslari). Those scholarships are available for postgraduate studies and are rarely offered at undergraduate level. In addition, many opportunities that were meant to be granted to Syrians inside Syria were diverted towards Syrian refugees (e.g., Erasmus Mundus program) as a result of the refugee crisis. Consequently, many scholarships are open to Syrian refugees while very few are made available to students inside Syria.

Since 2014, the Education, Audiovisual and Culture Executive Agency (EACEA), which is an agency of the European Union located in Brussels responsible for the management of certain parts of the EU's funding programmes in the fields of education, culture, audiovisual, sport, citizenship and volunteering, has developed a short-term mobility exchange programme to Europe and from Europe to other parts of the world for students, and both academic and administrative staff. The programme is called International Credit Mobility (ICM) programme. This two-way mobility programme allows students to study at both undergraduate and postgraduate levels in a foreign university for 3–12 months and obtain credits which are then recognised at the sending institution as part of their degree. There are also grants for staff mobility of 5 to 60 days. The official EU statistics indicate that the number of Syrian students and staff moving to Europe, as part of this program, increased from 35 in 2015 to 76 in 2018 and peaked in 2017 at 119 mobilities (European Commission, 2018b).

The majority of current research on Syrian displacement is centred on the mobility of displaced Syrians (World Bank, 2020) with little attention to mobilities of Syrian students who remained inside Syria. International student mobility constitutes an important part of such mobilities and has attracted increasing interest and popularity among Syrian students in the last few years. Several reasons contribute towards this observed interest, despite many obstacles that hinder the Syrian students' participation in these programmes.

This chapter aims to illustrate the status quo of international student mobilities between Syrian higher education institutions and EU universities. It explains the impact such mobility programme has on participating students and Syrian higher education institutions. It also discusses the challenges students and higher education institutions face when taking part in this programme and offer certain recommendations and venues for intervention to overcome such challenges. The data I draw on in this chapter are based on interviews conducted with students who are currently benefitting from the ICM programme or previously participated in it. By exploring the challenges that face mobilised students and how participating students experience international mobility, the chapter reveals specific representations of Syrian students and the assumptions that have been made about those students at the participating universities, as well as the very policies governing their mobility.

Background

Syria has always been a preferred destination for foreign undergraduate and postgraduate students who specialise in Arabic and Islamic studies. Damascus University, for example, has cooperated in 2003 with the University of Maryland in Arabic for Interactive Communication (AFIC) initiative to promote new methods and approaches to the study of Arabic at higher levels of proficiency. However, the overwhelming mobilities of Syrian students were at postgraduate level, motivated by the public universities delegations to qualify their academic staff. Undergraduate mobilities for Syrian students were only available on ad hoc basis and only as part of governmental exchange agreements.

The Syrian MoHESR has always supported student and staff mobilities. MoHESR encouraged Syrian public universities to sign agreements and memoranda of understanding with international universities. Also, MoHESR established the Syrian national committee of the International Association for the Exchange of Students for Technical Experience (IAESTE) to administer the mobility of Syrian students for training purposes. Moreover, private universities had until recently been required, as part of their accreditation process, to sign at least three agreements with international universities (MoHESR, 2020). However, war conditions that force the closure of some public universities and the relocation of many private universities to safe areas increase the financial burdens on Syrian universities and make them more concerned to survive than flourishing.

Another important outcome of the war conditions that have troubled Syria since 2011 and hit Syrian universities financially is the sharp decline in student mobilities from the United States, Europe and the rest of the world to Syria to study Arabic, Religion and other disciplines, as well as from Syria to Europe to obtain PhDs and qualify as university lecturers (Central Bureau of Statistics, 2019). Plenty of scholarships have been made available to Syrian refugees in host countries and through international donors. An evaluation report for a number of EU scholarships indicate that those scholarships target the most vulnerable youth who are more prone to financial stress but meet the legal and academic requirements; the scholarships aim to bring refugees back to higher education, improve their future perspectives and avoid social and political disruptions at host communities (European Commission, 2018a). However, a survey of Syrian scholars whose projects were funded by the EU's Madad Fund indicates that their scholarships were not enough to cover their day-to-day needs, forcing them to work while studying and affecting their academic performance (European Commission, 2017). Also, scholars in the same survey claim that the fundable subjects were very limited, leaving them studying subjects that were not their first choices and might not meet their abilities (European Commission, 2017). This could be due to the limited financial resources available and large number of applications for scholarships that obligate the management of such scholarships to exclude subjects such as medicine and dentistry from the funding list. Despite all these shortcomings, this new system where scholarships are available to Syrians, though in limited quantity and quality, encourages Syrian residents to apply for scholarships at both undergraduate and postgraduate levels and gradually created a culture that is mobility friendly.

The ICM programme inherited part of the well-known Erasmus Mundus programme that ended on 31 December 2013. In general, ICMs are run by both EU higher education institutions and their Syrian partners for their students and staff only and cover all available study cycles for common disciplines. The main differences between both programmes are that ICM programme is for short-term mobilities while Erasmus Mundus accommodated both short and long-term mobilities. Also, ICM programme does not fund degree-seeking mobilities and that sending institution has more power in selecting its candidates. In addition, ICM is managed directly by National Erasmus Offices (NEOs) in EU countries while Erasmus Mundus was centralised in Brussels. A recent development in student mobility is the possibility of developing jointly blended mobility curricula and activities amid the spread of COVID-19 and expected travel difficulties (European Commission, 2021).

The participation of Syrian higher education institutions in ICM is still modest. Partly because the Syrian war made EU universities reluctant to exchange students and staff with Syrian universities for fear that they will not return to Syria upon the completion of their mobilities. As a result, the Syrian share of the south-Mediterranean ICM budget for the period 2015–2018 was 1 percent compared to 8 percent for Lebanon (European Commission, 2018b). However, an increasing number of EU universities are now enthusiastic to engage with Syrian universities in such programme on a one-directional basis (host but not send staff and students). The number of staff and students moving to Syria from the EU has increased from 35 in 2015 to 119 in 2017 before it dropped to 76 in 2018 while mobilities in the other direction rose from zero in 2015 and 2016 to 15 in 2018 (European Commission, 2018b). The decline in the number of student mobilities to Europe may be attributed to that not only EU universities become selective in hosting Syrian students but also EU embassies became selective in granting visas to certain Syrian universities which their students have record of overstaying in Europe. Universities from Spain, Portugal and Italy are among the most active ones in ICM programmes hosting Syrian students and staff.

The European Commission (2021, p. 41) identifies the objectives of student mobilities as follow:

- ‘Expose students to different views, knowledge, teaching and research methods as well as work practices in the study field;
- Develop their transversal skills such as communication, language, problem-solving, inter-cultural skills and research skills;
- Develop their forward-looking skills; such as digital skills, that will enable them to tackle the challenges of today and tomorrow;
- Facilitate personal development such as the ability to adapt to new situations and self-confidence’.

The ICM programme appeals to students for a number of academic and personal reasons. The literature on students’ drives to apply for international mobility programmes within Europe identifies employment and residency opportunities and the quality of student experience (Amendola & Restaino, 2017; Verbik & Lasanowski, 2007) as well as test international life and study experiences (Amendola & Restaino, 2017; Novak et al., 2013) and to develop international competencies (Amendola & Restaino, 2017; Kumpikaite`& Duoba, 2011) and to improve their proficiency in foreign languages and academic knowledge (Amendola & Restaino, 2017; Caviezel et al., 2016; Cosciug, 2013), In addition, students perceive international mobilities as an important factor that would ease the way to find their first jobs (Severino et al., 2014).

Students’ Motives for Participating in the ICM Program

To explore Syrian students’ motives for participating in ICM, I conducted face-to-face interviews in addition to virtual interviews using Zoom application. These interviews took place from 15 March 2021 until 20 April 2021.

Interviews were conducted on a volunteer basis after an announcement to students. A total of twenty students directly participated in the interviews, of which 40 percent were females. Students eligible for interviews were those who participated or currently participating in ICM. Nine of them returned to Syria, while the remaining 11 are either continuing their post-graduate study, working or living in Europe. Students have been given pseudonyms here for reasons of anonymity.

The study found that motives can be classified into five main groups. Those motives are not mutually exclusive but complementary and together constitute the reasons behind Syrian students' desire to participate in the ICM programme. These are academic motives, professional motives, cultural and self-related motives and war-related motives.

Academic Motives

Academic motives comprise of a set of essential motives that are related to experiencing new curricula and teaching styles as well as taking advantage of the mobility to obtain a scholarship for further study. Loujy, for example, stated: 'I was interested in the opportunity of benefitting from an interesting curriculum that complemented my studies [....]'.

Many scholars take advantage of their mobilities to apply for master scholarships as they become closer to potential supervisors and can convince funding agencies of their potentials especially if they perform well in their attempted modules during the short-term mobility period (Huják, 2015). Saeed, who managed to obtain a scholarship to continue his master's degree, for example, stated: 'I want to continue my postgraduate study in Europe [...]'.

More importantly, passing their attempted modules eases the transfer process to the host university given that bachelor degrees, especially in Engineering and Business Administration, require studying fewer years in EU universities compared to Syrian universities. Jomana, for example, explained: 'I succeed in transferring the credits I obtained during my mobility and I am now targeting to graduate from my host university [...]'.

Professional Motives

There are a number of professional motives that encourage Syrian students to take part in ICM programme. First of all, they believe that spending a semester or two in EU universities will make a huge added value to their CVs and make a big difference to their future career. Laila, who is currently a full-time employee in Portugal, for example, said: 'I wanted to improve and widen my career prospects in the future, I wanted to enhance my future employability abroad, I wanted to try new things and have new experiences, I wanted to get to know the country better as I consider it as a future workplace, I wanted to improve my CV [...]'.

Cultural and Self-Related Motives

Studying in cosmopolitan culture also enhances intercultural skills and improves students' language skills. The intercultural and enhancing language skills motives represent the second and third main identified motives for students mobilised to Lisbon (Lampl, 2018). Raouf, for example, stated: 'I wanted to learn more about the culture of the destination, I wanted to meet people from different cultures [...]'. Mouyad, on the other hand, said: '[...] I wanted to live on my own for a period, I wanted to learn another language and improve my language skills [...]'. Self-motives are those related to develop personally in terms of skills and experience and which will increase students' self-confidence and self-esteem. Naya, for example, stated: 'I wanted to develop my soft skills, I wanted to try new things and have new experiences [...]'.

War-Related Motives

International credit mobilities allow students to move away from the war conditions and escape stress and anxiety that accompany such conditions, especially that those mobilities are financially covered and the monthly pay to students is enough to cover their living expenses without the need to their parent financial support. Saeed, for example, stated: 'I wanted to escape the difficult life conditions in Syria [...]'.

Universities' Motives for Participating in the ICM Program

Although Syrian public and private universities both wish to participate in the ICM program, they are in different administrative and financial positions regarding their willingness and reasons for participation. Some universities look at this programme as lucrative activity with not much added value. Others do not have the trained human resources or know how to access the programme especially with the absence of awareness sessions because there is no active Erasmus+ national office in Syria since 2016 as indicated by the list of active National Erasmus+ offices on EACEA website. In addition, some universities are afraid of bearing financial consequences if participating in this programme.

The motives for participation in ICM programme for public universities and private universities are also quite different. Public universities usually attract students with higher marks and from all financial backgrounds given their very cheap tuition fees. However, overcrowded classes resulted from displacements, and limited working hours at public universities redirected many wealthy and smart students toward private universities. Hence, the student community at private universities is dominated by financially better-off students. Private universities consider participating in ICM programme as a marketing tool to attract more students especially those who have the aspiration to study in the EU. More than half of all interviewed students mentioned that their universities use ICM programme as marketing tools.

The recent competition between private Syrian universities to rank higher according to ranking tools such as webometrics, which rate websites and give more weight to international activities and visibility, has changed their view of ICMs and made them keener to take part in ICM activities. Higher ranking position is also a marketing tool when attracting new students. In addition to this marketing motive, public and private universities believe that engaging in such programme exposes their students and staff to the opportunity to advanced teaching and research environment and enhances their internationalisation position. The internationalisation strategy at Arab International University, a private university in Syria, states that 'International Credit Mobility (ICM) programme fits very well in its internationalisation strategy and provides AIU students and staff with the right opportunity to experience different cultures and teaching environments'(Arab International University, 2020).

The main difference between participating public and private universities is in the study cycle that they exchange students at. Public universities prefer exchanging students at postgraduate level because public universities follow the semester system which makes it impossible to recognise credits at undergraduate level. On the contrary, private universities can only exchange students on undergraduate level because they do not have postgraduate studies and they follow the US credit hour system that accommodates recognition.

ICM – The Current Situation

Establishing partnerships in ICM programme is based on the EU partners' willingness to exchange students and staff with Syrian universities. However, the war conditions in Syria and the influx of Syrian refugees to Europe made EU universities reluctant to host more Syrian students and staff. However, few instances of participation in ICM can be traced back to previous relations in Erasmus Mundus programme where partners expanded their partnership after the end of Erasmus Mundus programme to ICM programme. Syrian universities approached EU universities requesting their partnerships in ICM programme but with little success.

Different practices can be observed in the applications of ICM programme by Syrian universities. Public universities request nominations for student mobilities by the designated faculties with no official public announcements. Postgraduate students are usually nominated by relevant faculties to gain research experience and attend workshops. However, difficulties in obtaining acceptance letters from the EU hosting university in addition to the delay in correspondences mean that better connected students may have more chances to apply and to be accepted. Private universities usually make public calls for student mobilities with certain conditions for applicants followed by interviews (see for example Arab International University and Al Andalus University websites). In certain cases, students submit their documents online with no need for interviews at the home university which gives the host university more power in selecting the candidates.

The Arab International University (AIU), a pioneer in Erasmus+ projects, has developed certain practices in announcing calls for interested students to participate in student mobilities. It develops the following set of conditions for students who wish to apply for ICMs (Arab International University, 2020)

- The student's Accumulated Grade Point Average (AGPA) should not be less than 3 out of 4.
- The student's level of English proficiency should not be lower than upper-intermediate.
- The student has not benefited from a similar scholarship during his/her university life.
- The number of credit hours completed should be at least 50.
- The number of credit hours remaining shall be 32 hours or more.
- The student has not received a university penalty of any kind during his/her university life.

The above-listed conditions aim at achieving certain purposes. The first condition of achieving certain AGPA aims at ensuring that the student has a minimum level of academic performance to pass modules during his/her mobility. Moreover, the second condition ensures that the student is able to understand lessons and communicate with academics and students. Furthermore, the third condition is meant to widen the student participation in the ICM programme and give more opportunities to students how do not benefit from previous mobilities to participate in future mobilities. The fourth and fifth conditions aim to nominate students with minimum knowledge in their disciplines and minimise the possibilities of leaving their home university for good. In case, a student would like to stay at the host institution after mobility period ends, the student will sacrifice at least two years of study at home institution. The last condition aims to select only students with sound conduct and behaviour during their study at home institution. Hence, an ideal candidate would be a third-year disciplined student who is English literate, and never participated in ICM before.

After meeting the conditions above, students are invited to interview by a committee that consists of academic and administrative staff to select the suitable students. The committee emphasises understanding their motives for participation in the program, any previous international experience, and personal characteristics. The committee informs the interviewees of the mobilities terms and conditions as determined by the Erasmus plus programme and the conditions set by MoHESR for credit recognition. Interviewed students are ranked on the basis of their AGPA, English fluency, motives, previous international experiences, and personal characteristics and then nominated to the host institution.

The communications between mobility students and their home institutions continue during their mobilities. International relations office ensures they are settled down at the host institution and follow up their performance during mobility. The office works with students on amending the learning agreements if pre-selected modules turn to be unavailable or if they wish to study additional modules.

ICM Assumptions and Policies

Clearly, EACEA has high expectations from ICM programme in terms of impact and participation. However, certain assumptions and misassumptions dramatically affect those who can participate in the ICM programme. This section reviews some of the assumptions that were flagged in the interviews with participants upon either starting or completing their mobilities.

English or Foreign Language Proficiency: The ICM programme requires that students, academic or administrative staff nominated for mobilities by the sending institution acquire the minimum language requirements to participate in the mobility which is B1. This condition, though realistic, does not consider the case of students at public universities who are unlikely to reach such level of foreign language proficiency with the majority of classes offered in Arabic. Therefore, students from lower-income backgrounds who cannot afford international or private schooling are less represented in ICM programme. Amr, for example, stated: 'I cannot imagine a student going into mobility with poor foreign language. I came across two Syrian PhD students that were unable to communicate with others and stayed most of the time at the dormitory rooms because their English was poor [...]'.

The closure of almost all EU consulates in Damascus and the boycott of many international airlines to Syria during the ongoing conflict reshape the process of obtaining visa and increases travel complexities. To obtain a visa, a student or staff has to travel to Beirut to apply for visa and then to collect it. Again, to travel to Europe, the nominated student or staff has to travel from Rafic Hariri Airport in Beirut. Moreover, the spread of COVID-19 added the extra costs of Polymerase Chain Reaction (PCR) testing. These extra costs and working days are not considered by EACEA within ICM programme, while EACEA compensates Syrian participants by one additional working day in its other programmes such as Capacity Building in Higher Education (CBHE). Such extra costs are totally ignored by EACEA within ICM programme and Syrian staff and students are not reimbursed for them. The natural consequence of this situation is that only students from rich backgrounds would apply for such mobilities which contradicts the equal opportunity principle clearly outlined by EACEA. Loujy, for example, stated; 'The visa process was a bit challenging for us as students, and I didn't get the expected assistance from the international office in the host university which consumed additional cost and time [...]'. Somar stated: 'The worst part was getting the visa it was a difficult process full of uncertainty, it took me a long waiting time which delayed my flight and I almost missed the scholarship [...] not knowing how is actually responsible for the process of getting the visa and who should help in this situation [...]'. Lana added: 'There should be consideration to allocate extra funding for Syrian students as they have to visit the corresponding embassy in Lebanon [...]'.

EACEA assumes that part or all credits passed during student mobilities will be recognised at the sending institutions. However, given that public universities are following the semester-based system, undergraduate students from public universities are less represented in ICM programme. In addition, the complications and long delay in recognising credits by MoHESR reduce the number of students from private universities who are interested in applying for ICM and disincentives students to attempt many credits while in mobility. As a result, some mobile students behave as if they are on tourist visa not giving much attention to passing the registered credits. Saeed, for example, stated: 'The recognition process of passed credits in my home institution took more than one year [...]'.

The ICM programme obligates the sending institution to prepare a public call for interest and advertise all mobility opportunities through sending institution websites and other social media. This obligation is necessary to ensure equal opportunities among all potential candidates. However, this requirement is not respected by all universities and favourism is still undermining the process of announcing the call and selecting the candidates. Those nominated students or staff are more likely to stay over and fail to return to Syria upon the completion of their mobilities. Somar added: 'From my experience, better connected students, in certain Syrian universities, are more likely to win the mobility [...]'.

The ICM programme assumes that staff taking part in academic or administrative mobilities should be rewarded or internally recognised through promotions or bonuses by their sending institutions. This is based on the correct belief that those staff will gain knowledge and/or experience during their mobilities that will be then transferred to the sending institution. However, this assumption is totally misjudged in the Syrian and developing countries' context. Syrian sending institutions consider nominating a particular person for a mobility as a reward per se and this person is neither promoted nor gets any bonus upon the completion of her/his mobility. On the contrary, such mobility will be a disadvantage in future applications. As a result, it is observable that nominated staff tends to be from the high hierarchy of the university and such mobilities have very little, if any, institutional impact.

The essence of the academic staff exchange for teaching within ICM programme is centred on the idea that this exchange will bring value to both universities. However, not all Syrian academic staff are able to lecture a class delivered in foreign language at an EU university especially as the educational gap has widened after nine years of conflict. Therefore, it is more likely that only Syrian academics with updated knowledge, usually western graduates, apply for teaching mobilities. Hence, Syrian sending institutions tend to prefer exchanging staff for training instead of teaching as they can accommodate more requests for participation.

EACEA assumes that participating in ICM activities will enhance the internationalisation position of participant organisations. Clearly, this is a legitimate assumption that expects further collaboration will start between universities in teaching, research, from initiating international joint projects, or from signing joint agreements. However, many EU universities are not enthusiastic to take this relationship further and are reluctant to strengthen their ties with Syrian universities. This could be due to the EU sanctions on Syria that put restrictions on EU travel to Syria and therefore such ICM projects turn to be a one-way road to EU without much benefit to EU universities.

EACEA assumes and permits sending institutions to charge mobile students the same fees they would have paid if they take the credits at their home institutions. However, Syrian universities sacrifice those fees and offer mobilities to their students free of charge as a tool to encourage them to participate in the available mobilities and allow extensions for their mobilities if necessary (e.g., during COVID-19 when travel conditions deteriorated).

To sum up, students and staff from wealthy backgrounds and who are English literate are more likely to take on such mobility opportunities with undergraduate students from private universities and postgraduate students from public universities. Academic staff who has a record of publications and updated knowledge get a better chance to obtain acceptance letter from host universities and therefore take part in the mobility. As a result, Syrian universities prefer exchanging administrative staff for training on exchanging academic staff for teaching because such mobilities do not require much English proficiency or updated knowledge.

Impact and Challenges

A recent impact study on students who participated in ICM conducted between 2017 and 2019 finds that students discover their ambitions while abroad and were able to re-orient their studies when they go back home to match their future careers. Students also experienced new teaching and learning methods and aim to continue to higher levels of education more than non-mobile students. In addition, mobile students improve their social cohesion as they developed their adaptability, cultural, communication and problem-solving skills which are all essential for employment. Mobile students seem to find a job quicker than non-mobile students (European Commission, 2019).

The Impact of ICM programme on both students and universities participating is enormous. The following is a discussion of the impact of this programme on both students and universities based on the above-mentioned interviews conducted with students and five years lived experience of working as international relations director at a private university in Syria;

ICM programme gives students the opportunity to develop academically. They explore diverse teaching approaches and evaluation methods that differ from the ones they used to. Although many students have high expectations from EU higher education institutions in terms of teaching quality and curricula content, some of them appreciate the flexibility they experience at host institutions while others were disappointed with teaching quality. The opportunity to experience different teaching styles makes them appreciate the quality of their education in Syria. Loujy said: 'Erasmus was a life changing experience for me, and besides any challenge I had during or after it, it was totally worth it. I'm overall grateful for my university for this chance [...]'.

ICM widens students' scope and helps them develop their intercultural skills. It enables them to establish friendships with students from all over the world and appreciate different views and habits. Also, many of them have never travelled abroad before and such opportunity makes them become more mobile, independent and self-confident. Students believe that participating in ICM programme will give them the opportunity to practice their English and may be gain another language.

ICM gives students the opportunity to use their mobilities as a tool to find scholarships for their postgraduate study (Bryła, 2015) through meeting potential supervisors and discussing proposals. Also, they are able to consult international relations office at host institution and gain knowledge on available scholarships whether offered by the host university or other sources. This enhances their employability and puts them in a better position in the job market.

ICM has significant impact on home institutions. Some universities require that nominated students achieve a minimum AGPA of 3 out of 4. This motivates students who would like to apply for ICM scholarships to study hard to obtain the required AGPA. This, in turn, is reflected in better student performance and increased students' engagement and seriousness. Also, students become more careful in their behaviour and conduct because any misbehaviour will mean that they will lose the opportunity to benefit from the ICM programme. In this regard, Lana stated: 'I wouldn't call that bias, as it is logical for the university to prioritize students with higher AGPA, had significant achievements, and familiar with the international context. This is the overall criteria that would give the participants a credit to be part of the mobility and deserve having this opportunity [...]'. In contrast, Jomana argued: 'AGPA is definitely a poor factor to select or reject a student, but I believe language skills should be more important [...]'.

Another impact the project has on participating Syrian higher education institutions is that they become more attractive to new students. Those institutions use student mobilities as a marketing tool directly in open days and conferences and indirectly through announcing calls for applications. Participating in the ICM programme is very important to the internationalisation strategy of Syrian higher education institutions and gives them the opportunity to find more EU partners for other programmes.

However, the culture of exchanging students while doing their studies at Syrian higher education institutions is still in its infancy. It faces the following challenges:

First, the public higher education system that is dominating the higher education system is not based on ECTS or American credit hours. Instead, it follows the French system where students study the same certain modules each semester. This system neither accommodates mobilities nor recognises modules passed during mobilities. This discourages undergraduate students from public universities from applying to ICM opportunities.

Second, Erasmus programme is a well-known and highly respected by European embassies and consulates. Usually, students, who are accepted for mobility by a European university to study within Erasmus programmes, are easily granted entry visas. However, the Syrian war causes the closure of almost all EU consulates working in Syria. This imposes travel difficulties to Syrian students who would like to apply for visa as they will need to travel to Lebanon to submit their visa applications. This causes extra financial burden on Syrian students. This burden is even amplified when the EU country has no consulate in Lebanon, which means that students have to travel to Cyprus to obtain visa to Portugal, for example. This increases their travel costs and is unobserved by Erasmus+ and cannot be therefore be reimbursed according to EACEA rules. On the contrary, the Italian consulate waives the visa fees for students who are apply for visa to participate in Erasmus activities.

Third, the majority of undergraduate programmes and course offering at EU universities are taught in local languages and not in English. Hence, mobility students have to acquire enough foreign language proficiency and pay extra efforts to understand course materials.

In situations where no English classes in the offering, one-to-one tutorials are arranged to enable them catch up with their colleagues. The limited availability of modules in English narrowed students choices and force them to repeat some modules already passed in home institutions which in turn reduces the number of recognised credits. Amal, for example, stated: 'My host university didn't have an English modules which limited my choices. Also, I had to take two modules on tutorial basis (one-to-one) because there were only 2 other registered Erasmus students in the class [...]'. Ghalia, who recently returned from her mobility, faced new challenges as she was forced to take her modules online due to COVID-19 lockdown. She reported: 'It should be noted that not all students have the same awareness of online education. Students should be taught how to deal with education via the Internet [...]'.

Fourth, the Syrian Ministry of Higher Education and Scientific Research's (MOHESR) process for recognising credits from foreign universities is very complicated and time consuming. MOHESR has not yet adopt Bologna process which makes it difficult to recognise mobility credits. Also, the Ministry keeps changing the conditions necessary for recognition. This causes too much confusion among students regarding the potential recognition and made them less willing to apply for ICM opportunities and to pay the effort to pass the registered modules. Even if they pass their modules at host institutions, they are reluctant to start the whole recognition process. Hence, students understand that participating in the ICM programme delay their graduation.

Fifth, Syrian higher education institutions are facing difficulties in selecting suitable candidates, those with genuine drive and how want to return to Syria upon finishing their mobilities. Some universities put strict criteria for nominating candidates to ensure they will return while others where less careful which resulted in brain drain. Syrian universities that do not apply strict selection criteria face huge brain drain and risk losing students and more importantly the trust of host institutions. Also, EU consulates and embassies become more cautious in giving visas to students that apply from those universities. That is, students or staff who failed to return to Syria upon completing their mobilities are risking no more visas to be given to their colleagues from the same university as it will be blacklisted.

Sixth, the closure of National Erasmus-plus office in Syria since 2016 contributes towards the lack of awareness of students and institution regarding mobilities terms and conditions and leads to the observed modest participation in the programme compared to other countries in the region. At the same time, this closure results in little support of the Ministry of higher education and scientific research of such programme.

Seventh, each EU host higher education institution has its own system for recruiting Syrian students which causes a lot of confusion to international relations staff at Syrian home institutions. Some EU universities require double selection process and online upload of documents while others are satisfied with home University sending them the list of selected students. Also, some host universities purchase insurance cover and provide it to students prior to their travel while others leave it to students to arrange it themselves.

Finally, the National Erasmus offices in host EU countries require documents that prove the full recognition of credits passed at their universities as part of their monitoring process. In addition, they condition granting future mobilities to the partner country by submitting documents, such as transcripts, that confirm such recognition. Until now, there is only one case of recognition of credits by the MOHESR that took around six months to be obtained.

Conclusions

The extended Syrian war has affected Syrian students' motives for participating in ICMs and consequently the representations of ICM students. Syrian students perceive the ICM as an opportunity to start a new life at EU university hoping to transfer their credits and start a new life in Europe as the maximum or just experience a new advanced teaching and learning environment that improves them personally and academically and put them in a better position in the job market at the minimum. Either way, mobile students are the winners. Generally speaking, private university students who take part in ICM programme are third-year undergraduate students who come from wealthy backgrounds and with high foreign language proficiency. Hence, they are more likely to return home once they finish their mobilities if they cannot find another scholarship to fund their study toward a full degree. However, students from public universities are more likely to be postgraduate students who have strong English proficiency and aim for permanent stay in Europe.

There is no doubt that the ICM programme represents a great opportunity for Syrian students as it changed their lives and helped them develop emotionally and academically. It also comes in a critical period of time where travel restrictions imposed on Syrian are very strong and when many Syrians are unable to fund learning journeys inside Syria not to mention to Europe. It surely meets EACEA objectives of improving mobile students' communication, language and inter-cultural skills and enabling them to gain soft skills highly valued by future employers. ICM programme also serves the reputational goals of Syrian sending institutions and improves their international positions.

However, certain suggestions can be presented to enhance the impact of this program;

1 There is an immense need to convince the higher education authorities in Syria of the importance of such programme and its crucial impact on Syrian students and institutions. Such understanding can be reached through holding workshops and meetings with the Ministry of Higher Education and Scientific Research to ease the recognition process of passed modules. Despite many attempts to convince the Ministry of adopting Bologna process, it still believes that such process is inapplicable to the Syrian higher education system. One suggestion is to designate certain number of credits in the curricula of each university as an elective module that can be filled with modules passed during student mobilities similar to the practice of Lebanese higher education institutions.
2 One possible method to overcome the issue of credit recognition is to offer more traineeship mobilities as part of ICM programme. Such training will have a long-lasting impact on the mobilised students and give them clear advantage in the job market without exposing students to the recognition dilemma. If such traineeships are made available in summer, it will attract more participants and magnify the benefits from such mobilities.
3 EACEA can recommend a unified set of selection criteria to all mobilities within ICM programme that should be applied when nominating students. The practice of certain European host universities of requiring online submission of application and documents ensure fair treatment of applicants and avoid any manipulation and conflict of interests that could arise in selecting candidates.
4 One ambitious step that will ease the recognition process and save time and costs associated with certifying documents and transcripts could be the establishment of a Blockchain platform that links host and home institutions together with related Ministries of Higher Education and that is administrated by EACEA. All certificates and transcripts can be exchanged through this platform without the need for certification and are automatically recognised. This platform can be further developed to issue a digital passport that represents student learning portfolio of both certificates and skills acquired.

References

Amendola, A., & Restaino, M. (2017). An evaluation study on students' international mobility experience. *Quality & Quantity*, *51*(2), 525–544. https://doi.org/10.1007/s11135-016-0421-3

Arab International University. (2020). Arab International University website. Retrieved March 2, 2020, from www.aiu.edu.sy

Bryła, P., (2015). Self-reported effects of and satisfaction with international student mobility: A large-scale survey among polish former Erasmus students. *Procedia-Social and Behavioral Sciences*, *191*, 2074–2082. https://doi.org/10.1016/j.sbspro.2015.04.248

Caviezel, V., Falzoni, A. M., & Vitali, S. (2016). *Esperienza erasmus: Motivazioni e timori prima della partenza*. Stat.Soc. http://www.rivista.sis-statistica.org/cms/?p=74

Central Bureau of Statistics. (2019). Syrian higher education statistics. Retrieved April 19, 2021, from http://cbssyr.sy/

Cosciug, A. (2013). The impacts of international student mobility in Romania. *Europolis*, *7*, 93–109.

Halkic, B., & Arnold, P. (2019). Refugees and online education: Student perspectives on need and support in the context of (Online) higher education. *Learning, Media and Technology*, *44*(3), 345–364. https://doi.org/10.1080/17439884.2019.1640739

Huják, J. (2015). The real benefit of an exchange programme: Moving from credit mobility to degree mobility. *In Central European Higher Education Cooperation Conference Proceedings*, July.

Kumpikaite`, V., & Duoba, K. (2011). Development of intercultural competencies by student mobility. *The Journal of the Knowledge Economy*, *4*, 41–50. https://dergipark.org.tr/en/pub/beyder/issue/3476/47289

Lampl, K. (2018). Educational tourism, Master thesis presented as part of the requirements for the Award of a Master Degree in Management from the Faculdade de Economia da Universidade Nova de Lisboa.

Ministry of Higher Education and Scientific Research. (2020). Ministry of Higher Education and Scientific Research website: Retrieved December 1, 2020, from http://www.mohe.gov.sy/mohe/

Novak, R., Slatinsek, A., & Devetak, G. (2013). Importance of motivating factors for international mobility of students: Empirical findings on selected higher education Institutions in Europe. *Organizacija*, *46*(6), 274–280. http://organizacija.fov.uni-mb.si/index.php/organizacija/article/view/515

European Commission. (2017). The report on the conference on higher education and refugees in the Mediterranean region. Beirut, Lebanon.

European Commission. (2018a). *Evaluation report: External monitoring and evaluation for the European Union regional trust fund in response to the Syrian crisis.* The 'Madad Fund'.

European Commission. (2018b). Erasmus+ for Higher Education in Syria. Brussels, Belgium.

European Commission. (2019). Erasmus+ Higher Education impact study: Study on the impact of Erasmus+ Higher Education Strategic partnerships and Knowledge Alliances. Brussels, Belgium.

European Commission. (2021). Erasmus+ Programme Guide, Version (1). Brussels, Belgium.

Severino, S., Messina, R., & Llorent, V. J. (2014). International student mobility: An identity development task? *International Journal of Humanities and Social Science*, *4*(3), 89–103. http://hdl.handle.net/10396/14973

Verbik, L., & Lasanowski, V. (2007). *International student mobility: Patterns and trends. Observatory of borderless higher education*, BULLETIN National Higher Education Research Institute (IPPTN), https://core.ac.uk/download/pdf/83543455.pdf

World Bank. (2020). *The mobility of displaced Syrians: An economic and social analysis (2020), international bank for reconstruction and development.*

Author biography

Dr Sulaiman Mouselli is Senior Lecturer in Finance, Dean of the Faculty of Business Administration, Arab International University, Ghabagheb, Daraa, Syrian Arab Republic. Sulaiman has published widely in areas of business and higher education, and most recently has worked on projects related to mobility of Syrian people during the crisis and higher education opportunities for Internally Displaced People (IDP). Sulaiman combines his expertise from the areas of business with higher education research and has a number of high impact publications, in journals such as *Business, Management and Education* and *International Journal of Educational Management.*

Part II

Representations of Internationally (and Intra-Regionally) Mobile Students in and from the Middle East

Chapter 6

Between Foreigners and Family

Social Media Representations of International Students in Israeli Universities

Annette Bamberger

Introduction

International student mobility is one of the defining features of global higher education (Choudaha, 2017; Larsen, 2016). To attract such students, nations and institutions have increasingly crafted policies, recruitment plans and marketing campaigns (Findlay et al., 2017). Research into the representations of international students has focused primarily on the major Anglo-Saxon destinations for international students (e.g. Lomer, 2017; Robertson, 2011; Stein & de Andreotti, 2016). This research reveals a confusing mix of ambiguous representations and attitudes towards international students. Importantly, scholars argue that discursive representations of international students shape student expectations and attitudes towards the academic experience, and even pedagogy (Koehne, 2006; Stein, 2018). Rather less research has explored the representations of international students in more diverse contexts; the few studies which have done so indicate divergent representations from those in the Global North (e.g. Mulvey & Lo, 2020). Context, is of course, highly important to understand how this emerging phenomenon of the 'international student recruitment business' influences students, academics and institutions. Thus, a critical study of representations of international students in diverse settings is worthwhile and important.

The Middle East is a region in which internationalisation is commonly argued to be linked to individual countries' economic and human capital development (e.g. Findlow & Hayes, 2016; Hayes & Al-Abri, 2019). However, Israel, founded as the nation-state of the Jewish people and locked in intractable conflict with the Palestinians and many of its neighbours, has a particular set of historical, economic, political and social influences which affect the purposes and representations of international students that challenge such a depiction. In this chapter, I analyse how international students are represented in two Israeli higher education institutions (HEIs) in a highly stratified and differentiated system of Higher Education (HE). I analyse their social media posts to understand how they represent international students and consider the implications of these representations for

DOI: 10.4324/9781003138457-9

the students' agency and academic experience. I examine Technion Israel Institute of Technology (Technion) and Interdisciplinary Center Herzliya (IDC)[1]. Technion, an elite public research-intensive global top-100 university has prestigious branch campus collaborations in China (Guangdong Institute, (GTIIT) and the United States (Cornell University). It specialises in scientific degrees, with students from the United States and Asia as its main target international demographic. IDC, an unranked academic college, that does not receive public funding, offers mainly undergraduate degrees in the social sciences and has the largest international student body in Israel, chiefly consisting of students from the Jewish diaspora. These HEIs represent diverse missions, disciplines and capabilities, and are differently placed in global and local hierarchies of HE. Peruta and Shields' (2018) study reveals that different types of HEIs (e.g. liberal arts, public universities) in the US context, employ different strategies to market and engage with students on Facebook. In the Israeli context, Mizrahi-Shtelman and Drori (2020) argue that different sectors of HEIs (universities, colleges and teacher training colleges) form fields with distinctive characteristics. Thus, the initial proposition underlying this chapter is that an analysis of diverse HEIs social media posts could reveal different representations of international students with implications for understanding representations of international students in Israel more broadly, and shedding light on this phenomenon globally.

I pursued the following lines of inquiry: How are international students represented? How might these representations shape international student agency and expectations? To address these questions, I analysed Facebook (FB) posts because this was the social media platform that both HEIs used intensively in English. Both institutions maintain FB pages in Hebrew and international pages in English; I analysed the latter because these would contain representations of and content for international students. FB posts from the international pages of Technion (95) and IDC (500) were collected over one year (March 2018 – March 2019), a period of time that reflects the scope of an annual marketing cycle. As suggested by the disparity in the number of posts between the institutions, IDC had a more strategic approach, posting often, around particular events and with professionally (and student) designed videos, photos and graphics. This chapter focuses on one of two inter-related studies; in the first, conducted with my colleagues Yifat Bronshetin and Miri Yemini, we employed Qualitative Content Analysis methodology (Schreier, 2012) to inductively determine the type of the posts (e.g. student recruitment; campus events), the format used (e.g. personal testimonials; videos; pictures) and appeals made (e.g. 'rankings', 'excellence'). This resulted in valuable insights not only about how the institutions portrayed themselves to international students, but importantly, the manner in which they did so. IDC relied considerably on a *personal approach* to marketing on FB, using students and staff testimonials to 'sell' the institution, whereas Technion relied more on an *institutional approach*, which highlighted institutional achievements in rankings, research, etc. (see Bamberger et al., 2020). This is an important distinction because, in the personal approach of IDC, students are actively owning their own stories, and representing themselves as such, whereas in Technion posts the university portrays the students. This study prompted me to take our analysis further, and employ an alternative lens, that of discourse analysis to investigate international student representations. In this chapter, I applied discourse analysis to the research corpus of FB posts to reveal the ways in which international students were represented (Fairclough et al., 2011). While the analysis revealed several representations common in the literature (e.g. consumers; future global knowledge workers; elites), it revealed two novel and contradictory representations. Illustrative posts are referenced by date and can be located on the publicly available international FB pages of both universities.

I begin by establishing the widespread constructions of international students, with a particular focus on Israel's distinctive and contested position within the Middle East and the internationalisation literature. I then proceed to analyse the two representations. I conclude with a discussion of the wider implications of the study for understanding representations of international students.

Ambiguous Representations of International Students

In recent years, research has focused on critiquing and analysing the discursive representations of international students, particularly in national and institutional policies (Brooks, 2021; Karram, 2013; Lomer, 2017; Stein, 2018). These representations are ambiguous and often contradictory in nature. While students are represented as valuable economic contributors to host societies (Cantwell, 2019), they are likewise a drain on local resources and competitors for local jobs, housing, etc. (Robertson, 2011; Stein & de Andreotti, 2016). International students have been viewed as intellectual and cultural resources; however, they have also been condemned for plagiarism and associated with a decline of academic standards (Amsberry, 2009; Divan et al., 2015). They are viewed as possessing important global skills, which ostensibly they impart to their fellow students (Lomer, 2017); however, these skills are often deprecated and are also connected with deficit discourses, in which students are belittled for inadequate English skills, different knowledge and educational practices (Lee & Rice, 2007). International students are viewed as economic elites, capable of paying high tuition and maintenance fees and as national elites, capable of advocating for the 'host' nations interests back home after the study programme (Mulvey & Lo, 2020; Sidhu, 2006); however, they are also viewed as scourges, coming into the country to exploit welfare programmes, work opportunities and public charity (Lomer, 2017; Robertson, 2011). They are viewed as desirable immigrants and as making a positive impact on local communities; however, they are likewise viewed as criminals and radicals, in need of supervision and securitisation (Marginson et al., 2010; Sawir et al., 2012).

International students are frequently represented as passive, and recipients of university and government care and support services (e.g. Askehave, 2007; Leyland, 2011; Robertson, 2011). This passivity is only interrupted when they are represented as discerning consumers, useful (informal) recruitment agents (Ammigan, 2019) or as criminal agents (Sawir et al., 2012). In this way, they are viewed more as passive subjects to be manipulated by nations/institutions than important partners in HE and as actively shaping their own life course (Waters, 2018). This passivity is echoed in research which reveals submissiveness in international students, and a reluctance to participate in classroom discussions and challenge superiors (Liu, 2009). This portrayal of passivity thus extends into questions of pedagogy, supervision and student evaluation. Critical research increasingly connects these portrayals, particularly of passivity, deficits and economic objects, to exploitation, marginalisation and new forms of colonial power relations enacted in and through the university (Rhee & Sagaria, 2004; Suspitsyna & Shalka, 2019). These accounts argue that international students are constructed as an often racialised/ethnicised 'other'.

While scholars such as Lomer (2017) reveal the often faulty assumptions behind these representations (and rationales for international student recruitment), they are nonetheless important because she and others argue that these representations impact on international students' expectations and academic experiences both creating the situations in which they describe and shape the conditions for student agency (i.e. the acceptance/resistance of such representations) (Koehne, 2006; Stein, 2018). In this way, representations of international students are increasingly connected to issues of marginalisation, pedagogy, student agency, equality and social justice.

While much of the previous research looks at policies, this study analyses FB posts, which target the 'desired' and 'assumed' international students. In line with studies, which emphasise the power of discourse to create the conditions it purportedly describes (Bacchi, 2009), it is my contention that these portrayals shape the actual profile of the international student recruit and their academic experience. This is an important distinction because unlike some policies, which may not be readily or widely available to international students, FB posts are part of the official communications of the university with these students, and moreover, are expected to resonate with these students (i.e. to attract them and form relationships). Thus, these portrayals are likely – perhaps more so than those found in policy – to have an impact on international student expectations and experiences, making the representations in FB posts worthy of study. Moreover, in this empirical research, based on the previous study (Bamberger et al., 2020) which revealed the divergent institutional/individual approaches used on FB by the two institutions, these FB posts were co-produced by students and thus can be considered to reflect student agency in their own representations, as opposed to how institutions represent them or how they are represented in national-level policies. This will have theoretical implications, contributing a new understanding of how various sources of representations may shape student experience and agency. However, this form of data does have some limitations, perhaps most notably, that it would initially seem unlikely that universities would overtly represent students in a derogatory fashion (e.g. 'cash cows' see Lomer, 2017), which has proven to be the case in policy documents; however, latent derogatory representations through consumer choice and service tropes are likely to be in evidence – and indeed, were found in this research.

Overall, from previous studies, there is a strong sense of the representations of 'international students' (as an ostensibly homogenous group) in Anglophone contexts. As I have endeavoured to show, these representations are ambiguous. While these studies are helpful to understand the complex nature of international student representations in some of the largest 'host' countries, there is rather less understanding of how such students are perceived and represented in diverse societies, particularly in the Middle East and more specifically in Israel. There has tended to be an assumption of generalising from the 'Global North' to other regions and contexts in the world (i.e. 'West to the Rest'). Given the vastly different contexts, values and purposes of internationalisation in these regions, it is important to study and understand these representations to build a global tapestry of understanding of international student representations. Particularly, the use of FB posts and the opportunity to analyse student's own representations of themselves. I propose that a study of Israel could provide such a view.

Israel

Since its inception in 1948, Israel has been embroiled in an intractable geopolitical conflict. With its roots in sectarian violence in British Mandatory Palestine (Bar-Tal, 2007), the conflict has been fought in sporadic wars, military operations and violent struggles. While Israel was established by the Zionist movement as the nation-state of the Jewish people, there is a substantial Palestinian Arab minority in the country, and about 4.8 million Palestinian Arabs in the Occupied Territories of Gaza and the West Bank (OCHA, 2017). The legitimacy of the state is the subject of continuing contestation in the region. It is a state comprised of deeply divided societies with diverse national, ethnic, religious and social groups. Albeit military and political in nature, this conflict affects all spheres of Israeli life, including IIE and international student recruitment. International student flows are affected by various factors including the unpredictable security situation in Israel, instability in Jewish communities around the world, regulations that restrict movement and possibilities for collaboration both among groups in Israel and across the Middle East, Hebrew as the primary language of instruction, the Boycott, Divestation and Sanctions movement (BDS), and the founding values of the state as the Jewish nation which dictates who may live, work and immigrate to the country (Bamberger et al., 2019; Yemini, 2017). Thus, while the Israeli HE system has at least three universities regularly placed in the top global university rankings, and demonstrates strong performance in research, with high publication, citation and patent rates (Weinberger & Zhitomirsky-Geffet, 2021), in the realm of international students, with only 1.4% of its student population coming from overseas, Israel performs poorly compared to the OECD average of 9% (Bamberger et al., 2019; Maoz, 2016). This has attracted the attention of the Council for Higher Education (CHE) – Israel's central body charged with coordinating the HE system. In a multi-year plan announced in July 2017, internationalisation – understood primarily as international student recruitment[2] – was identified as one of the key foci, with the goal of doubling international student numbers to 25,000 within five years. Despite low numbers of international students, there is a long history of engagement with international students, who have been fostered for particular reasons, and in distinctive ways (Bamberger, 2019).

Jewish students from the diaspora have been catered to in Israeli universities since their founding in the pre-state period. Beginning in 1955, special programmes aimed at bringing Jewish diaspora youth to Israel in an academic framework have been fostered to encourage immigration, combat assimilation, build Jewish leadership in the diaspora, and promote a relationship with Israel (Bamberger, 2020b). Over time, these international programmes developed separate infrastructures, and while open to all, and students from a variety of backgrounds have attended, they were created for a Jewish population including marketing and recruitment, funding, support services, and formal and informal curriculum. International degree-seeking students – at the undergraduate and post-graduate (without thesis) level – continue to be predominately Jewish and are broadly enrolled in programmes taught in English (Maoz, 2016). While these international programmes may be revenue ventures for some HEIs, the state, non-profit organisations and Jewish Diaspora organisations provide financial support for international Jewish students with an eye towards promoting solidarity, Jewish identity and Israel-Diaspora relations throughout the world (Bamberger, 2019). In addition to the traditional Jewish population of international programmes, Israel has also historically fostered exchanges and partnerships for student mobility, particularly with countries identified as of strategic economic and political importance. More recently, beginning in 2008 with the opening of a national TEMPUS office and the subsequent expansion of Erasmus +, there has been an influx of European students to Israeli campuses. Furthermore, since 2012 there have been significant government initiatives to bring closer collaboration with China and India – including sponsorship of Chinese and Indian research students (MA thesis, PhD, and post-doctorate) – with academic cooperation forming a basis for partnership. It remains to be seen if the newly forged diplomatic relations with several of the Arabian Gulf states (United Arab Emirates, Bahrain) and Morocco will foster new forms of academic collaboration in the region.

The CHE plan builds on these established patterns and aims to expand the intake of two categories of international students: (1) research students with a special focus on China and India; and (2) excellent Jewish students, particularly from the United States and Canada. The policy documents emanating from the CHE reveal the drivers behind these new policies: Israel hopes to build close economic and political relationships with these countries while strengthening the academic level of its HEIs and its research and development capabilities to compete in the 'global knowledge economy' (Bamberger, 2019; Maoz, 2016). The overall outcome is that Israel targets two distinct strands of international students: (1) research students, particularly from countries with which Israel wants to improve economic and political ties; and (2), students from the Jewish Diaspora, connecting to the identity of the state as the Jewish homeland. Increasingly these patterns are framed by the purposefully hierarchical and stratified nature of the Israeli HE system: universities as elite research institutions that view the creation of knowledge as their primary mission; and colleges, as second-tier institutions that are primarily oriented towards teaching (Shavit et al., 2003; Yogev, 2000). Little is understood about how diverse Israeli HEIs market their programmes to international students, particularly through new digital platforms, such as social media. As attracting international students becomes an institutional and national aim, and marketing efforts increase system-wide, an investigation of the representations of international students on social media of different HEIs is particularly timely. In the following sections, I present my analysis.

Cautious and Hesitant Foreigners in Need of Support

International students were represented as cautious and hesitant to study in Israel. The reason for this hesitancy was portrayed by the Technion as a fear of studying in a 'foreign country'. Other more sensitive issues such as security issues, institutional reputation and financial obligations were not addressed. The remedy proposed to conquer this fear, was for students to familiarise themselves with Israel and to avail themselves of university support systems.

> Worried about traveling to a foreign country? Fear not! We provide a comprehensive Orientation day in which you'll get familiarized with

> the campus and surrounding neighbourhoods. We'll also provide you with the survival tips you need to get settled in, such as opening an Israeli bank account, getting a cell phone plan, and more...
>
> (Technion, December 6, 2018)

> Having a bit of an understanding of the culture upon arrival can be a useful thing for students who want to study in Israel. It can help you become comfortable with the local people, and establish a routine that will help you flourish. Want to learn a little about Israel? Here are a few important things to know.
>
> (Technion, December 11, 2018)

The representation of international students as cautious and hesitant was reinforced through posts which encouraged international students to 'Always try! #GoForIt #TakeChances' (Technion, December 13, 2018), extorting students to 'Face situations head on and don't back down!' and not to 'worry about failures. Worry about the chances you miss when you don't even try' (Technion, December 21, 2018). These representations likely reflected the more diverse target market for international students that Technion wished to attract.

IDC portrayed international students as vulnerable and in need of care, because of geographical distance from home/family. This representation of vulnerability necessitated special support and care services for international students. IDC created a programme in which first-year students are assigned an Israeli counsellor. Counsellors, introducing themselves on FB as experienced and empathetic advisors, concerned for the welfare and adaptation of the students:

> I decided to become a counselor because I understand how hard it may be to adapt in a new place and I believe I can assist new students in the RRIS [Raphael Recanati International School, the department of IDC which caters to international students] with their new path here in Israel.
>
> (IDC, September 6, 2018)

> I became an RRIS Counselor because I am dedicated to helping people reach their full potential and conquer their goals. I believe that with the right tools, support and mindset you can accomplish incredible things in this tiny, crazy and amazing country. I am here to help students coming to IDC from across the globe to do exactly that.
>
> (IDC, October 4, 2018)

> I decided to join the program and assist new students because I want everyone to have a soft landing in the best country in the world!:)
>
> (IDC, September 16, 2018)

These quotes from counsellors followed a similar pattern with superlative references to Israel (e.g. 'crazy and amazing country', 'best country in the world'). These may be aimed at combating against/speaking back to some of the socio-political tensions that characterise Israel, particularly as viewed through international media.

Notably, international students are represented as 'foreign' in that they were not part of or familiar with the society. This necessitated them to familiarise themselves with the culture and to avail themselves of special care/support services. There was however an important difference between the literature that portrays international students as passive recipients of care (e.g. Askehave, 2007; Leyland, 2011; Robertson, 2011) and this study. In the IDC posts, given its personal approach to social media communications, international students were afforded a level of agency in telling their stories:

> Packing my bags up at such a young age and moving to another country alone was not a simple decision and throughout this process, I had to learn to overcome many challenges.
>
> (IDC, December 26, 2018)

> Not only did I want to further my knowledge in Business Administration, in particular, finance, I also wanted to get to know a country that has had a huge impact on my life. Being able to study in English in a country like Israel showed me that when there is a will to achieve something greater than yourself, there is a way if you just put your heart into it.
>
> (IDC, December 19, 2018)

While emphasising that the decision was not 'simple' echoing the themes of hesitancy and that it was a 'challenge', in these accounts, students highlighted their own agency in deciding to study abroad and their own accomplishments and determination in the face of adversity. In this way, students portrayed themselves as capable, strong and determined – and eventually successful.

Part of the Family

The portrayal of international students as 'family' was salient throughout the posts at IDC (absent in Technion). This idea of 'family' and 'home' represented international students as belonging in Israel and at IDC. Despite the diverse backgrounds of the students, they belonged in the country – perceived as a homeland – and at the university because of their ethnoreligious identity and ancestry.

> In truth, my family is to thank for this, from my grandparents down to me, Zionism and a love for the Jewish homeland has always been a

> part of who I am and I am thankful for my family who still supports my dream of living here in Israel .... To me it is just the beginning, and I hope that Israel continues to be not just my home, but the home of the Jewish people for the next 80 years and for all time after that.
>
> (IDC, July 19, 2018)

> I chose to come to Israel as I feel it is my true home, I love the culture, the people, the vibe and I couldn't see myself anywhere else ...
>
> (IDC, February 3, 2019)

> ... Since childhood, I visited Israel frequently and identified strongly as a secular Jew. I'm not religiously observant, but have always been a Jew before all else. To me, being Jewish is to be part of a proud history, culture, a people who have survived and thrived despite the odds. And even in the face of adversity that I personally can scarcely imagine, my ancestors dreamed of establishing a Jewish homeland in Israel. I came to Israel to be part of something bigger than myself, bigger than one individual. To be part of a generational effort. I derive a sense of common purpose from being in Israel. I chose to study at IDC because of it's beautiful, dynamic campus, the accomplished professors, and the myriad activities and organizations in which I can partake on campus.
>
> (IDC, January, 16, 2019)

This representation dovetails with official Israeli immigration policy – according to Israeli law, anyone with one Jewish grandparent has a right to Israeli citizenship – and the contested state-sponsored national identity of Israel as the Jewish nation-state.

While the previous discourse of Israel as 'home' and 'family' could be perceived as exclusive to Jewish students, some student profiles, who were readily identifiable as non-Jewish, focused on advocacy for Israel, indicating inclusion in the family, along political/ideological as opposed to ethnoreligious lines.

> I am here to further my knowledge, to publicly advocate for Israel correctly and diplomatically in order to keep Israel safe and on the map forever .... With over 80 representing countries there is a strong growing love for Israel showed from every student studying here, regardless of their heritage. The most important is the message they will bring back to their countries about Israel, and I'm glad to be a small part of it.
>
> (IDC, August 26, 2018)

In either case, the 'family' representation, was closely intertwined with advocacy and affection for the (Jewish) nation-state of Israel. This representation at once embraces those who have strong Jewish identities and connections with Israel as a (Jewish) ancestral home; and those who support Israel as the nation-state of the Jewish people, while excluding others, particularly those critical of the state. It likewise serves to represent the desired and successful international student, as one who is connected to this family – and loyal to it.

Discussion and Conclusion

In this study, my aim was twofold: to understand how international students are represented outside of the dominant Anglo-American destinations; and to consider the implications of these representations, particularly for student agency. This study confirms findings from the literature which reveal ambiguity in the representations of international students (e.g. Lomer, 2017; Stein & de Andreotti, 2016); it also advances our understanding of international student representations in several ways.

My analysis revealed a set of novel international student representations: that of cautious and hesitant foreigners in need of support; and that of family members. International students are represented as hesitant and cautious 'foreigners' in that they were not actually part of the society and needed to familiarise themselves with the culture and avail themselves of special care services. Complementing this representation, IDC represented international students as part of the extended (Jewish, Israel-advocate) family – a representation that is advanced by international students themselves. Thus, while they were represented as 'at home' in Israel, their perceived ancestral homeland, they were also represented as vulnerable and in need of support because of an unfamiliarity with this homeland and distance from their families and communities abroad. This indicated that IDC's target audience was primarily Jewish diaspora youth. It indicates a novel way of representing international students – that of part of an extended 'family' of a diaspora nation. Through this representation, we see a novel positioning of international higher education – to create and cement a national community, reinforcing diaspora identities and bonds with a perceived national homeland. In this way, international higher education becomes part of the process of nation-building, creating imagined communities (Anderson, 1983). However, this study indicated an invitation to international higher education that extended beyond those associated with the ethnoreligious (Jewish) 'nation' – inclusion based on political affiliations/ideological support of the nation-state.

The representation of 'family', like others in the literature is not straightforward; rather, distinctions are made between affective attachment to people and land, and actual familiarity, acquaintance, and competence. Indeed, the international programme thrives on this duality; Jewish diaspora students can 'Study in English, Live in Israel' or study in the homeland without sufficient (heritage) language skills to study alongside Israelis in Hebrew.

They can likewise study in English, earning a degree (in highly mobile disciplines such as business, communities, international relations), increasing their cosmopolitan capital without any obligation to stay in Israel, keeping their options open. These representations – created in part by students themselves – may reflect the desire of international students to blend the pursuit of ethnic identity capital and cosmopolitan capital (Bamberger, 2020a) in their international study decisions. IDC attracts significantly more international students than Technion (which does not employ the 'family' representation) – despite its lower status in global/local hierarchies. Thus, this study suggests that affective representations may be appealing to some (diaspora) international students, perhaps more than the 'global academic speak' of rankings, prestige and 'excellence'. It also indicates that this type of affective representation may be a strategy employed for lower-ranking HEIs to compete for international students. In this way, this depiction turns prevailing market discourses and rational decision-making models of international student mobility on their head. The fact that the Technion does not attract more students, and that the overt representation of 'family' was absent – using the institutional as opposed to personal approach – likewise indicates that HEIs which are plugged into the global system, are possibly less *able* to speak in the way that IDC did (i.e. particularistic). Notably, the Technion used the more common representations of international students: elites, consumers, global, etc. Thus, this study supports emerging literature (e.g. Mizrahi-Shtelman & Drori, 2020) which indicates that the type of HEI has a significant impact on the ways in which it 'speaks to the global', while indicating that its intended audience – and its approach (i.e. institutional or personal) – is highly influential in the way in which it speaks.

This study adds nuance to our understanding of international student agencies and sources of international student representations. IDC posts were heavily constructed through a *personal approach*, in which students told their own stories (Bamberger et al., 2020). While the institution coordinated the posts, students provided narratives, which presumably they wanted to share and that they thought would be appealing to other potential students. This dovetails with the literature which indicates that international students are often viewed as passive, except for their marketing/recruiting activities (e.g. Ammigan, 2019). Notably, there was a divergence between the two institutions. While Technion and IDC both represented students as hesitant and cautious foreigners, international students also represented themselves as determined, strong and capable of meeting the challenges of studying in a 'foreign' country, which was enabled by the fact that IDC employed a personal approach – a representation absent in Technion. On the one hand, the personal approach represents a more agentic practice, empowering international students to represent themselves and their experiences on their own terms. It also allows for alternative representation of students (e.g. instead of foreigners in need of support;

determined students capable of succeeding, given the right supports). On the other hand, students used tropes like 'family' and 'home' while parroting meritocratic discourses about 'working hard'. In this way, student posts overlooked structural issues (e.g. class, ethnicity, religion) which enabled their successes in international higher education, and clung to simplistic forms of national affectation, without subjecting their views and state narratives to critical scrutiny. Importantly, these student representations are likely to have a greater influence on international student recruitment and expectations, as opposed to policies, given their public nature. Moreover, Bamberger et al. (2020), indicate that the possibility of tagging students, and circulation of posts through friends' networks, would likewise increase the reach and influence of such representations.

While this study has several limitations, and it is important not to generalise (nor was this the purpose), it nonetheless sheds light on representations of international students from diverse societies. It highlights issues of international student agency, institutional approaches and the important role of social media – and other publicly circulated sources – in international student representations. In this way, it contributes to a new understanding of how various sources of representations may shape student experience and agency.

Acknowledgments

This chapter is based in part on a research project conducted with my colleagues Yifat Bronshtein and Miri Yemini and the resulting publication:

Bamberger, A., Bronshtein, Y., & Yemini, Y. (2020). Marketing universities and targeting international students: A comparative analysis of social media data trails. *Teaching in Higher Education*. DOI: 10.1080/13562517.2020.1712353.

Notes

1 Given that this study is based on publicly available documents, the names of the HEIs are used. This study received ethical approval from Tel Aviv University.

2 When it was first announced, it focused almost exclusively on international student recruitment; however, as the plan developed, other areas were included in the budgeting mechanism, such as research collaborations and 'internationalization at home' activities (see Bamberger, 2020b).

References

Ammigan, R. (2019). Institutional satisfaction and recommendation: What really matters to international students. *Journal of International Students*, *9*(1), 262–281. https://doi.org/10.32674/jis.v9i1.260

Amsberry, D. (2009). Deconstructing plagiarism: International students and textual borrowing practices. *The Reference Librarian*, *51*(1), 31–44.

Anderson, B. (1983). *Imagined communities: Reflections on the origin and spread of nationalism*. Verso.

Askehave, I. (2007). The impact of marketization on higher education genres – The international student prospectus as a case in point. *Discourse studies*, *9*(6), 723–742. https://doi.org/10.1177/1461445607082576

Bacchi, C. (2009). *Analysing policy: What the problem represented to be?* Pearson Higher Education.

Bamberger, A. (2019). International student mobility in Israel. *International Higher Education*, *96*, 9–10.

Bamberger, A. (2020a). Accumulating cosmopolitan and ethnic identity capital through international student mobility. *Studies in Higher Education*, *45*(7), 1367–1379. https://doi.org/10.1080/03075079.2019.1597037

Bamberger, A. (2020b). *Diaspora, state and university: An analysis of internationalisation of higher education in Israel* (Doctoral dissertation, University College London).

Bamberger, A., Bronshtein, Y., & Yemini, Y. (2020). Marketing universities and targeting international students: A comparative analysis of social media data trails. *Teaching in Higher Education*, *25*(4), 476–492. https://doi.org/10.1080/13562517.2020.1712353

Bamberger, A., Morris, P., Weinreb, Y., & Yemini, M. (2019). Hyperpoliticised internationalisation in a pariah university: An Israeli institution in the occupied West Bank.*International Journal of Educational Development*, *66*, 119–128.

Bar-Tal, D. (2007). Sociopsychological foundations of intractable conflicts. *American Behavioral Scientist*, *50*(11), 1430–1453. https://doi.org/10.1177/00027642073 02462

Brooks, R. (2021). The construction of higher education students within national policy: A cross-European comparison. *Compare: A Journal of Comparative and International Education*, *2*(51), 161–180. https://doi.org/10.1080/03057925.2019.1604118

Cantwell, B. (2019). Are international students cash cows? Examining the relationship between new international undergraduate enrollments and institutional revenue at public colleges and universities in the US. *Journal of International Students*, *5*(4), 512–525.

Choudaha, R. (2017). Three waves of international student mobility (1999–2020). *Studies in Higher Education*, *42*(5), 825–832. https://doi.org/10.1080/03075079.2017.1293872

Divan, A., Bowman, M., & Seabourne, A. (2015). Reducing unintentional plagiarism amongst international students in the biological sciences: An embedded academic writing development programme. *Journal of Further and Higher Education*, *39*(3), 358–378. https://doi.org/10.1080/0309877X.2013.858674

Fairclough, N., Mulderrig, J., & Wodak, R. (2011). Critical discourse analysis. In T. A. Van Dijk (Ed.), *Discourse studies: A multidisciplinary introduction* (pp. 357–378). SAGE Publications Ltd. https://www.doi.org/10.4135/9781446289068.n17

Findlay, A., McCollum, D., & Packwood, H. (2017). Marketization, marketing and the production of international student migration. *International Migration*, *55*(3), 139–155. https://doi.org/10.1111/imig.12330

Findlow, S., & Hayes, A. (2016). Transnational academic capitalism in the Arab Gulf: Balancing global and local, public and private, capitals. *British Journal of Sociology of Education*, 110–128.

Hayes, A., & Al'Abri, K. M. (2019). Regional solidarity undermined? Higher education developments in the Arabian gulf, economy and time. *Comparative Education*, *55*(2), 157–174. https://doi.org/10.1080/03050068.2018.1504884

Karram, G. L. (2013). International students as lucrative markets or vulnerable populations: A critical discourse analysis of national and institutional events in four nations. *Canadian and International Education*, *42*(1), 1–14. https://doi.org/10.5206/cie-eci.v42i1.9223

Koehne, N. (2006). (Be) Coming,(Be) Longing: Ways in which international students talk about themselves. *Discourse: Studies in the Cultural Politics of Education*, *27*(2), 241–257.

Larsen, M. (2016). *Internationalization of higher education: An Analysis through spatial, network, and mobilities theories*. Palgrave MacMillan.

Lee, J. J., & Rice, C. (2007). Welcome to America? International student perceptions of discrimination. *Higher Education*, *53*(3), 381–409. https://doi.org/10.1007/s10734-005-4508-3

Leyland, C. (2011). Does the rebranding of British universities reduce international students to economic resources? A critical discourse analysis. *NOVITAS-ROYAL*, *5*(2) 199–214.

Liu, J. (2009). From learner passive to learner active? The case of Chinese postgraduate students studying marketing in the UK. *International Journal of Management Education*, 7(2), 33–40. https://doi.org/10.3794/ijme.72.187

Lomer, S. (2017). Soft power as a policy rational for international education in the UK: A critical analysis. *Higher Education*, *74*(4), 581–585. https://doi.org/10/1007/s10734-0160060-6

Maoz, L. (2016). *Internationalism in higher education: International students in Israel. Suggestions for policy*. CHE (Hebrew).

Marginson, S., Nyland, C., Sawir, E., & Forbes-Mewett, H. (2010). *International student security*. Cambridge University Press.

Mizrahi-Shtelman, R., & Drori, G. S. (2020). World-rank and/or locally relevant? Organizational identity in the mission statements of higher education organizations in Israel, 2008–2018. *Minerva*, 1–25. https://doi.org/10.1007/s11024-020-09414-5

Mulvey, B., & Lo, W. Y. W. (2020). Learning to 'tell China's story well': The constructions of international students in Chinese higher education policy. *Globalisation, Societies and Education*, 1–13. https://doi.org/10.1080/14767724.2020.1835465

OCHA. (May, 2017). Occupied Palestinian Territory Fragmented Lives Humanitarian Overview 2016. https://www.ochaopt.org/sites/default/files/fragmented_lives_2016_english.pdf

Peruta, A., & Shields, A. B. (2018). Marketing your university on social media: A content analysis of Facebook post types and formats. *Journal of Marketing for Higher Education*, *28*(2), 175–191. https://doi.org/10.1080/08841241.2018.1442896

Rhee, J. E., & Sagaria, M. A. D. (2004). International students: Constructions of imperialism in the chronicle of higher education. *The Review of Higher Education*, *28*(1), 77–96. https://doi.org/10.1353/rhe.2004.0031

Robertson, S. (2011). Cash cows, backdoor migrants, or activist citizens? International students, citizenship, and rights in Australia. *Ethnic and Racial Studies*, *34*(12), 2192–2211. https://doi.org/10.1080/01419870.2011.558590

Sawir, E., Marginson, S., Forbes-Mewett, H., Nyland, C., & Ramia, G. (2012). International student security and English language proficiency. *Journal of Studies in International Education*, *16*(5), 434–454. https://doi.org/10.1177/1028315311435418

Schreier, M. (2012). *Qualitative content analysis in practice*. Sage.

Shavit, Y., Ayalon, H., Bolotin-Chachashvili, S., Menahem, G., & Shwed, U. (2003). The diversification of higher education and it's consequences for social stratification in Israel. *10es Journées d'études Céreq—Lasmas-IdL, Caen,«Les données longitudinales dans l'analyse du march du travail.*

Sidhu, R. K. (2006). *Universities and globalization: To market, to market*. Routledge.

Stein, S. (2018). National exceptionalism in the 'EduCanada'brand: Unpacking the ethics of internationalization marketing in Canada. *Discourse: Studies in the Cultural Politics of Education*, *39*(3), 461–477.

Stein, S., & de Andreotti, V. O. (2016). Cash, competition, or charity: International students and the global imaginary. *Higher Education*, *72*(2), 225–239. https://doi.org/10.1007/s10734-015-9949-8

Suspitsyna, T., & Shalka, T. R. (2019). The Chinese international student as a (Post) colonial other: An analysis of cultural representations of a US media discourse. *The Review of Higher Education*, *42*(5), 287–308. https://doi.org/10.1353/rhe.2019.0053

Waters, J. L. (2018). International education is political! Exploring the politics of international student mobilities. *Journal of International Students*, *8*(3), 1459–1478. https://doi.org/10.32674/jis.v8i3.66

Weinberger, M., & Zhitomirsky-Geffet, M. (2021). Diversity of success: Measuring the scholarly performance diversity of tenured professors in the Israeli academia. *Scientometrics*, *126*(4), 2931–2970. https://doi.org/10.1007/s11192-020-03823-9

Yemini, M. (2017). Internationalization under intractable conflict: The influence of national conflict on Israeli higher education institutions' internationalization efforts. *European Education*, *49*(4), 293–303. https://doi.org/10.1080/10564934.2017.1392249

Yogev, A. (2000). The stratification of Israeli universities: Implications for higher education policy. *Higher Education*, *40*(2), 183–201. https://doi.org/10.1023/A:1004049331498

Chapter 7

Constructing Self through Transnational Nursing Education in the Middle East

Wendy Maddison

Introduction

Transnational education (TNE) is commonly defined as the mobility of educational programmes across international borders, provided to learners located in a different country from that of the awarding institution (Knight, 2016). It is described as a complex process that entwines technology, people, cultures, economies, knowledge, and ideas globally (Altbach, 2007; Donn & Al Manthri, 2010). However, there has been little regionally sensitive research conducted into what TNE *does* from a learner's perspective – how local students attending an international branch campus of TNE in their own country make sense of engaging with a global learning environment at home. Such students have been described as 'glocals', shaped as members of a global educational community (Choudaha, 2013) and comfortably inhabiting both global and local arenas. A process of 'glocalisation' is viewed as empowering and transformational (Patel & Lynch, 2013). However, this conceptualisation does not adequately explore how students learning in very different cultural contexts construct their sense of self – or selves – through their encounters with the phenomena of TNE. Issues such as culture, belief systems, gendered ways of knowing and power relations create a distinct and multi-layered landscape which requires meticulous unpacking to understand the impact of TNE on the construction of self.

It is estimated that over one-third of all international branch campuses have been established in the affluent Middle Eastern countries of the Gulf Cooperation Council (GCC) (The Quality Assurance Agency for Higher Education, UK, 2014; Wilkins & Huisman, 2012). The GCC comprises Saudi Arabia, the Kingdom of Bahrain, Oman, United Arab Emirates, Kuwait and Qatar, and remains a top destination for TNE (JISC, 2018). One of the drivers in attracting international branch campuses to the GCC region was a response by local governments to develop national strategies of economic diversification, with the objective of moving away from dependence on the oil industry (OECD, 2015). Another key driver was

DOI: 10.4324/9781003138457-10

consideration of high local population growths in the region, estimated at having increased by 30% over the past decade to over 50 million people, with a majority under 25 years of age (Abdul Salam et al., 2015). To create employment opportunities, nationalisation programmes were introduced for specific jobs previously occupied by expatriates (Ernst & Young, 2015), such as nursing. Intricately linked to the demographics in this region was also the requirement for a tremendous increase in the provision of health-care services (Feuilherade, 2014) and the professional education of local healthcare professionals (ILO, 2018). In an Arab Islamic country such as Bahrain, there is demand specifically for globally oriented female nurses to provide culturally appropriate care for female patients (Kain, 2015; Mackay et al., 2016; The World Health Organisation, 2013).

In light of the above trends, and as part of its strategy of internationalisation, an Irish medical university established an international branch campus in the Kingdom of Bahrain in 2004. The university opened the doors of its state-of-the-art branch campus to its first medical students, followed in 2006 by its first 40 Bahraini nursing students, 34 of whom were females. Today, total enrolment in the four-year nursing degree course is approximately 400 students, of which approximately 85% are Bahraini females. The nursing programme is delivered in English, and the BSc degree is awarded by the Higher Education Council of the Kingdom of Bahrain and the National University of Ireland.

This Chapter draws on findings from doctoral degree research conducted by the author. The research explored how a transnational programme of nursing education delivered in the Kingdom of Bahrain impacted the life-world and sense of self of a small group of Bahraini females as they became Irish-qualified nurses in Bahrain. A lifeworld (Smith et al., 2009) comprises the lived subjective experiences, relationships and networks of belief systems that root and situate an individual within their world; a grounded reality that provides a sense of identity.

Literature Review Summary

Local students attending an international branch campus (IBC) 'at home' are positioned within a specific global-local nexus (Giddens, 1999), a global contact zone (Kadiwal & Rind, 2013), of TNE. Experiences of TNE cannot be separated from the particular geo-political and socio-cultural context in which local students are nested (Anderson-Levitt, 2003; Davey & Bredemeyer, 2011; Donn & Al Manthri, 2010; Maddison, 2015). In the Arab world, the pervading influence of Islam frames students' lifeworlds, informs the pedagogical environment and shapes gendered ways of knowing (Elsaadda et al., 2010; Khine, 2008). Despite the rapid increase of TNE in the Arab states (Miller-Idriss & Hanauer, 2011), little is known of local students' experiences of attending an IBC (Hussin, 2007; Pincas, 2001).

This is an important dimension of the TNE phenomenon, but as yet not fully investigated (Chapman & Pyvis, 2007; Zembylas, 2012).

There is scant literature addressing the TNE experiences of Middle Eastern females attending an IBC in their home country, and how these educational experiences have impacted their sense of self. Of the few studies conducted in the GCC region, Khine and Hayes (2010) investigated a female way of knowing with 167 Emirati females commencing a degree programme in the United Arab Emirates. The authors recommend that in order to be successful, a TNE programme must be filtered through the local culture of students in the host country, with attention paid to language and how students construct meaning (Tubin & Lapidot, 2008). Gargano (2009) emphasises that students' expressions of their experience should be amplified as they negotiate and inhabit their transnational space. Examining local student experiences of an IBC in Dubai, Kadiwal and Rind (2013) refer to this group of students as 'selective cosmopolitans' (p. 689) as they exercise agency in brokering contiguous intercultural influences and local-global tensions along their educational journey (Singh & Doherty, 2004). Local students attending an IBC are viewed as responding reflexively to their TNE experiences (Marginson, 2014) and are not merely passive consumers of TNE (Kadiwal & Rind, 2013). This suggests an array of 'glocal' possible selves under construction (Stevenson & Clegg, 2010; Tran, 2011) as TNE shapes hybrid identities (Edwards & Usher, 2000; Faist, 2010; Marginson, 2014; Pirc, 2014).

There are calls to know more about the long-term impact of IBCs and the outcomes of TNE experiences through regionally sensitive studies (Miller-Idriss & Hanauer, 2011) of local students who are positioned in specific discursive contexts (Fail et al., 2004; Oikonomidoy & Williams, 2013; Stevenson & Clegg, 2010). For example, female Arab students are expected to conform to local embedded patriarchal socio-cultural norms (Elsaadda et al., 2010) and embody a situated lifeworld within an educational environment (Miriam et al., 2013). Issues such as gender and power relations within a pedagogical framework of TNE in the Middle East have not been adequately explored (Welikala, 2011). There are calls to listen to the female voice in context (Barbaria et al., 2011) and to consider female lived experiences as valid knowledge (Plummer & Young, 2010; Lazar, 2007). However, there is scant reference in the literature to how female Arab students attending an IBC in the Middle East construct their sense of self along their TNE journey.

Background to the Study

The study is situated in the Kingdom of Bahrain. Socio-cultural norms and values are grounded in Arab Islamic culture and Bahraini family units are traditionally headed by a male. Bahraini females marry on average at around 22 years old (Kingdom of Bahrain, Supreme Council for Women, 2015), and many female nursing students at the Irish medical university, where the study takes place become engaged to be married during their programme of study. It is reported that the traditional patriarchal structure of Middle Eastern society poses challenges to female empowerment (Hafez, 2018; Moghadam, 2010; World Economic Forum, 2014b), although in Bahrain no legal reasons exist to hinder female movement, employment, political participation, or education (The Economist Intelligence Unit, 2012; Young, 2016). However, there is somewhat of a dichotomy regarding the social status of a Bahraini female. On one hand, she is expected to contribute towards building an economically progressive society, but on the other she is socially situated in an Arab Islamic context to occupy traditional roles such as wife, homemaker and mother. This 'double-burden syndrome' (McKinsey & Co., 2014, p. 18) reflects conflicting possibilities of being, summarised by The Kingdom of Bahrain Supreme Council for Women (2015):

> Bahraini women today are at a more advanced stage in the process to build a sustainable society and have a greater ability to attain the highest positions in the Kingdom, whereby women in Bahrain today are Ministers, Judges and Business Women, while maintaining their natural presence as a family nurturer, which in turn is a nurturer of the nation as a whole.
>
> (p. 5)

Bahraini government secondary schools are segregated by gender, with female students typically outperforming male students (Kingdom of Bahrain, Ministry of Education, 2020). The curriculum is delivered in Arabic, Islamic studies are integrated throughout all years, and English is taught as a second language. Education is free of charge at government schools for all Bahrainis. There are also many mixed gender private schools in Bahrain, which follow an English curriculum. However, the cost of private education is out of the reach of many Bahraini families. The majority of Bahraini nursing students who enter the Irish medical university have studied at Bahraini government secondary schools through the medium of Arabic and are financially sponsored to study nursing by the Bahraini government.

Situated within a particular socio-economic and cultural context, the study reported here explores the impact of a transnational programme of nursing education on the sense of self of a small group of Bahraini nurses who attended an IBC of an Irish medical university in Bahrain. The rationale of this research was to understand how this small group of nurses scaffolded a sense of self through the experiences of their TNE programme and to investigate the meanings they made as their lived TNE experiences impacted their lifeworlds.

The Study Design

Exploring the impact of a TNE experience on a learner's construction of self was the focus of the study. In order to achieve in-depth and rich accounts through which learners' perspectives, experiences and meaning-making could be explored, Interpretative Phenomenological Analysis (IPA) (Smith et al., 2009) was employed as the methodological framework of analysis. As a qualitative methodology, IPA does not seek to make generalised claims using a large number of participants but favours very small numbers. It follows an idiographic method, its gaze focused within the psychological realm (Smith & Osborn, 2003), exploring details of unique experiences which underpin individual sense-making and self-formation. From an IPA perspective, an individual's sense of self evolves, influenced not only by surrounding socio-cultural positioning but also through experience and the conscious assertion of agency. IPA is based on hermeneutics and employs a phenomenological approach. It lends itself to inter-subjective understanding (Standing, 2009) as the researcher has a central, reflexive and subjective role in an IPA study.

Reflexivity is also considered a pillar of feminist methods (Hesse-Biber, 2007; Probyn, 1993; Shope, 2006). Employing IPA as a methodology and postmodern feminism as a theoretical framework provided a set of distinctive tools and researcher positioning through which Bahraini female nursing students' self-formation within the phenomenon of TNE could be explored. A postmodern perspective considers concepts such as identity and reality as being fluid and socially constructed (Harvey, 1990), reproduced over time through language, culture, gender and power relations (Bender-Slack, 2010; Bohan, 2002; Enns, 2010; Snyder, 2008). Multiple ways of knowing and being arise from a discursive disruption of different bracketing of identity (Hinds & Sparks, 2008; Snyder, 2008). Postmodern feminism, therefore, suggests that female identities can be braided into a sense of self, which is not bound by place or time, nor can be neatly slotted into one particular category (American Psychological Association, 2007; Chowdhury, 2009). Hence, 'locational feminisms' (Enns, 2010; Jasper, 2013) define the rich and complex diversity of many forms of feminism worldwide, reflecting multifarious possibilities of female situated knowledge and identities, and representing many distinct individual standpoints, or perspectives (Clark Mane, 2012; Harding, 2004).

In the study reported here, Bahraini female participants were randomly recruited based on criteria of having recently graduated from the School of Nursing of the Irish transnational medical university in Bahrain; having attended Arabic government secondary school; and speaking English as a second language. Nine Bahraini female graduates participated, sufficient for a qualitative study (Cresswell, 2013) and IPA research specifically. Data was obtained from a focus group discussion with the participants who critically reflected on their TNE journey, followed by individual semi-structured in-depth interviews focusing on individual meaning making of experiences. Data was analysed through the methodology of IPA, and findings were interpreted through the theoretical framework of postmodern feminism.

It could be argued that findings from the study, summarised below, only relate to a small group of female participants in a specific context, therefore may not be generalisable to a wider and larger population of both genders located elsewhere in the world. However, from an IPA perspective, this is also one of the study's strengths, as detailed investigation into the impact of the phenomenon of TNE on the lifeworlds and identities of individuals enables us to better understand their situated positions as learners. Such methodology could therefore be usefully adopted to provide comparative insights into other groups of learners in different TNE contexts.

Discussion of Findings

Findings from the study are summarised through four master themes that have emerged through the analysis of interview data, discussed below:

- The Transition: Minding the Gaps
- A Transnational Community of Practice: Construction of a Collective Consciousness
- Embodied Agency: The Shaping of Persona
- Becoming: The Same Yet Different – A New Standpoint

The Transition: Minding the Gaps

The participants in the study reported that their first step on the path of 'becoming' a transnationally qualified nurse involved bridging gaps, some wider than others. This period of critical adaptation was defined as the Transition (Tawash et al., 2019), and occurred early in the first semester of the first year of their programme of study. Table 7.1 highlights the differences and complexities involved in the Transition as participants moved from the known learning environment of a Bahraini government high school with a prescriptive, passive learning style and didactic method of instruction (Hayes et al., 2011) to an independent and flexible learning model in the unknown context of a western medical university.

Both academic and cultural gaps were identified during the Transition. These gaps presented intricate ontological and epistemological challenges and obstacles (Holden et al., 2017; Wilson, 2002) that needed to be bridged, or overcome, in order for the participants to succeed academically. Table 7.2 identifies the academic and cultural gaps that required bridging by the participants during the Transition period.

Table 7.1 Minding the Gaps: Differences in Learning Environments between Local Government Arabic High School and Western Medical University in Bahrain (Maddison, 2016)

Bahraini Government High School	*Western Medical University in Bahrain*
Didactic, structured learning	Reflective, active learning
Individual effort, segregated schooling	Teamwork, mixed gender groups
Learning in Arabic	Learning in English
Rote learning, dependent on teachers	Critical thinking, independent learning
Limited intercultural exposure	Wide intercultural exposure
Externally regulated and motivated (through families, teachers, religious leaders, authority figures such as fathers)	Internally regulated and motivated (through self-efficacy, self-determination and personal agency)
Fixed mindset – in the moment	Growth mindset – forward thinking
Strong family influence/collectivistic focus	Looser family influence/individualistic focus
Arab Islamic values and norms inform, drive and maintain embedded traditional beliefs and behaviours; cultural and religious conformity	Western culture pervades; encouragement of personal development and change; cultural and religious diversity

The Transition required the participants to navigate a complex process of acculturation during which they had to disengage from previous ways of learning, being and doing. A process of internal acclimatisation (Pyvis & Chapman, 2005) took place as the participants grasped new norms and values embedded within the university and made sense of new experiences. These experiences were often described by the participants as 'shocking', meaning strange, for example being taught by a native English speaker; the Irish accent; studying with males in the classroom; and exposure to the different cultures of the international medical students. A major challenge reported by all participants during the Transition was studying in English

Table 7.2 Academic and Cultural Gaps Bridged by the Participants during the Transition Period (Maddison, 2016)

Academic Bridging	*Cultural Bridging*
Overcoming English language challenges	Overcoming culture 'shock'
Adapting to new ways of learning and knowing	Adapting to new ways of being
Developing self-determination and self-efficacy as a learner	Developing skills of reflexivity and personal agency
Redefining relationships in the classroom: • Faculty members as role models • Male classmates as peers and colleagues	Redefining social relationships: • Reconciling Arab Islamic values with difference • Reshaping gendered boundaries
Moving in new spaces: Campus as a transnational habitus	Moving in new places: Cognitive and conceptual stretching

as the *lingua franca* of learning (Kane, 2014). Early in the Transition period many of the participants reported that they translated lectures delivered in English back into their native Arabic language in order to synthesise meaning. Language presented a barrier to both academic success and social interaction within the English language milieu of the university.

Apart from epistemological considerations, there were also ontological issues of how the students' educational experiences impacted their sense of being in the world. An awareness of changing subjectively was noted at this stage. Successfully passing through the Transition represented the start of a process of reframing and recontextualising of self.

A Transnational Community of Practice: Construction of a Collective Consciousness

Moving through the Transition, a sense of belongingness was fostered as the participants shared goals, knowledge, experience and engaged reciprocally with other nursing students. The concept of a Community of Practice (Wenger, 1998) as a specific type of learning community can be usefully employed here to understand the emerging sense of belongingness and cohesiveness being moulded by the participants within their new transnational learning environment. As a member of a community, people are linked through a common interest and shared beliefs and values, with a sense of identity formed through the roles they occupy and relationships they share with others in the group (Lave & Wenger, 1991; Takase et al., 2002). A community's focus is on providing a safe environment conducive to establishing trust, sharing knowledge and shaping identities through socialisation of its members into the community's norms and values. Three interrelated dimensions comprise a definition of a specific Community of Practice: Mutual engagement of members leading to a collective meaning; working towards a common objective in joint enterprise with others; and a shared repertoire, which operationalises meaning made within the group and facilitates learning. These dimensions were extended and applied to the participants' experiences of TNE in this study, defining a specific 'Transnational Community of Practice' (TCP) (Guldberg et al., 2019; Maddison, 2016) as a conceptual space and comfortable place, favourable to transformative learning (Mezirow, 2009).

With their peers, the participants mapped their shared TCP on to the Irish educational landscape they had come to inhabit. Their TCP represented a new social system of their own making which fostered a sense of belongingness and interaction with other nursing students, empowering the construction of a professional self-concept (Ohlen & Segesten, 1998). The TCP also supported the development of self-efficacy and self-determination for personal growth, bolstered mastery of challenges and facilitated cognitive processing of new experiences. It also reflected expectations of who the participants were becoming: a professional western-educated nurse in the Middle East.

As a result of shared experiences within their TCP, a collective identity among the student nurses emerged. Even after graduation, the participants referred to themselves individually as 'we' in an inclusive sense, as a member of a specifically situated group. However, the 'we' did not homogenise: The participants still retained a clear individuality which was evident in terms of their choices and opinions. The collective bonding that occurred was described by one participant as being 'one hand together'. The participants' unique TCP could be said to reflect the desired norms and values of a 'generalised other' (Mead, 1934), which shaped this new collective sense of self. The concept of the 'generalised other' can be described as a social formation representing specific desired behaviours and conduct, perspectives, norms, values and expectations that are internalised over time by a person in order to become a member of the generalised other. The transnational 'we' expressed by the participants can thus be deconstructed to represent both a socialised 'me' as a member of the 'generalised other' – a Transnational Community of Practice – which steadily moulded a professional self, and an active 'I' which progressively empowered and directed personal choice and ambition. When the participants expressed themselves as 'we', it could be interpreted that they were representing themselves as a socialised 'me' – the collective consciousness of their TCP. This is supported by findings from the study that when the participants graduated, they all defined their primary self as a nurse, then a Bahraini, Muslim, female – in that order.

Embodied Agency: The Shaping of Persona

By their third year of study, the participants had stretched existing embedded and embodied socio-cultural norms through the exercise of a growing sense of personal agency, such as becoming friends with their male classmates, culturally not acceptable, but which they justified by calling the male students their 'study brothers' rather than 'boy' friends. Their agency was also expressed through decision-making processes in their daily lives, such as whether to wear 'hejab' (a large headscarf covering the hair and neck, part of an Islamic female dress code), or not. However, their Islamic religion continued to provide the participants with a fixed and important reference point of self as an Arab female. It continued to furnish them with a cultural framework of boundaries they referred to as 'red lines', which they could negotiate and reshape on their own terms, but not erase or cross, such as drinking alcohol or eating pork.

The process of acquiring the persona of a transnationally educated nurse was a dynamic one. The participants reported that there were many socio-cultural barriers to surmount which caused them distress. For example, families were reported as both a source of stress, as well as support. Nursing as a career option for Bahraini females is still in its nascency, and the participants described a general lack of understanding about the profession in Bahrain. Families expressed concerns about reputation – both that of the family and their daughter – and how they would be perceived in Bahraini society if their daughter worked as a nurse. Reluctance was expressed by families concerning participants studying alongside male classmates, working night shifts and having to care for and touch male patients – considered 'haram' or taboo for a modest Muslim female (Hamzeh & Oliver, 2009). At this stage of self-formation, the participants expressed firm views on what they expected of their career, as well as future partners. Only one of the participants had agreed to an arranged marriage, during the third year of her programme, and had stopped working as a nurse at the request of her husband.

Dress code was an issue of contention; many families initially insisted that their daughters retain the traditional form-concealing 'abaya' (a long, loose black cloak worn as an outer garment) and not wear a uniform. However, over time the university nursing uniform (a smart, long, white tunic displaying the university crest and white trousers) eventually came to be accepted as culturally appropriate, embodying a professional self by the wearer, and symbolising a source of pride and identity not only among those who wore it but also their families. The participants reported that family opinion gradually shifted from resistance to encouragement of their new professional persona.

The participants found that they could change perceptions of the nursing profession within their communities, and became confident agents of change in the hospitals where they worked, positively influencing nursing practice such as encouraging other nurses to read research. However, dress codes were important signifiers of their status as transnationally educated local nurses. Their university uniform marked them as different. This difference drew a specific gaze towards them when they were training in the hospitals. 'The Look', as they all called it, signified difference and was a judgemental gaze which implied intangible power relations, a form of social imposition which questioned the way they were presenting themselves – and it expected conformity to local cultural norms. The participants' gendered performativity (Butler, 2010) as Bahraini western-educated nurses attracted The Look. The Look perceived these young women to be bold and immodest: They did not avoid the male gaze nor did they shirk from physical contact according to cultural requirements, nor did they always speak quietly. As social practice is expressed through discourse, The Look can be conceptualised as a discursive practice (Foucault, 1972). The Look, therefore, represents assumptions of dominant patriarchal relations within a Bahraini clinical environment, and can also be considered as part of the hidden curriculum of transnational nursing education in this context, limiting and challenging possibilities of self-construction.

The Look also projected a jealous gaze. There were negative incidents reported on the hospital wards. Other Bahraini nurses who had graduated from a local nursing college were not so welcoming to the transnationally educated student nurses, and harassment was reported. Opinion was expressed by participants that the transnational nursing students were perceived as a threat by other local Bahraini nurses. The Look, therefore, marked the participants as different from other Bahraini females and defined who they were not. It served to reinforce a knitting of a transnational professional self as competencies were developed in both the Bahraini clinical and western academic contexts. Bolstered by the confidence gained from their educational experience, the participants learnt to deflect, reject and fracture The Look. However, through a sense of empowered agency, they could also redirect and transform the focus of The Look from negative to positive connotations. Once a Looker realised that these young women were very capable and confident in performing their professional duties, despite not conforming to embedded cultural expectations, the participants reported that the Look could also signify approval of difference, confirming their competence as transnationally educated nurses.

Becoming: The Same Yet Different – A New Standpoint

By graduation, meanings had shifted in the participants' lifeworld as their sense of being in, and relatedness to, the world changed. However, all the participants in the study firmly retained Islam as a frame of reference which defined their cultural self. The participants emphasised that their religious beliefs and values had not changed, but had been enhanced as a result of their educational experiences.

An alternative way of knowing was articulated, bound to a cultural self and grounded in the tenets of Islam, but placed within an agenda of transnational nursing education. Participants nourished a professional self as a western-educated nurse, were empowered to contest claims of dominant patriarchal knowledge such as those exercised through The Look and could change perceptions of gender norms within their communities. These facets of self, however, were not mutually exclusive nor contested, but were synthesised to support a reconceptualisation of the participants' lifeworld that provided them with a firm view of their new situated positioning in Bahraini society. The participants expressed strong beliefs that they could drive change through the projection of their professional personas as transnationally educated nurses. They viewed themselves driving winds of change, as more Bahraini transnationally educated nurses would follow their steps into the local hospitals.

The study identified the emergence of a distinct and particular Bahraini locational feminism (Enns, 2010), the shaping of a new Arab feminist reflexivity. The participants' situated knowledge proved to be fertile terrain for developing a feminist understanding of a unique Bahraini female standpoint (Harding, 2004) or positioning. As a particular standpoint is achieved through a collective identity that promotes a sense of belongingness (Zarshenas et al., 2013), the participants' experience of an Irish transnational nursing educational experience in Bahrain supported a new discursive positioning in this context (Baker & Wiseman, 2009). Adherence to the Islamic faith was not incompatible with a feminist perspective, representing the basis of feminist principles (Chowdhury, 2009) of working towards gender equality, expanding opportunity and empowering choice. From a postmodern feminist perspective, this is a new conceptualisation of TNE as it presents the subject of a Bahraini locational feminism in the Middle East, operationalised through the participants' transnational learning experiences and extended into the public space of the hospital, as well as the private spheres of individual lives. Through the medium of their educational programme, the participants constructed an intricate situated self as a Bahraini female transnationally educated nurse, sui generis. As a result of the impact of their TNE programme, the participants defined themselves as being 'the same, but different'.

Conclusion

This chapter adds to existing knowledge on what the phenomenon of TNE *does*, and how a TNE experience can shape the lifeworld and sense of self of local learners in situated cultural and geographical contexts. It reports findings from a small-scale study focusing on the impact of transnational nursing education on a group of Bahraini female nursing graduates of an Irish transnational medical university in the Kingdom of Bahrain and explores how they constructed themselves to become western-educated nurses in the Middle East.

'Becoming' (Marginson, 2014; Monrouxe et al., 2011) a transnationally educated nurse was not always a smooth passage; however, by graduation the participants had developed a professional persona that could move fluidly and comfortably between a Bahraini clinical environment and an Irish academic setting. Along their TNE journey, the participants honed skills of agency and self-determination which provided them with confidence to contest dominant patriarchal knowledge, such as that embedded in 'The Look'. The emergence of a new and empowering locational feminism was identified in this context, supported through the participants' constructed Transnational Community of Practice.

There was no evidence from the findings of this study that a western transnational nursing education was a homogenising learning experience, nor that the young women who participated in this study were passive consumers of transnational knowledge. Rather, it highlights that a constellation of possible reflexive positions (Brannick & Coghlan, 2007; Pillow, 2003) are possible for local students attending an IBC of TNE. In this particular study, the participants' TNE experience was transformational in character. Upon graduation, the participants demonstrated strong insight into their own subjectivities, identities and positioning in their lifeworld. Occupying a particular standpoint (Harding, 2004) as a Bahraini female, they had navigated complex issues of gender, power relations and sociocultural values during the lengthy socialisation into the professional persona of a western-educated nurse.

Attention is drawn to the intricate ontological and epistemological challenges that confront local students in a TNE environment, such as those outlined in this chapter. To gain an in-depth understanding of how TNE impacts individual learners' lifeworlds in diverse cultural contexts, the voice of local students' experiences must be listened to. It is recommended that providers of TNE create an environment compatible with the sociocultural and linguistic experiences of local learners, conducive to transformational learning.

This study extends the scope of feminist research in TNE and has unpacked an empowering journey of self-construction as a small group of female Bahraini students became Irish qualified professional nurses at home in Bahrain. Although conducted with a very small number of homogenous participants who had attended an IBC in one particular context in the Middle East, the methodology employed could be usefully transferred to other groups of TNE learners in different situated contexts. It is recommended that further small-scale in-depth studies are conducted in other diverse TNE environments in order to deepen understanding of the impact of the phenomenon of TNE on learners' sense of self.

References

Abdul Salam, A., Elsegaey, I., Khraif, R., AlMutairi, A., & Aldosari, A. (2015). Components and public health impact of population growth in the Arab world. *Plos ONE*, *10*(5), 1–15. 10.1371/journal.pone.0124944

Altbach, P. G. (2007). Globalization and the university: Realities in an unequal world. In F. Forest, & P. G. Altbach (Eds.), *International handbook of higher education* (pp. 121–139). Springer.

American Psychological Association (2007). Guidelines for psychological practice with girls and women. *American Psychologist*, *62*(9), 949–979. 10.1037/0003-066X.62.9.949

Anderson-Levitt, K. (2003). *Local meanings, global schooling: Anthropology and world culture*. Palgrave MacMillan.

Baker, D., & Wiseman, A. W. (2009). *Gender, equality and education from international comparative perspectives*. [Electronic book]. Emerald Group Pub.

Barbaria, P., Bernheim, S., & Nunez-Smith, M. (2011). Gender and the pre-clinical experiences of female medical students: A taxonomy. *Medical Education*, *45*(3), 249–260.

Bender-Slack, D. (2010). The role of gender in making meaning of texts: Bodies, discourses, and ways of Reading. *Feminist Teacher*, *20*(1), 15–27.

Bohan, J. S. (2002). Sex differences and/in the self: Classic themes, feminist variations, postmodern challenges. *Psychology of Women Quarterly*, *26*, 74–88.

Brannick, T., & Coghlan, D. (2007). In defense of being "Native": The case for insider academic research. *Organizational Research Methods*, *10*(1), 59–74.

Butler, J. (2010). Performative agency. *Journal of Cultural Economy*, *3*(2), 147–161. 10.1080/17530350.2010.494117

Chapman, A., & Pyvis, D. (2007). Dilemmas in the formation of student identity in offshore higher education: A case study in Hong Kong. *Educational Review*, *58*(3), 291–302.

Clark Mane, R. L. (2012). Transmuting grammars of whiteness in third-wave feminism: Interrogating postrace histories, postmodern abstraction, and the proliferation of difference in third-wave texts. *Signs*, *38*(1), 71–98.

Cresswell, J. W. (2013). *Qualitative inquiry and research design: Choosing among five traditions* (3rd ed.). SAGE.

Choudaha, R. (2013). Know your international student–Global or glocal? *University World News*, *269*(28).

Chowdhury, E. H. (2009). Locating global feminisms elsewhere: Braiding US women of color and transnational feminisms. *Cultural Dynamics*, *21*(51), 51–78

Davey, J., & Bredemeyer, S. (2011) Becoming a professional nurse. In L. Scanlon (Ed.) *"Becoming" a professional: Lifelong learning book series* (Vol. 16). Springer. https://doi.org/10.1007/978-94-007-1378-9_10

Donn, G., & Al Manthri, Y. (2010). *Globalisation and higher education in the Arab gulf States*. Symposium Books.

Edwards, R., & Usher, R. (2000). *Globalisation and pedagogy: Space, place and identity*. Routledge.

Elsaadda, H., Moghissi, H., Cooke, M., & Valassopoulos, A. (2010). Dialogue section: Arab Feminist research and activism: Bridging the gap between the theoretical and the practical. *Feminist Theory*, *11*, 121–127.

Enns, C. Z. (2010). Locational feminisms and feminist social identity analysis. *Professional Psychology: Research and Practice*, *41*(4), 333–339.

Ernst, & Young (2015). How will the GCC close the skills gap? http://www.ey.com/Publication/vwLUAssets/EY-gcc-education-report-how-will-the-gcc-close-theskills-gap/$FILE/GCC%20Education%20report%20FINAL%20AU3093.pdf

Fail, H., Thompson, J., & Walker, G. (2004). Belonging, identity and third culture kids: Life histories of former international school students. *Journal of Research in International Education*, *3*(3), 319–338.

Faist, T. (2010). Towards transnational studies: World theories, transnationalisation and changing Institutions. *Journal of Ethics and Migration Studies*, *36*(10), 1665–1687.

Feuilherade, P. (2014). GCC healthcare spending surges as demand soars. *Middle East*, (*453*), 38–39.

Foucault, M. (1972). *The archaeology of knowledge and the discourse on language* (A.M. Sheridan Smith, Trans.). Pantheon.

Gargano, T. (2009). (Re)conceptualizing international student mobility: The potential of transnational social fields. *Journal of Studies in International Education*, *13*(3), 331–346.

Giddens, A. (1999). *Runaway world: How globalization is reshaping our lives.* Profile.

Guldberg, K., Achtypi, A., D'Alonzo, L., Laskaridou, K., Milton, D., Molteni, P., & Wood, R. (2019). Using the value creation framework to capture knowledge co-creation and pathways to impact in a transnational community of practice in autism education. *International Journal of Research & Method in Education.* 10.1080/1743727X.2019.1706466

Hafez, S. (2018). Women and education in Muslim context. In Daun H., & Arjmand R. (Eds.) *Handbook of Islamic education: International handbooks of religion and education* (Vol. 7). Springer. 10.1007/978-3-319-64683-1_14

Hamzeh, M. Z., & Oliver, K. (2009). Gaining research access into the lives of Muslim girls: Researchers negotiating Muslimness, modesty, inshallah, and haram. *International Journal of Qualitative Studies in Education*, *23*(2), 165–180. 10.1080/09518390903120369

Harding, S. (Ed.). (2004). *The feminist standpoint theory reader.* Routledge.

Harvey, D. (1990). *The condition of postmodernity. An enquiry into the origins of cultural change.* Blackwell.

Hayes, A., Holden-Rachiotis, C., Kavanagh, B., & Otoom, S. (2011). Bridging the gap: On easing the transition from Arab secondary school to Western third level learning. *Evaluation & Research in Education*, *24*(2), 105–120. 10.1080/09500790.2010.550281.

Hesse-Biber, S. N. (2007). The practice of feminist in-depth interviewing. In S. N. Hesse-Biber, & P. L. Leavy (Eds.), *Feminist research practice: A primer.* Sage Publications.

Hinds, J., & Sparks, P. (2008). Engaging with the natural environment: The role of affective connection and identity. *Environmental Psychology*, *28*(2), 109–120.

Holden, C., Anand, E., Maddison, W., Tawash, E., & Hughes, J. (2017). Epistemological and ontological challenges of transnational foundation year medical students. *International Journal of Learning and Development*, *7*(4). 10.5296/ijld.v7i4.11863

Hussin, V. (2007). Supporting off-shore students: A preliminary study. *Innovations in Education and Teaching International*, *44*(4), 363–376.

International Labour Organisation (ILO) (2018). Labour Migration, Skills Development and the Future of Work in the Gulf. Retrieved December 14, 2020, from http://apmigration.ilo.org/resources/labour-migration-skills-development-and-the-future-of-work-in-the-gulf-cooperation-council-gcc-countries

Jasper, A. (2013). Feminism, religion and this incredible need to believe: Working with Julia Kristeva again. *Feminist Theology*, *21*(3), 279–294. 10.1177/0966735013484218

JISC (2018). Transnational education (TNE). Retrieved February 1, 2021 from https://www.jisc.ac.uk/rd/projects/transnational-education

Kadiwal, L., & Rind, I. (2013). 'Selective cosmopolitans': Tutors' and students' experience of offshore higher education in Dubai. *Compare: A Journal of Comparative and International Education*, *43*(5), 689–711.

Kain, V. J. (2015). Internationalisation of the curriculum in an undergraduate nursing degree. In W., Green, & C. Witsed (Eds.) *Critical perspectives on internationalising the curriculum in disciplines. Global perspectives on higher education* (Vol. 28). Sense Publishers.

Kane, T. (2014). Whose lingua Franca? The politics of language in transnational medical education. *Journal of Medical Education*, *63*(2), 94–112.

Khine, M. S. (Ed.) (2008). *Knowing, knowledge and beliefs: Epistemological studies across cultures*. Dorchert.

Khine, M. S., & Hayes, B. (2010). Investigating women's ways of knowing: An explanatory study in the UAE. *Issues in Educational Research*, *20*(2), 105–117.

Kingdom of Bahrain, Ministry of Education (2020). Statistics Reports. Retrieved November 1, 2020 from https://www.moe.gov.bh/statistics.aspx

Kingdom of Bahrain, Supreme Council for Women (2015). Bahraini Women in Numbers. Retrieved November 1, 2020, from https://www.scw.bh/en/MediaCenter/Publications/SupremeCouncilforWomen/SupremeCouncilforWomenPublication/Final-Numbers_En-May-2015.pdf

Knight, J. (2016). Transnational education remodeled: Toward a common TNE framework and definitions. *Journal of Studies in International Education*, *20*(1), 34–47. https://doi.org/10.1177/1028315315602927

Lave, J., & Wenger, E. (1991). *Situated learning. Legitimate peripheral participation*. Cambridge University Press.

Lazar, M. M. (2007). feminist critical discourse analysis: Articulating a feminist discourse praxis. *Critical Discourse Studies*, *4*(2), 141–164.

Mackay, M., Joyce-McCoach, J., Stephens, M., Cutler, N., Brown, R., Fernandez, Froggat, T., Heaton, L., Moxham, L., Sim, J., Traynor, V., & Bourgeois, S. (2016) Review of transnational nursing education programme curricula: Process, findings and recommendation. *Nurse Educ. Today*, *42*, 73–77. 10.1016/j.nedt.2016.04.004

Maddison, W. (2015). Developing a transnational student success 'Signature'. *World Academy of Science, Engineering and Technology: Educational and Pedagogical Sciences*, *9*(5). http://waset.org/publications/10001127/transnational-higher-education-developing-a-transnational-student-success-signature-for-pre-clinical-medical-students-an-action-research-project

Maddison, W. (2016). *Transnational Medical and Nursing Education: An exploration of its impact on Bahraini females* [EdD Thesis for University of Liverpool]. https://livrepository.liverpool.ac.uk/3000920/1/200874979_Oct2015.pdf

Marginson, S. (2014). Student self-formation in international education. *Journal of Studies in International Education*, *18*(1), 6–22. 10.1177/1028315313513036

McKinsey & Company (2014). Women Matter. GCC Women in Leadership – from the first to the norm. Retrieved 1/11/20 from: https://es.uefa.com/MultimediaFiles/Download/uefaorg/CaptainsofChange/02/20/42/36/2204236_DOWNLOAD.pdf

Mead, G. H. (1934). *Mind, self and society*. Chicago University Press.

Mezirow, J. (2009). Transformative learning theory. In J. Mezirow, & E. W. Taylor (Eds.), *Transformative learning in practice: Insights from community, workplace, and higher education*, (pp. 18–32). Jossey-Bass.

Miller-Idriss, C., & Hanauer, E. (2011). Transnational higher education: Offshore campuses in the middle East. *Comparative Education*, *47*(2), 181–207.

Miriam, E., Alon, L., Raveh, H., Ella, G., Rikki, N., & Erfat, S. (2013). Going global: Developing management Students' cultural intelligence and global identity in culturally diverse virtual teams. *Academy of Management Learning & Education*, *12*(13), 330–335. 10.5465/amle.2012.0200

Moghadam, V. M. (2010). Women, structure, and agency in the Middle East: Introduction and overview to feminist formations' special issue on women in the Middle East. *Feminist Formations*, *3*(2), 1–9.

Monrouxe, L. V., Rees, C. E., & Hu, W. (2011). Differences in medical students' explicit discourses of professionalism: Acting, representing, becoming. *Medical Education*, *45*, 585–602.

OECD (2015). Better Skills, Better Jobs, and Better Lives: A Strategic Approach to Education and Skills Policies for the United Arab Emirates. http://www.oecd.org/countries/unitedarabemirates/A-Strategic-Approach-to-Education-and%20SkillsPolicies-for-the-United-Arab-Emirates.pdf

Ohlen, J., & Segesten, K. (1998). The professional identity of the nurse: Concept analysis and development. *Journal of Advanced Nursing*, *28*(4), 720–727.

Oikonomidoy, E., & Williams, G. (2013). Enriched or latent cosmopolitanism? Identity negotiations of female international students from Japan in the US. *Discourse: Studies in the Cultural Politics of Education*. 10.1080/01596306.2012.71719.

Patel, F., & Lynch, H. (2013). Globalization as an alternative to internationalization in higher education: Embedding positive glocal learning experiences. *International Journal of Teaching & Learning in Higher Education*, *24*(2), 223–230.

Pillow, W. (2003). Confession, catharsis, or cure? Rethinking the uses of reflexivity as methodological power in qualitative research. *Qualitative Studies in Education*, *16*(2), 175–196.

Pincas, A. (2001). Culture, cognition and communication in global education. *Distance Education*, *22*, 30–51.

Pirc, T. (2014). Nation state and cosmopolitan identity in a postmodern world of globalization. *Limes; Borderland Studies*, *6*(2), 132–148.

Plummer, & M. Young, L. E. (2010). Grounded theory and feminist inquiry: Revitalizing links to the past. *Western Journal of Nursing Research*, *32*(3), 305–321.

Probyn, E. (1993). *Sexing the self: Gendered positions in cultural studies*. Routledge.

Pyvis, D., & Chapman, A. (2005). Culture shock and the international student "offshore". *Journal of Research in International Education*, *4*, 23–42.

Shope, J. H. (2006). "You Can't cross a River without getting wet": A feminist standpoint on the dilemmas of cross-cultural research. *Qualitative Inquiry*, *12*(1), 163–184.

Singh, P., & Doherty, C. (2004). Global cultural flows and pedagogic dilemmas: Teaching in the global university contact zone. *TESOL Quarterly*, *38(*1), 9–42.

Smith, J. A., Flowers, P., & Larkin, M. (2009). *Interpretative phenomenological analysis: Theory, method and research*. SAGE Publications.

Smith, J. A., & Osborn, M. (2003). Interpretative phenomenological analysis. In J. A. Smith (Ed.), *Qualitative psychology: A practical guide to methods*. SAGE.

Snyder, R. C. (2008). What is third-wave feminism? A new directions essay. *Signs: Journal of Women in Culture and Society*, *34*(1), 175–196.

Standing, M. (2009). A new critical framework for applying hermeneutic phenomenology. *Nurse Researcher*, *16(*4), 20–30.

Stevenson, J., & Clegg, S. (2010). Possible selves: Students orientating themselves toward the future through extracurricular activity. *British Educational Research Journal*, *37*(2), 231–246.

Takase, M., Kershaw, E., & Burt, L. (2002). Does public image of nurse's matter? *Journal of Professional Nursing*, *18*(4), 196–205.

Tawash, E., Anand, E., Holden, C., Hughes, J., & Maddison, W. (2019). From Arabic high school graduate to Western qualified nurse: The challenge of transition (A discussion paper). *Studies in Higher Education*. 10.1080/03075079.2019.1623774

The Economist Intelligence Unit. (2012). *Women's Economic Opportunity Index 2012*. Retrieved November 1, 2020, from https://www.eiu.com/public/topical_report.aspx?campaignid=weoindex2012

The Quality Assurance Agency for Higher Education, UK. (2014). *Review of UK Transnational Education in the UAE: Overview*. Retrieved November 1, 2020, from https://www.qaa.ac.uk/docs/qaa/international/review-transnational-education-uae-14.pdf?sfvrsn=1407f481_2

The World Bank. (2020). Labour force participation rate, female (% of female population ages 15+). https://data.worldbank.org/indicator/SL.TLF.CACT.FE.ZS?locations=BHThe%20World%20Bank,%202020

The World Health Organisation (WHO). (2013). *A universal truth: No health without a workforce: Third Global Forum on Human Resources for Health report*. Retrieved November 1, 2020, from http://www.who.int/workforcealliance/knowledge/resources/hrhreport2013/en/

Tran, L. T. (2011). Committed, face-value, hybrid or mutual adaptation? The experiences of international students in higher education. *Educational Review*, *63*, 79–94.

Tubin, D., & Lapidot, O. (2008). Construction of 'Glocal' (global-local) identity among Israeli graduate students in the USA. *Higher Education*, *55*, 203–217. 10.1007/s10734-006-9049-x

Welikala, T. (2011). *Rethinking international higher education curriculum: Mapping the research landscape*. Universitas 21.

Wenger, E. (1998). *Communities of practice: Learning, meaning and identity*. Cambridge University Press.

Wilkins, W., & Huisman, J. (2012). The international branch campus as transnational strategy in higher education. *Higher Education*, *64*, 627–645.

Wilson, M. (2002). Transnational nursing program: Models, advantages and challenges. *Nurse Education Today*, *22*, 417–426.

World Economic Forum (2014b). Global Gender Gap Report. Global Gender Gap Index Bahrain. Retrieved November 1, 2020, from http://reports.weforum.org/global-gender-gap-report-2014/economies/#economy=BHR.

Young, K. E. (2016) Women's labor force participation across the GCC. *Arab Gulf States Institute in Washington*. www.agsiw.org.

Zarshenas, L., Farkhondeh, S. S., Molazem, Z., Khayyer, M., Zare, N., & Ebadt, A. (2013). Professional socialization in nursing: A qualitative content analysis. *Iranian Journal of Nursing and Midwifery Research*, *19*(4), 432–439.

Zembylas, M. (2012). Transnationalism, migration and emotions: Implications for education. *Globalisation, Societies and Education*, *10*(2), 163–179.

Author biography

Dr Wendy Maddison is the Head of Student Development & Wellbeing at RCSI Bahrain. Her areas of expertise include transnational higher education; student experience, provision of student support in different cultural contexts, personal and professional development strategies; student well-being; development of extra-curricular and informal learning opportunities. She has published in high impact journals such as *Studies in Higher Education* and *International Journal of Learning and Development*, covering topics to do with educational, identity and professional transitions of local (female) Middle Eastern students as they begin their educational journeys at an overseas campus of an international university.

Chapter 8

Ready, Willing, and Able? Exploring the Relationships and Experiences of International Students at a Federal University in the United Arab Emirates

Natalie I. Cruz, Jobila W. Sy, Cassandra Shukla, and Alisha Tysor

Introduction

The United Arab Emirates (UAE) is one of the most diverse and globally minded countries in the world, which has demonstrated exemplified by its education system (Ahmad & Hussain, 2017). As of 2019, over 77,000 international students (IS) studied in the UAE, or almost 50% of the total number of tertiary students in the UAE (UNESCO, 2019). Research has been conducted in recent years to understand the experiences of students at international branch campuses (IBCs) and international schools (Ahmad & Hussain, 2017; Wilkins et al., 2012), but very little is known about the experiences of IS at UAE federal universities. This empirical study examines the experiences of IS at a federal higher education institution (HEI) in the UAE, by aiming to understand their relationships with national students, adjustment experiences, and perception of institutional support systems, through the lens of the intergroup contact theory (ICT). The study highlights perceptions, experiences, and barriers that impact engagement between the two populations and how IS are engaged and supported on campus. Highlighting these perceptions, barriers and experiences will be used to understand the type of 'image' of an international student that has been shaped at a federal university in the UAE, making visible the assumptions that have been made about these students, and how these assumptions may impact international students' experiences.

Problem and Purpose

This descriptive, exploratory study empirically analyses the experiences of IS and their connections with national students at a federal UAE university. The research site is referred to as Emirati Dunes University

DOI: 10.4324/9781003138457-11

(EDU). Researchers utilised survey methods to answer the following questions:

a How do national students describe their interactions and perceptions of IS?
b How do IS describe their interactions and perceptions of national students?
c How do IS describe their adjustment experiences at EDU?
d How do IS perceive institutional support services at EDU?

EDU is referred to as a federal institution in this chapter, and non-international students are referred to as national or Emirati students. An international student is defined as someone enrolled in a degree program in the UAE who does not have Emirati citizenship. This definition aligns with the unique citizenship and residence rules of the UAE. This rigid and unique definition of IS will be problematised in subsequent sections. This chapter provides relevant background and context of the UAE and its higher education system, problematises the term 'international student', describes the theoretical framework, and provides a brief review of the relevant literature. The methodology, findings, discussion, and recommendations for future research are also shared.

Higher Education and International Student Context within the United Arab Emirates

The UAE is a young and wealthy nation in the Gulf region of the Middle East. Approximately 88% of the 9.3 million residents are expatriates or non-national, and the language of business is English although citizens primarily speak Arabic (UAE, n.d.). In the 2015–2016 academic year, close to 140,000 students were enrolled in higher education institutions (United Arab Emirates Ministry of Education [MOE], 2018). Federal institutions enrol 33% of all students, but only 9% of IS (Ministry of Higher Education & Scientific Research, 2016). There are three federal universities and 72 private universities or colleges (Cruz & Shukla, 2020). In 2019, about 50% of tertiary students were international, or 77,463 students (UNESCO, 2019). India and Middle-Eastern/North African countries like Yemen, Jordan, and Egypt are the most popular senders of IS to the UAE (UNESCO, 2019). A study into the motivations of IS in the UAE found that it is an attractive destination amongst international students due to its security, political stability, hospitality, and tolerance of multiculturalism (Ahmad & Hussain, 2017). The UAE receives only 1.5% of the globally mobile student population, but it is considered a growing 'higher education hub' due to its investment in education and international branch campuses (IBCs) (Knight & Morshidi, 2011). Many private institutions are IBCs, which are HEIs that are owned, operated, and provide degrees by an international provider, such as New York University-Abu Dhabi (C-BERT, n.d.).

Although the majority of Emiratis attend private institutions, federal HEIs serve mostly Emiratis (Ashour & Fatima, 2016). Small numbers of IS attend federal institutions, and increasing numbers of national students attend IBCs (Wilkins et al., 2012). Even so, many federal universities have pushed to enrol more IS to capitalise on the UAE's global appeal. Federal universities offer free tuition to citizens, and most of the classes are in English although most Emirati students' native language is Arabic. The main mission of federal universities is to educate citizens, although HEIs have tried to recruit more IS in recent years. The oldest university was established in 1976 (Cruz & Shukla, 2020), so the higher education system is relatively young. The federal HEIs are typically segregated by gender for all students, and the curriculum and structure have been developed in close conjunction with the federal government (Al Ali, 2014).

Research about IS in the UAE is almost exclusively focused on students in IBCs, lacking insights into the experiences of students who attend federal universities. The increasing number of IS in the country warrants a deeper exploration of their relationships with Emirati students, which can also help HEIs better support and understand IS' experiences. For the purposes of this book, it also provides critical insights into how the IS and Emirati students are constructed by each other.

Complexities in the Definition, Assumptions, and Constructions of International Students

Mobility and circulation of people have become a mainstream experience as more people live in multiple countries and identify with different cultures. Globalisation has rapidly increased in the emergence of the modern nation-state and development of many countries, which presents tensions for national leaders between cultivating a global presence and promoting a national agenda (Marginson, 2013). The notion of categorising a student as either international or domestic has become more complicated in a globalised world, as mobile individuals often identify as transnational, global, or beyond a particular nation-state. Tertiary students may be classified as nationals who have never lived for a substantial time in their country of citizenship. Likewise, students classified as international may have lived a significant portion of their lives in the country of their HEI, but may not have citizenship (Jones, 2017). The binary view of international or national is particularly problematic in the UAE.

In the UAE, people may be classified as 'international' because their father does not have Emirati citizenship, but they have lived their entire lives in the UAE (UAE, n.d.). Classifying a student as 'international' is further complicated because 87.9% of the UAE resident population is from another country (UAE, n.d.). For example, if university personnel assume that most IS have prolonged experiences living in the UAE, they may be reluctant to provide specialised services for IS. On the other hand, students who have lived their entire life in the UAE may have to go through an international orientation, which may not be necessary and not appreciated.

The multicultural context of the UAE juxtaposed with the insular nature of local culture and family structures makes for an interesting case study for IS at a federal institution. Emirati female students are strongly encouraged to wear the local traditional dress: a black head-covering, known as a shayla, and a black abaya, or loose-fitting robe-like dress. Non-Muslim international students who do not wear the local dress are more readily identified, which may impact local students' assumptions of them. It is important to note that Emiratis pride themselves on the UAE's diversity, while also attempting to preserve their cultural identity and traditions. These contradictions are also seen in many other countries with an open and welcoming nature for international students, but also with restrictive structures, limited employment opportunities, and a need to pacify a fear that national students are neglected (Marginson, 2013).

Previous literature has found that within Anglophone societies like the United Kingdom, Australia, and the United States, implicit assumptions of IS can lead to challenges with the way they are received in the university context (Harrison, 2015; Harrison & Peacock, 2010). The deficit model that is often ascribed to IS due to language and cultural barriers does not play out in the same way at federal institutions in the UAE. In the context of the UAE, many international students' English skills may be better than Emirati students, and thus may be desired group mates in-class projects. This may run counter to other contexts, where some studies have found that in other countries where national students may be weary to partner with international students due to fear of lower marks or causing offence (Harrison & Peacock, 2010). Another assumption that is made about IS is that they should adapt or assimilate – indeed a whole strand of research describes how IS can effectively assimilate (Jindal-Snape & Rienties, 2016). However, it remains to be seen how this translates to a multicultural society like the UAE where people of many different cultures live alongside each other, although often leading very distinct lives.

This study brings nuance to the idea of who is classified as 'international' and how this impacts their university experience. It also suggests implications for the assumptions that underlie the definition of an international student in the UAE. The experiences of an international student need to be problematised and reimagined as society changes and educational research critically evolves.

Theoretical Framework

The intergroup contact theory (ICT) is described in international literature as an effective means to understand prejudice and build relationships among different groups of people (Allport, 1954; Chavous, 2005; Pettigrew, 1998; Pettigrew et al., 2011). Allport (1954) hypothesised that four conditions are necessary for optimal intergroup contact: *equal status*, *cooperation*, *common goals*, and *institutional support*. These conditions incorporate both relational conditions (*cooperation* and *common goals*), as well as structural conditions (*equal status* and *institutional support*) (Chavous, 2005). According to Pettigrew (1998), *equal status* can be defined as members interacting in a situation where equality is expected and perceived. *Common goals* require that members of both groups are interdependent to achieve shared goals. *Cooperation* refers to members of both groups working together collaboratively and not competitively. Lastly, *institutional support* or *support of authorities* means that at an institutional, authoritative, or societal level, positive intergroup contact and harmony are not restricted and are fostered as an accepted norm. Previous literature (Harrison & Peacock, 2010) has shown that classroom settings can fulfil the condition where international and domestic student participants have *equal status* as students share *common goals* and demonstrate *cooperation* in situations that require academic and social collaboration (e.g. group projects, class assignments, student organisations/club participation, etc.). IS also have diverse experiences that influence their perceptions of *institutional support*.

Allport (1954) posits that when members of cross-cultural groups engage under the aforementioned conditions, these interactions can result in decreased prejudice and intergroup discrimination, improved relations, and tolerance. Some studies have shown that even when Allport's (1954) four conditions are not met, prejudice still decreases, and empathy, mutual understanding, and perspective-taking increase (Lytle, 2018; Pettigrew & Tropp, 2006). However, the mere presence of diversity and intergroup proximity does not equate to increased intergroup interactions, nor does it decrease group conflict (Chavous, 2005; Pettigrew & Tropp, 2006). It is possible that mere contact without structure and guidance could even lead to negative experiences (Harrison & Peacock, 2010). It is incumbent upon institutional environments to actively promote intergroup interaction, particularly friendship formation through influences from policy, campus cultural inclusiveness, infrastructure, program interventions (e.g. intercultural competence training), professional development, curricula, and other societal priorities that influence university culture and identity (Chavous, 2005; Tawagi & Mak, 2015).

A study by Tawagi and Mak (2015) examined applications of intergroup contact among international and national students and found that improving campus cultural climate also improved intercultural attitudes of IS and the quality of intergroup interactions. Tawagi and Mak (2015) stated, 'A culturally inclusive educational environment may make international students feel more comfortable and respected; they may then be more open to interacting with domestic students in equal and positive ways, resulting in improved intercultural attitudes' (p. 350). They confirmed that there is little research available that explores these topics from the perspective of IS and recommend future research that examines perceptions of cultural inclusivity and relations from international and domestic students' perspectives.

This study utilised intergroup contact as its theoretical framework to guide data collection and analysis of international and domestic students' previous experiences, intergroup interactions, and university engagement as a means to understanding institutional support. ICT is heavily influenced by a student's prior experience and the quantity and quality of the interaction (Chavous, 2005; Tawagi & Mak, 2015). Capturing international and domestic student experiences and perspectives in the study discussed in this chapter provided a holistic understanding of ICT currently underrepresented in the research literature. It also revealed how IS have been understood by the domestic students and the institution where they were studying. Such insights provided a window into the assumptions that have been previously made about IS. The data from IS have additionally shaped an understanding of the types of things that were not said or assumed about them, making these silences an important lens through which their experiences of university education could be understood.

Literature Review

This brief literature review focuses on challenges and opportunities associated with the relational conditions of international and domestic student engagement (i.e. *cooperation* and *common goals)*, and how structural conditions (i.e. *equal status* and *institutional support*) impact adjustment and engagement for IS.

Relational Conditions That Impact International and Domestic Student Engagement

The presence of IS provides opportunities for students, faculty, and the wider community to expand their global awareness. Local peer interaction is an essential component of the international student experience (Trice, 2007). Research has shown that IS who engage in meaningful relationships with national students often perform better academically and have higher life satisfaction (Quinton, 2020; Trice, 2007). From the lens of ICT, these relationships are enhanced by the presence of amicable collaboration and the achievement of shared goals. Nevertheless, there are documented challenges that threaten these optimal conditions that support positive intergroup contact, like perceptions, cultural differences, and language (AlSahafi & Shin, 2017; Marginson, 2013; Quinton, 2020; Trice, 2007).

Perceptions and Prior Experiences

A recent study in the United States evaluated self-esteem, university identity, and perceived discrimination as predictors of adjustment issues and indicated the likelihood to interact with domestic students (Quinton, 2020). The outcomes highlighted that low self-esteem correlated with less interaction with nationals, and IS who had a better sense of institutional identification fostered more meaningful relationships with national and IS (Quinton, 2020).

While studies have found that international students often desire stronger relationships with local students, domestic students do not always have those same feelings (Marginson, 2013; Quinton, 2020; Harrison, 2015). Harrison and Peacock (2010) classified domestic students in their study in the UK as embodying 'informed cosmopolitanism' or 'passive xenophobia', although students certainly fall along a continuum. If students had multicultural families, prior travel experience, or spoke other languages, it often led to a greater desire to engage with international students (Harrison & Peacock, 2010). However, these precursors and desires often do not trans late into automatic or inevitable connections among students – intentionality is critical (Harrison, 2015).

Cultural Differences and Established Networks

While the literature supports the value of establishing international-national peer relationships, opportunities for positive interactions and relationship formation can be challenging due to barriers such as available time to engage with other students socially, different cultural practices and perspectives, established networks, and language difficulties (Trice, 2007). National students often enter the university with an established network of family, friends, and secondary school acquaintances. Conversely, IS may not have the same type of local network. This network, or lack thereof, may affect their desire to create deep, meaningful relationships with new individuals (Marginson, 2013).

Different cultural practices and perspectives can be challenging for students, faculty, and staff. The cognitive dissonance, or inconsistency between thought and action, often associated with the cross-cultural experience can be overwhelming for some individuals with limited experience with other cultures. While some national students find different cultural practices and perspectives an opportunity for personal growth, others may not have the skills nor interest to overcome adversity (Harrison, 2015). Real or perceived cultural distance and difference can lead students to assume that friendships with those from different backgrounds will not work due to fear, unfamiliarity, or lack of similar interests (Harrison, 2015). The resulting adverse reactions of some national students can leave IS feeling discriminated against or unwanted (Marginson, 2013; Trice, 2007). Research has shown these feelings can then result in dissatisfaction with the academic experience, reduced interest in interacting with nationals, and correlated with increased chances of homesickness amongst other emotional issues (Quinton, 2020; Trice, 2007).

Structural Conditions that Impact IS and Domestic Student Adjustment and Engagement

Optimal intergroup contact requires structural conditions which promote member equality and institutional support that fosters these positive exchanges (Pettigrew et al., 2011). In relation to the ICT, these structural conditions can often be developed through activities and classroom settings, which support students' ability to have positive exchanges (Chavous, 2005). In the context of international and domestic student adjustment and engagement, the literature often highlights language barriers as a major challenge (AlSahafi & Shin, 2017; Lin & Scherz, 2014). Overcoming language barriers not only impacts relational conditions but can also at times define one's level of equality within an environment where communication is key to navigating academic and social interactions (Ozer, 2015). Therefore, the extent to which institutions can support more positive interactions becomes a critical component in IS and domestic student adjustment and engagement (Pettigrew et al., 2011).

Language Barriers

One of the primary challenges associated with international student adjustment and engagement is that of language barriers (AlSahafi & Shin, 2017; Ozer, 2015). Primarily, this issue is examined from the perspective of IS' ability to demonstrate language proficiency in the host country's official language. A study by AlSahafi and Shin (2017) found that expressive and written language were predictive barriers to institutional adjustment, while improving language proficiency was found to be an effective coping mechanism to improve academic and social engagement. Other studies have examined increasing opportunities for intercultural interactions in the face of globalisation and the important role language proficiency plays to help prevent social isolation (Ozer, 2015). Language levels have been found to impact IS' academic and engagement levels with the locals. Several studies have found that IS can be anxious when speaking with local students

(Lin & Scherz, 2014) and were more likely to experience discrimination and struggle to form meaningful relationships with domestic students (Poyrazli & Lopez, 2007). Language adjustment in international education has not fully captured the complexity of linguistic diversity found in multilingual communities such as the UAE.

Although the official language is Arabic in the UAE, the medium of instruction is English. In this case, local students engage and interact in a language that is not their native language in formal classroom settings. On the other hand, informal social interactions may be a mixture of languages. This can leave IS with potentially stronger English skills in an odd situation as they may excel in the classroom but struggle with connecting with local students in their native language. With expanding exposure to linguistic diversity, navigating multilingual interactions brings an added layer of challenges to academic and social adjustment for all participants, particularly IS, which impacts levels of peer-to-peer and peer-to-institution engagement.

In this study, IS may or may not be studying and interacting in a non-native language, just as local students engage in curricular experiences in a non-native language. AlSahafi and Shin (2017) state: 'Proficiency in the target language is a fundamental factor that enhances [IS'] academic achievement and cultural adjustment' (p. 54). However, in this case, the target language is not fixed in an explicitly monolingual context. Overall, research supports that successful adjustment and engagement requires fluency in both academic and social language (AlSahafi & Shin, 2017). Language proficiency for classroom performance is distinct from colloquial communication found in social interactions.

Institutional Support

IS come from a variety of backgrounds and experiences. However, there are some common needs that IS typically have, and HEIs should provide requisite levels of support. The literature about IS often highlights several important domains of student needs, including academic/language, socio-cultural, and practical needs (Arthur, 2017; Bartram, 2008). In particular, faculty, counsellors, and local students are an important part of the institutional support systems for IS (Arthur, 2017; Glass et al., 2017).

Although HEI administrators readily recruit and welcome IS to their campus, appropriate levels and structures of support have not always been a priority. In terms of academic support, HEIs should provide academic and language support like tutors, language centres, and faculty engagement (Lin & Scherz, 2014). Faculty members are critical to ensuring that IS connect on campus and reach their full academic potential (Arthur, 2017; Glass et al., 2017). Sociocultural needs can be met by facilitating intentional connections between domestic and IS, providing ongoing support related to the host country culture, engaging with community members and local residents, and connecting students with on-campus opportunities (Bartram, 2008). IS are often more motivated to build cross-cultural relationships (Harrison, 2015; Quinton, 2020), so it is important for the HEI administrators to support these relationships in both structured and unstructured ways (Arthur, 2017). Lastly, transition or adjustment support services are critical. Many HEIs have international student offices that connect students to resources, but it should be a campus-wide effort. This can include programs or services like orientation, career counsellors, housing assistance, campus engagement, campus resources, and immigration services (Arthur, 2017; Bartram, 2008). The levels of institutional support will vary at each HEI depending on the international student numbers, demographics, and campus culture. However, faculty and staff need to consider the unique academic, sociocultural, and practical needs of IS.

An inherent contradiction is that services may be provided (or not provided) for international students based on what it is assumed that they need. This may be particularly relevant in a multicultural context like the UAE. Starr-Glass et al. (2017) offers a perspective from the viewpoint of a transnational campus in Europe. He says that by labelling students as international, they may take on the negative assumptions that are made about international students. He offers the solution to provide basic immigration services, and instead dovetail any other initiatives into general student services that all students can access. Marginson (2013) advocates for the recognition of the agency of international students to understand their own needs without encumbering them with restrictions and expectations. This can also extend to services that may benefit all students – even domestic students who may have some of the same needs as international students – such as a desire for increased academic support or programs to transition on campus. If international students are recruited to increase the diversity and internationalisation of college campuses (Marginson, 2013), but research demonstrates that these impactful relationships do not often develop organically (Harrison & Peacock, 2010), then a program to increase intercultural engagements is, therefore, a justified service that benefits all students and should be branded as such.

Assumptions and constructions of international students are often problematic, and faculty and staff need to understand and deconstruct these narratives to best support transnational students in a globalised higher education context. This brief literature review has focused on research complementing the elements of the ICT, and included institutional support, language barriers, cultural differences, established networks, and perceptions and prior experiences. This intersects with the focus of this study, which is to understand how IS and Emirati students perceive and engage with each other, as well as how IS are supported and transition to the case study campus.

Methodology and Research Design

This descriptive study used survey data to understand national students' perceptions and engagement with IS, as well as IS' experiences at a federal university in the UAE. Given the dearth of prior research, the primarily open-ended survey questions were important to establish a baseline of understanding of IS in this context.

Research Site

The study took place at a national, federally funded university in the UAE, referred to by the pseudonym Emirati Dunes University (EDU). At EDU, all students take most of their classes in English, and there is even an English immersion program to help UAE students learn English. In 2018, EDU overall enrolled 90% female/10% male students, and 86% undergraduate/14% graduate students. Although EDU has residence halls, the vast majority of students commute to campus and live with their families in the local area. As the findings show, most IS have strong prior connections with the UAE, and also commute to school. However, the small residence halls are primarily filled with IS and smaller numbers of Emirati males.

Participants and Sampling

At the time of data collection, IS represented 1.3% of EDU's student population (n = 121). In Fall 2017, all IS were sent an electronic survey that requested feedback about their experiences at EDU. Forty-three IS responded to the survey, which was 35.5% of the population. National students were also recruited to complete a questionnaire about their intercultural experiences and interactions with IS. Researchers strove to minimise bias by recruiting a random sample of students. Mostly first and second-year national students enrolled in advising courses were sent an email with the opportunity to participate in the survey. This recruitment was due to the positionality of the authors as instructors of first-and-second-year courses. Approximately 250 national students were sent an email and 83 responded to the survey, which was a response rate of 33%. While the smaller participant sample, predominantly female respondents, and open-ended questions do not provide the opportunity to extrapolate beyond this study, it provides a good baseline for this context and sets the stage for future research.

Measures

The UAE international and national student surveys were developed specifically for the study to answer the research questions about the engagement and institutional support of IS, and national and IS interactions and perceptions. Several steps were taken to strengthen the validity and reliability. Survey questions were constructed from the literature, such as the ICT framework (Allport, 1954), and literature that examines international and national students engagement (Trice, 2007), language challenges (AlSahafi & Shin, 2017; Ozer, 2015), and the importance of institutional programs and support systems (Arthur, 2017; Bartram, 2008). The pilot version of the survey was reviewed by other faculty members and edited accordingly. Lastly, the survey was vetted through the institutional research office. The surveys contained a variety of open and closed-ended questions, and both surveys collected basic demographic data. Twelve questions from the national student survey were used for this chapter, which related to their background and intercultural experiences, their perceptions and experiences with IS, and their feelings about the UAE as a globalised country. Most questions were open-ended, but several utilised a five-point Likert scale. Additionally, 14 questions from the IS survey were used in this chapter, related to institutional support systems, adjustment, and experiences with Emirati students.

Data Collection and Analysis

Surveys were distributed through the Qualtrics platform. Data collection took place in late Fall 2017 and early Spring 2018. All participants consented to the terms of the study before proceeding to answer the questionnaire. Statistical analyses were conducted using SPSS, and open-ended questions were coded by researchers using descriptive coding to collate the answers. Pairwise deletion methods were used for missing data so that each question could stand on its own. Because researchers examined questions in the aggregate and did not attempt to make connections between different questions for a specific case, pairwise deletion methods worked well and allowed more robust data analysis.

Findings

There is little research about IS at federal HEIs in the UAE, so one of the aims of this study was to provide descriptive and explanatory data. The surveys had a total of 126 participants: 83 national and 43 international students. Due to attrition or skipped answers, numbers did not total 83 or 43 for each question. Tables 8.1 and 8.2 summarise relevant demographic data for participants. Emirati male students were solicited for this study, but only female students responded. The lack of Emirati male respondents undoubtedly skewed the findings, and more research should be focused on Emirati males' experiences in the future. The IS survey participants represented a greater gender and academic diversity at EDU compared to the national students. The UAE categorises anyone whose father does not hold

Table 8.1 National Student Demographic Data (*N* = 83)

Characteristic	N	%
Gender		
Female	83	100
Male	0	0.00
Age		
18–21	77	92.77
22–26	5	6.02
27–30	0	0.00
31–35	0	0.00
36–40	1	1.20
Academic Classification (Undergraduate)		
First Year	24	28.92
Second Year	42	50.60
Third Year	17	20.48
Fourth Year	0	0.00

UAE citizenship as foreign, so many IS had actually lived in the UAE for much of their lives but were considered international. This is an important distinction about the international student context in the UAE. In this study, 40% of the IS respondents had lived in the UAE for at least four years prior to enrolling at EDU.

Table 8.2 International Student Demographic Data (*N* = 43)

Characteristic	N	%
Gender		
Female	31	72.09
Male	11	25.58
Unknown	1	2.33
Age		
18–21	33	76.25
22–26	7	16.28
27–30	1	2.33
31–35	2	4.65
Academic Classification		
First Year	1	2.33
Second Year	21	48.84
Third Year	9	20.93
Fourth Year	8	18.60
Graduate	4	9.30

National Students' Perceptions and Experiences with International Students

Research question one focused on how national students described their interactions and perceptions of IS. UAE federal universities do not have large numbers of IS, but national students often have intercultural experiences through secondary school, travelling, and living in a highly internationalised country. Ninety-eight percent of participants reported that they had travelled to a foreign country, with the vast majority of participants listing at least three different countries. In general, surveyed Emirati students were open to people from different cultural backgrounds. Almost 84% of students said that they were extremely or somewhat interested in 'learning about other nationalities and cultures'. Based on survey results and experience working at the institution, the reasoning for this interest likely stems from concerns regarding communicating with relatives in other countries, interest in cultures and travelling, and even increased future employment. One student notably remarked that knowing more about other cultures, including foreign languages, could help them 'communicate better with the foreign [people]', which is a significant population in the country.

Most survey questions focused on students' perceptions and experiences with IS. Sixty-three percent of participants reported that they were aware that they had IS in at least one of their classes, although 13% were unsure. Students who reported having IS in their classes enjoyed the students because they heard new perspectives and learned about other cultures. One student reflected that the presence of IS positively affected her global awareness and knowledge through exposure to 'new ideas due to their different cultural backgrounds. In addition, they introduce new perspectives which help create more ideas and understand global problems even further'. In these cases, the national students saw the presence of IS as a positive element of their community for the knowledge and perspective that they can share. In terms of interactions with IS outside of the classroom, only 40% of Emirati students said that they had interacted with IS. Given that EDU is a predominately commuter campus and does not have a robust campus life, this is expected. This may have also been due to the fact that some students remarked that EDU enrols few IS or students were unclear on who IS were. It also seemed like they had few opportunities for interaction. One student went as far as to remark that 'Emirati society is very dominating' on-campus due to the perception that many IS, as well as national students, wear the Emirati-style abaya and shayla.

Eighty-eight percent of students expressed a desire to interact with IS more often, while an additional 10% were content with their level of interaction. The majority of students felt that they did not face any difficulties with interacting with IS, but the main difficulties were related to culture (19%) or language (15%). When asked what impact IS have on-campus life,

46% of national students felt they had a positive impact as IS were seen to increase global awareness and encourage students to be more studious. 26% felt they had no impact as they are 'the same as us' or unseen, and the remaining 28% were unsure or gave unclear answers. No one felt they had a negative impact. When asked if there should be more IS at EDU, 88% of students said yes, 7% were unsure, and 5% said no. One student even remarked 'Yes, why have one type of rose when you can have a bouquet of different roses?' reflecting on the diversity and vibrancy she felt they brought to the campus community. The top reason for wanting more IS was to learn more about different cultures, which seemed to be the dominating value national students felt the IS brought. Additionally, the perceived positive impact beyond encouraging diversity can be seen in another student's response that IS 'motivate me to study more and be a good student because they do so'. When asked how more IS would impact the classroom culture, only 2% of respondents thought they would negatively impact the classroom experience. Reflections focusing on not wanting more IS at the institution included that having more IS would result in fewer Emirati students being able to study at the university. Additionally, due to cultural differences IS 'would have certain ways to do things that national students wouldn't'; possibly making some students uncomfortable. However, these views were not widespread.

The survey also asked about the international composition of the UAE resident population in general and respondents' feelings about how expatriates impact the cultural identity of the UAE. Ninety-three percent of respondents felt positive about international residents in the UAE. The three most common answers were coded as learning how to cooperate with others, contributing to the development of the UAE, and learning about other cultures. This aligns with the positive constructions Emirati students have about IS at EDU helping them to learn more about other cultures, or as vectors toward cultural development. The survey also asked about the negative impact of expatriates. Two-thirds of respondents listed at least one negative impact, and the most common themes were the loss of culture, expatriate overpopulation, and cultural differences. It is interesting to recognise the tension expressed by national students alongside the appreciation of other cultures and the impact of cultural diffusion on their own culture. Research has found in other countries like the United Kingdom that high levels of IS can lead to fear and bitterness from domestic students (Harrison, 2015). More research is needed to understand the depth of this tension amongst national students in the UAE.

In summary, the results from the survey for national students found that the majority of Emirati students had international experiences, were open to having more IS on campus, and had mostly positive perceptions of both IS and expatriates in the UAE. However, it is important to note the possibility of response bias towards a socially desirable answer regarding the positive and negative impacts of international students and expatriates. The UAE's current 2021 National Agenda prioritises the responsibility of its citizens to maintain a 'cohesive society and preserved national identity' with an overall vision of being among the best countries in the world (UAE Vision 2021, 2018). This vision is integrated throughout Emirati life and thus may lead national students to feel the tension of being welcoming to others without losing their identity to an expat-majority society.

International Students' Perceptions and Experiences with National Students

One of the major goals of this study was to understand the relationships between Emirati and IS, and research question two focused on how IS described their interactions and perceptions of national students. Seventy-six percent of IS felt that their Emirati peers had been welcoming inside class, compared to 56% outside of class. Within the respondents, there were two distinct groups. For students who identified as Arabic speaking or from another Gulf country, there was a stronger sense of belonging and many students reported also growing up in the country. Other students, identifying as non-Arabic speaking often reflected on lack of ability to build relationships and inability to connect due to the language issues. Among these students, one reflected that they felt 'outcast[ed] from students and staff', whereas another said they dealt 'with me but at the same time I was feared'. These reflections and others like them spoke to the need for non-Arabic speaking IS to feel more included in the community and understood. Forty-four percent of IS reported that most of their friends were international, 21% reported that they had an equal number of international and national friends, and 35% reported that they had more Emirati friends. Considering nearly 42% of the IS respondents had lived in the country prior to enrolling at EDU, likely attended international schools with Emiratis, and had completed at least one year at the institution, it is surprising to see that such a high percentage of IS reported no Emirati friends.

Another question asked how satisfied they were with their interactions with Emiratis. Forty-four percent of IS reported that they wanted to interact more, 50% were satisfied with their levels of interaction, and only 6% of IS participants said they wanted to interact with Emirati students less. There can be barriers to interacting with Emirati students which may inhibit IS from reaching out. Twenty-one percent of IS reported that they did not face any difficulties, which is almost the same as the number of students that reported having more Emirati friends. The top four specified barriers that IS shared were cultural differences (18%), they don't know what to talk about (18%), language difficulties (13%), and that Emirati students didn't seem interested in being friends with them (13%). In addition to the perceived communication problems impeding friendships formation among IS and national students, some IS remarked on being unable to relate to their Emirati peers as they face different pressures and had different educational goals. One student shared that:

> My experience in [EDU] is much easier than national Emirati peers in terms of education and responsibilities where I find the fact that we get educated in English is much easier for me, however, they find it somewhat difficult and struggle with it.

This is in line with the finding discussed in the previous section and illustrates there is a shared understanding among IS and national students that IS are generally more academically focused. Conversely, IS did not see themselves as sources of knowledge and cultural awareness as perceived by the Emirati students. However, IS also remarked on enjoying learning about other cultures.

International Students' Adjustment Experiences

The third research question examined how IS described their adjustment experiences at EDU, which included language, cultural, and emotional adjustment.

Language Adjustment

Federal universities in the UAE are unique because although the majority of students are non-native English speakers, most of the classes are in English. Both Emirati and international students are required to obtain a certain score on English proficiency exams. In reality, it is more important for IS to know English, but they also must know or learn Arabic for several required classes or certain majors. Over a third of IS rated themselves as having no experience or a beginning level in speaking (37%), reading (38%), writing (43%), and listening (33%) to Arabic. This is even more profound considering that 98% of international student respondents were at least a second-year undergraduate or graduate student. While 23% of IS expressed that Arabic is their native language, 30% of students shared that their lack of Arabic skills affected their ability to connect to Emirati students. One student described her experience struggling to connect with students in Arabic: 'Most of the UAE students speak in Arabic and due to this it is not easy to make friends in this university'. This factor also extended to non-Arabic speaking IS's interaction with faculty. One student wrote, 'when real explanation is needed from the professor and he speaks in Arabic, that's a real problem for those of us who don't listen to Arabic good'. Considering the university operates in English and does not require admitted IS to speak Arabic, the use of Arabic in the classrooms, the prevalence of Arabic among students, and the lack of cultural awareness could alienate non-Arabic speaking IS and may give the impression that the academic experience is not a good fit. However, many IS did not seem to be deterred by lower-level Arabic skills in their classes. Forty-five percent of IS thought that the classes at EDU were moderately or extremely easy, compared to about 12% of Emirati students. It may be that Emirati students have more difficulties as most classes are taught in English.

Cultural/Emotional Adjustment

IS often struggle with adjustment challenges that may go unseen or unheard. For the international student survey respondents at EDU, 33% of respondents explained that cultural adjustment was either moderately or very difficult, while 38% of students expressed that connecting with peers and making friends was difficult. Table 8.3 shows further analysis. In an open-ended question that asked students to explain their difficulties related to their adjustment experiences, some of the responses related to challenges with cultural adjustment such as the lack of visibility of IS, isolation of being the only non-Emirati in classes, and a desired larger international student body. One student recalled feeling 'overwhelm[ed] being the only

Table 8.3 Adjustment Experiences at EDU

	Very Difficult		*Moderately Difficult*		*Neither Difficult Nor Easy*		*Moderately Easy*		*Extremely Easy*			
Variable	*N*	*%*	*N*	*%*	*N*	*%*	*N*	*%*	*N*	*%*	*Total (N)*	*Mean*
Academic adjustment	0	0.00	5	13.16	17	44.74	9	23.68	7	18.42	38	3.47
Language adjustment (speaking English and/ or Arabic)	0	0.00	7	17.95	11	28.21	9	23.08	12	30.77	39	3.63
Cultural Adjustment	3	7.69	10	25.64	7	17.95	8	20.51	11	28.21	39	3.31
Connecting with peers and making friends	8	20.51	7	17.95	10	25.64	6	15.38	8	20.51	39	2.92
Living in the United Arab Emirates	1	2.56	3	7.69	8	20.51	8	20.51	19	48.72	39	4.02

Note: This 5-point Likert scale ranged from 1 (very difficult) to 5 (very easy).

non local in all of my classes, also I felt uncomfortable being the only one not wearing an abaya (i almost never saw a non local)'. This also feeds into the assumptions that IS may not be able to identify each other at EDU, as IS often assumed that only local students wear the national attire, which is not always the case.

However, 46% of students who responded to the open-ended question stated that they did not have any major adjustment difficulties. They cited reasons such as they felt integrated within the campus community, that living on campus helped them feel connected, and that citizens were kind. Overall, students rated academic, language, and location adjustments as moderately or extremely easy, and less than 18% of students expressed that the aforementioned factors were moderately or very difficult. Therefore, while some students felt disconnected from their peers, few found it to really impede their success.

Institutional Support

An important component of ICT is institutional support. Research question four sought to discover how IS perceived institutional support services at EDU. Institutional support as constructed in this study consists of both support services and individuals like faculty and staff. EDU is predominantly a commuter campus, but on-campus residence halls are provided for IS and Emirati students with unique circumstances. In regard to the IS who participated in this survey, 33% lived on campus, and 67% lived off-campus. Given the small number of IS at EDU, most students desired more programs and support. When asked if they would utilise certain programs or services, the vast majority of respondents said they would be extremely or somewhat likely to take advantage of them. This included: (a) A staff member to support IS (79%); (b) more online resources prior to beginning at EDU (74%); (c) English language program (71%); (d) Arabic language program (68%); (e) Ongoing orientation course (67%); and (f) A mentoring program to be matched with Emirati students (65%). EDU does not have robust campus services like many IBCs in the UAE, and the highest utilised office or service on campus was the Athletic Centre, utilised by 31% of participants. Next was Career Services at 17%. In terms of engagement outside of classes, 30% of students reported that they were not involved in any activities outside of classes, and the highest levels of involvement were through sports teams at 23%, and university events and programs at 27%.

About 70% of IS felt that faculty and staff understood their needs as an international student, and 62% of students felt that they received an adequate amount of support from faculty and staff. Interestingly, one student said 'I don't think most of my professors knew I was an international student', and therefore did not judge the professors for not providing extra support, but reinforced that some IS students seemed to feel invisible for better or worse. For the 38% of students who felt that support was inadequate, they cited reasons like a lack of social or emotional support, or that very few professors reached out or showed interest. In regards to emotional support, a student shared they felt EDU 'support[ed] us in stuff like renewing our visa, our Emirates ID and some necessary things but overall, they do not support me in social or emotional aspects'. Even with the strong desire for more Emirati friendships and institutional support, 91% of students felt accepted as a part of the campus community.

Discussion

The purpose of this study was to understand the experiences of IS studying in a federal university in the UAE. The analysis was framed through the ICT (Allport, 1954), and the research questions focused on IS's relationships with Emirati students, the support structures at the university, their adjustment experiences, and Emirati students' assumptions and perceptions of IS. This focus has enabled us to reveal how IS are constructed and how they perceive Emirati students, suggesting a number of assumptions on which these interactions are based.

Relational Conditions that Impact International and Domestic Student Engagement

The first research question focused on national students' interactions and perceptions of IS. The UAE prides itself on its tolerance, diversity, and welcoming nature and has residents from virtually every country in the world (UAE, n.d.). Overall, Emirati students took pride in their country's openness, highlighting their ideas that expatriates made the UAE better. One student expressed her feelings about expatriates in the UAE as such: 'They helped in having more cultural exchange, tolerance, respect and showed how the different nationalities are living together in peace and harmony'. Emirati students were well travelled and expressed a desire to learn about other cultures. Given the small numbers of IS at EDU, it is not surprising that only 40% of Emirati students reported interactions with IS outside of the classroom. It is also possible that IS are not considered as international or recognised by their national colleagues as such, particularly since many are from the Middle East and North Africa region, speak Arabic, and dress in national attire. The Emirati student participants seem ready and willing for more IS at EDU, given that 84% desired more interaction with IS, and 88% thought that there should be a greater number of IS at their university. One student shared why she thought there should be more IS at EDU: 'Yes, because it's good to hear opinions about the subject from students that have different perspectives'. As Harrison (2015) noted, even when domestic students are open to interacting with IS, it often doesn't organically happen.

Even though Emiratis overwhelmingly wanted to engage more with IS, EDU needs to facilitate the connections between students.

The second research question focused on how IS described their experiences and relationships with national students. IS felt that Emirati students were more welcoming inside than outside of class, which aligns with the response from national students about how they interacted with IS more inside of the classroom. This also speaks to the benefit that structured interactions and common goals can play in the engagement of international and national students, which is one of the main conditions of the ICT (Pettigrew, 1998). Emirati students surveyed had a stronger desire for more IS relationships as compared to IS toward Emiratis, which could be due to the complicated definition of an international student at EDU and in the UAE in general. Higher desire for connections from national students contrasts the sentiment found in many other studies in other contexts (Harrison, 2015). About a third of the IS lived in the UAE for at least four years before beginning EDU and may feel that they have plenty of Emirati friends. Although the findings showed that many Emirati students viewed IS as ways to improve their cultural understanding, IS did not appear to always feel welcomed, particularly outside of the classroom.

Structural Conditions That Impact IS and Domestic Student Adjustment and Engagement

Language difficulties continued to arise as a main challenge that impeded IS from developing stronger relationships with Emirati students. Almost a third of IS shared that their lack of Arabic language skills made it difficult to engage with national students, and more than a third rated themselves as a beginning Arabic speaker. This also speaks to the unique nature of the UAE and the federal institutions – the vast majority of students are native Arabic speakers and prefer to speak Arabic, but almost all classes are in English. This is different from the experiences of IS in many other countries where they may struggle to learn the language used inside and outside of the classroom (Lin & Scherz, 2014).

Questions three and four related to students' adjustment experiences and engagement with institutional support services and structures on campus. Students struggled with cultural adjustment and making friends primarily, which is common for IS (Lin & Scherz, 2014; Quinton, 2020). The vast majority of students felt supported or understood by faculty and staff, but many students desired more on-campus support services and structures. Given that EDU is predominantly a commuter university and many IS live on campus, it may be that university staff may not be fully aware of the unique needs and situations of these IS. This connects to assumptions that faculty and staff may also have of IS at EDU. Since the majority of IS are from nearby countries with similar cultures, staff may feel that IS are mostly able to adjust with minimal support. Overall, however, IS felt like they were accepted in the campus community and had adjusted, but the majority of students desired more support and programs from EDU.

Through the framework of the ICT, we find that several conditions are met or partially met to encourage engagement among international and national students in the UAE. In particular, *institutional support* is important for IS to feel supported and engaged at EDU. While there is room for improvement, IS at least felt welcomed into the community and supported by faculty and staff. Emirati students rated their interactions positively with IS and desired to have more IS on campus, and IS felt that Emiratis were welcoming in class, which can meet the conditions of *equal status, cooperation, and common goals*. The nature of students' interactions and connections on campus are positive and show potential. More intentional programming and engagement could provide the desired interactions and engagement that both international and national student's desire.

Conclusion

This descriptive study explored the experiences of IS studying at a federal HEI in the United Arab Emirates through the lens of the intergroup contact theory (Allport, 1954). Surveys of national students and IS were used to examine research questions that related to national and international student interactions, IS' adjustment to college, and institutional support. An analysis of the results showed that students desired more engagement with each other, and overall had positive perceptions of each other. Some of the main barriers to adjustment and engagement related to language or cultural differences, and although IS generally felt supported on campus by faculty and staff, many desired more intentional on-campus programs and support.

Constructions and assumptions of IS by Emirati students seemed to impact their rationale and willingness to engage with IS. Similarly, the unique nature and assumptions of what needs IS have at the case study institution, seemed to impact what services were provided to students. Future studies should push the narrative beyond internationalised universities in other higher education contexts, and explore the experiences of students who do not neatly fit the 'international student' label. This book chapter represents one of the few empirical studies about IS studying at federal universities in the UAE where this label is contested, and more research should be conducted that explores IS' experiences in unique contexts.

References

Ahmad, S. Z., & Hussain, M. (2017). An investigation of the factors determining student destination choice for higher education in the United Arab Emirates. *Studies in Higher Education*, *42*(7), 1324–1343. https://doi.org/10.1080/03075079.2015.1099622

Al Ali, M. (2014). *The development of the UAE federal higher education system: Main characteristics and influences (10048148)* [Doctoral thesis, University of Bath]. ProQuest.

Allport, G. W. (1954). *The nature of prejudice*. Addison Wesley.

AlSahafi, N., & Shin, S. (2017). Factors affecting the academic and cultural adjustment of Saudi international students in Australian universities. *Journal of International Students*, *7*(1), 53–72. https://doi.org/10.32674/jis.v7i1.245

Arthur, N. (2017). Supporting international students through strengthening their social resources. *Studies in Higher Education*, *42*(5), 887–894. http://dx.doi.org/10.1080/03075079.2017.1293876

Ashour, S., & Fatima, S. K. (2016). Factors favouring or impeding building a stronger higher education system in the United Arab Emirates. *Journal of Higher Education Policy and Management*, *38*(5), 576–591. https://doi.org/10.1080/1360080X.2016.1196925

Bartram, B. (2008). Supporting international students in higher education: Constructions, cultures and clashes. *Teaching in Higher Education*, *13*(6), 657–668. https://doi.org/10.1080/13562510802452384

Chavous, T. (2005). An intergroup contact-theory framework for evaluating racial climate on predominantly white college campuses. *American Journal of Community Psychology*, *36*(3/4), 239–257. https://doi.org/10.1007/s10464-005-8623-1

Cross-Border Education Research Team [C-BERT] (n.d.). *International Campuses*. http://cbert.org/resources-data/intl-campus/

Cruz, N., & Shukla, C. (2020). United Arab Emirates. In R. D. Ludeman et al. (Eds.), *Student affairs and services in higher education: Global foundations, issues, and best practices* (3rd ed., pp. 566–569), International Association of Student Affairs and Services (IASAS) in cooperation with the Deutsches Studentenwerk (DSW).

Glass, C. R., Gesing, P., Hales, A., & Cong, C. (2017). Faculty as bridges to co-curricular engagement and community for first-generation international students. *Studies in Higher Education*, *42*(5), 895–910. https://www.doi.org/10.1080/03075079.2017.1293877

Harrison, N. (2015). Practice, problems and power in 'internationalisation at home': Critical reflections on recent research evidence. *Teaching in Higher Education*, *20*(4), 412–430. https://www.doi.org/10.1080/13562517.2015.1022147

Harrison, N., & Peacock, N. (2010). Cultural distance, mindfulness and passive xenophobia: Using integrated threat theory to explore home higher education students' perspectives on 'internationalisation at home'. *British Educational Research Journal*, *36*(6), 877–902. https://www.doi.org/10.1080/01411920903191047

Jindal-Snape, D., & Rienties, B. (2016). *Multi-dimensional transitions of international students to higher education*. Routledge.

Jones, E. (2017). Problematising and reimagining the notion of 'international student experience'. *Studies in Higher Education*, *42*(5), 933–943. http://dx.doi.org/10.1080/03075079.2017.1293880

Knight, J., & Morshidi, S. (2011). The complexities and challenges of regional education hubs: Focus on Malaysia. *Higher Education*, *62*(5), 593–606. https://www.doi.org/10.1007/s10734-011-9467-2

Lin, S. Y., & Scherz, S. D. (2014). Challenges facing Asian international graduate students in the US: Pedagogical considerations in higher education. *Journal of International Students*, *4(*1), 16–33. https://doi.org/10.32674/jis.v4i1

Lytle, A. (2018). Intergroup contact theory: Recent developments and future directions. *Social Justice Research*, *31*, 374–385. https://doi.org/10.1007/s11211-018-0314-9

Marginson, S. (2013). Equals or others? Mobile Students in a nationally bordered world. In Sovic, S., & Blythman, M. (Eds.), *International students negotiating higher education* (pp. 9–27). Routledge. https://doi.org/10.4324/9780203817483

Ministry of Higher Education & Scientific Research. (2016). *Higher education, 2016*. [Data set]. Federal Competitiveness and Statistics Authority. https://fcsa.gov.ae/en-us/Pages/Statistics/Statistics-bySubject.aspx#/%3Ffolder=Demography%20and%20Social/Education/Higher%20Education&subject=Demography%20and%20Social

Ozer, S. (2015). Predictors of international students' psychological and sociocultural adjustment to the concept of reception while studying at Aarhus university, Denmark. *Scandinavian Journal of Psychology*, *56*, 717–725. https://doi.org/10.1111/sjop.12258

Pettigrew, T. (1998). Intergroup contact theory. *Annual Review of Psychology*, *49*, 65–85. https://doi.org/10.1146/annurev.psych.49.1.65

Pettigrew, T., & Tropp, L. (2006). A meta-analytic test of intergroup contact theory. *Journal of Personality and Social Psychology*, *90*(5), 751–783. https://doi.org/10.1037/0022-3514.90.5.751

Pettigrew, T., Tropp, L., Wagner, U., & Christ, O. (2011). Recent advances in intergroup contact theory. *International Journal of Intercultural Relations*, *35*(2011), 271–280. https://doi.org/10.1016/j.ijintrel.2011.03.001

Poyrazli, S., & Lopez, M. D. (2007). An exploratory study of perceived discrimination and homesickness: A comparison of international students and American students. *Journal of Psychology*, *141*(3), 263–280. https://doi.org/10.3200/jrlp.141.3.263-280

Quinton, W. (2020). So close and yet so far? Predictors of international students' socialization with host nationals. *International Journal of Intercultural Relations*, *74*, 7–16. https://doi.org/10.1016/j.ijintrel.2019.10.003

Starr-Glass, D. (2017). Troubling metaphors and international student adjustment: Reflections from a transnational place. *Journal of International Students*, *7(*4), 1126–1134. https://www.doi.org/10.5281/zenodo.1035979

Tawagi, A., & Mak, A. (2015). Cultural inclusiveness contributing to international students' intercultural attitudes: Mediating role of intergroup contact variables. *Journal of Community & Applied Social Psychology*, *25*, 340–354. https://doi.org/10.1002/casp.2218

Trice, A. (2007). Faculty perspectives regarding graduate international students' isolation from host national students. *International Education Journal*, *8*(1), 108–117.

UAE. (n.d.). *Fact sheet*. UAE Government. https://u.ae/en/about-the-uae/fact-sheet

UAE Vision 2021. (2018). *National agenda 2021: Cohesive society and preserved identity*. https://www.vision2021.ae/en/national-agenda-2021/list/identity-circle

UNESCO Institute of Statistics. (2019). *Global flow of tertiary-level students*. http://uis.unesco.org/en/uis-student-flow

United Arab Emirates Ministry of Education [MOE]. (2018, March 11). *List of licensed institutions in UAE*. https://www.moe.gov.ae/En/MediaCenter/News/Pages/licensedInstitutions.aspx

Wilkins, S., Stephens, M., & Huisman, J. (2012). Student satisfaction and student perceptions of quality at international branch campuses in the UAE. *Journal of Higher Education Policy and Management*, *34*(5), 543–556. https://doi.org/10.1080/1360080x.2012.716003

Author biographies

Natalie I. Cruz is Assistant Professor of Education at Charleston Southern University. Her research interests include global student mobility, the international student experience in under researched contexts, as well as ways to promote access for intercultural opportunities.

Dr Jobila W. Sy is at the American University of Antigua College of Medicine, Antigua & Barbuda. She is Associate Professor and Chair of the Education Enhancement Department. Her research interests focus on factors that impact student success with an emphasis on international higher education, multicultural education, learning strategies, academic achievement, educational policy, student development theory and academic advising.

Cassandra Shukla is Instructor at Zayed University in the United Arab Emirates. She has worked in first year experience, advising, and cultural education in the United States, UAE, and India. Cassandra's research areas lie in student success, learning-communities, and academic-partnership programs.

Alisha Tysor is Student Support and Engagement Coach for Noodle, a leading online higher education network in the United States. She has worked on projects and grants in the United States and UAE that focus on holistic student development and academic achievement. Her research interests include building student self-efficacy and grit through positive psychology.

Chapter 9

Syrian Students' Academic Mobility Struggle and Alternative Options

Ranwa Korsheed, Susan Deeb, and Rasha al-Dahhan

Syrian Higher Education before and during the Syrian Crisis

Before the 2011 Syrian crisis, many state universities in Syria engaged in improving their curricula, quality control and linkages with the market, in order to earn the 'credits' needed to facilitate international student mobility. Additionally, in 2001, private universities were allowed in the education sector in a further effort to offer opportunities for student and staff mobility. By law, these private universities are smaller, allowing a maximum of 10,000 students each. Dr Asa'ad Lotfi, the president of Kalamoon University, the first private university to open, said: 'We are changing the teaching methods by having classes with a maximum of 40 students; they are interactive and rely on a range of materials. We are also using the credit system to align ourselves with educational institutions outside of Syria'. Credits are one standard that contributes to better opportunities for gaining grants enabling students to pursue study abroad. Another favourable criterion that promotes grant opportunities is English. Private universities such as the Arab International University, teach at least some of their classes in English.

However, these pedagogical and structural developments reached their demise when the Syrian war broke out in 2011. The beginning of 2011 brought about the start of large-scale devastation to Syria and its people. This destruction inevitably took its toll on Syria's intellectual and cultural life. Schools, universities and teaching hospitals were targeted and destroyed. Teachers, academics and students alike were forced to flee their schools, their universities and their homes. The destruction of the higher education infrastructure and the disruption of education and academic mobility are a testimonial to the effects of the war on Syrian intellectual capital.

Consequently, the lack of accreditation and integrity of post-2011 universities compromised internationalisation. Widespread fake certification and general corruption raised distrust and international scepticism

DOI: 10.4324/9781003138457-12

and diminished social mobility for those who carried Syrian credentials. Moreover, the collaborations with the West and Europe that existed before 2011 were lost due to political realignment and the regional divisions that were created following the 2011 turmoil.

Academics further faced constrained mobility when education became a casualty of the economic sanctions. Naturally, the poor suffered more in this aspect. This was because the wealthy could afford to go abroad for education and gain access to whatever scarce resources were left in Syria. The economic sanctions led to dire working conditions for staff at educational institutions manifested in the lack of security and safety, scantiness and damage to learning spaces due to the fact that many schools were used as shelters or taken over by the military. This in turn led to the migration of 52,500 (22%) teachers and 532 (18%) school counsellors, therefore impacting the educational sector. These sanctions have also prevented Syrian academics from attending conferences and collaborating with international colleagues (Syria Crisis Education Strategic Paper, 2016).

Syrian students' despair was compounded when US universities and NGOs refused to offer scholarships to displaced students and higher education inside Syria. Similarly, EU countries and many other countries followed the same approach and had concerns about working with universities in Syria in fear of violating Washington's rigid sanctions regime. Europe first imposed sanctions at the beginning of 2011 and has extended them several times since then. Collaboration with Syrian academics has thus been happening through establishing informal professional networks and communities of practice, where exchange of knowledge and training was taking place, through organisations such as the British Council (based in Beirut). Another obstacle that Syrian students face post-2011 sanctions is the inability of Syrian students to make online payments, as a result, Udemy, one of Syrians' favourite course providers has recently been banning Syrian students from signing up in its courses.

These restrictions are not limited to online courses. Students in Syria have endless hurdles to clear to be able to secure a place in universities even when awarded prestigious fellowships, such as the Chevening scholarships. These students have to take the IELTS test of English language proficiency. After 2011, the British Council in Syria (which jointly owns IELTS) closed down and students have had to travel to another place, usually Beirut, to take the test. The expenses involved in such a trip, including the cost of the test itself, which totals a sum far beyond the income of an average family (approximately $400 in mid-March 2011, $40 in 2019 according to the Dollar exchange rate), was another hurdle to overcome. Lebanon security measures imposed on Syrians who wanted entry into Lebanon to have $2000 in cash and a valid hotel reservation (Al-Fanar, 2019). If and when a student is fortunate enough to financially bear the enormous expenses of the IELTS test and passes it, he or she has to reserve a place in the university accommodation. The only way to do this is to make an online deposit. But due to international sanctions, online payments for Syrians have been shut down.

All these roadblocks have left students yearning for a higher education, in the United States or United Kingdom. These students, as we will explain in the following sections of this chapter, experience total despair and an overwhelming state of helplessness. The salvaged educational system post-2011, coupled with international sanctions, has crippled student mobility.

International Students

The term 'international student/s' has somehow remained contested and variously defined in academic and policy literature. In the United Kingdom, the term is applied to students who are not 'domiciled' in the country and come from countries within the European Union 'other European' and 'non-European Economic Area (EEA)' countries, as well as 'non-EU' countries. Students who study for a UK HE degree, outside the United Kingdom, are generally referred to as 'overseas' students by national HE statistics and advisory bodies (HESA, 2016; UKCISA, 2018), although the term is also widely associated with non-European students studying in the United Kingdom (Taylor & Ali, 2017. In line with the above definitions, this study employs the term 'international' for EU, EEA as well as non-EU students.

Scholars have explored how international students' mobility ties in with concurrent forms of the global movement, diaspora and migration (Brooks and Waters, 2010; Ploner, 2017), reproduce cultural capital and social (dis)advantages (Waters, 2006), or reshape notions of place, belonging and community (Nada & Araújo, 2018). Likewise, research has focused on experiences of 'transition', 'orientation' or 'adjustment' of international students and looked at the ways equality and inclusion are played out within increasingly diverse academic environments. Scholars have also emphasised the 'internationalisation of curricula' as a way to enhance students' intercultural skills development, world-mindedness and employability (Leask, 2016).

Becker and Kolster (2012) discovered significant factors of a country, which make a study destination attractive and mobility between countries possible. These factors include mutual recognition of degrees/qualifications (by the host country and the domestic country), costs of higher education and living in a country (tuition fee, availability of financial aid, travel expenses, living costs), governance of higher education institutions (public vs. private), internationalisation of a country (number of foreign students, availability and diversity of international programmers, stringency of immigration policies), the living, study and work environment of a country (climate, research facilities, ambience, employment and immigration opportunities/regulations during and after study, demographic growth/decline), and social and geographical linkages (friends/relatives living or studying in the same country, geographical proximity). These, as explained in the previous section have been adversely affected by the Syrian conflict, affecting international students enrolment in Syrian universities and vice versa.

International and Arab Students' Enrolments Abroad

Although statistics of international student enrolment in British universities' post-graduate programmes are shown clearly on the top ten universities' websites, statistics of international students joining distance learning programmes are limited. Consequently, this chapter recommends transparent publication of the percentage of international students joining distance learning programmes. Total numbers and percentages of learners joining distance programmes can be found; however, the number of Arab international students studying online, in general, and Syrian students, is not found (Kemp, 2019).

Scholarships for students in the Middle East are provided under the condition of English language proficiency. Moreover, British universities are collaborating with different institutions in the Arab World, (for instance, the University of Warwick, one of the top British universities, works with Knowledge Horizon, and STEPS in the United Arab Emirates). Unfortunately, such collaborations do not include all Arab countries, especially not in Syria. Syrian students are facing hardships when it comes to applying to foreign universities' programmes and specifically British universities programmes being the most desired. In order for Syrian students to join British universities, they have to apply for an English language proficiency test. Students living in Syria have to travel to another country in order to do the test. In addition, after the outbreak of COVID-19, Duolingo, an American language-learning website and a digital language proficiency exam, launched an online English language proficiency test that was banned in Syria due to international logistic sanctions mostly by the United States. Unfortunately, English language tests were not the only learning opportunities banned. Access was banned also from Coursera (online education website), international research databases and grants through Syrian universities, professional certificates, i.e., CFA (charted financial analyst), CMA (certified management accountant), FRM (financial risk manager). This shows that education is being politicised by academic institutions when it comes to students who live in Syria which undermines the notions of equality and inclusion raised by international organisations and many universities around the world.

Students' Views Regarding Online Postgraduate Programmes

Given the status and context of Syrian higher education described in the sections above, a questionnaire was devised to elicit responses from university students in Syria with regard to their attitudes and willingness to join online post-graduate programmes at British universities, in light of the limited available chances to study on these universities' campuses. This questionnaire consisted of a demographic section, seven closed items and three open items. It collected data on students' desires and attitudes towards joining online programmes at British universities, the anticipated obstacles, and suggestions to help Syrian students further pursue their postgraduate studies at British universities.

The questionnaire was administered online to a group of students enrolled in different faculties at Damascus University, being the most distinguished university of the Syrian state universities. The group consisted of 26 female students and 30 male students. The students belong to the age group of 19–25 years old. The questionnaire did not target a specific faculty, it was rather open to any student from any faculty as its link was posted online in a group for students at Damascus University. Ninety percent of the participants are undergraduate students who were enrolled at scientific faculties at Damascus University. Only 3% had jobs. On the other hand, the remaining 10% were postgraduate students. The questionnaire was written in Arabic and used a seven-item Likert scale. The questionnaire was tested for internal consistency (reliability) using SPSS (V.16.0) and a Cronbach's alpha test was carried out. The result of the test can be seen below:

According to Table 9.1, the questionnaire shows an internal consistency value of (.94) which indicates a high value of internal consistency for the Likert-Scale items.

Piloting

The main research tool of this paper, the aforementioned questionnaire, was piloted on a group of 37 students at Damascus university enrolled in different faculties which were not specifically targeted. The items showed a high degree of clarity and relatedness as the participants have stated in the comment box in the questionnaire. In addition, the results of the pilot

Table 9.1 Reliability Statistics

Cronbach's Alpha	*Cronbach's Alpha Based on Standardised Items*	*No. of Items*
.949	.959	7

test had close percentages to the actual test. Those will be presented in the coming sections.

Results Analysis

A significant percentage of 94.6% of the participants have stated their desire to pursue post-graduate studies at British Universities. About 94.7% of the participants anticipated that getting a visa was one of the obstacles that would face students who want to pursue post-graduate studies at traditional British Universities. In addition, 92.9% of the students agreed that the absence of certified language testing centres in Syria and the difficulty of reaching other centres in neighbouring countries were also major obstacles that face students.

With regard to pursuing post-graduate studies at British Universities by joining available online programmes, 66.1% of the participants expressed their desire to join these programmes. 80.3% of the students stated that joining such programmes would save the Syrian students the trouble of getting a visa and securing convenient accommodation. However, only 57.1% of the students thought that for Syrian students living in Syria, this kind of education would be a preferred choice than joining traditional on-campus programmes. In addition, 75% of the students agreed that online postgraduate studies programmes at British universities would offer them accredited and internationally recognised diplomas. When asked about the programmes they would like to join, answers have varied according to students' majors. The most desired programmes are those of medicine, dentistry, surgery, education, physics, social studies, design, engineering, and technology. Furthermore, the students listed some of the anticipated obstacles that might be faced while pursuing postgraduate studies online. The most frequently mentioned obstacles were logistic and financial. Finally, the students listed some suggestions to help them pursue their postgraduate studies. The most frequently mentioned ones were about creating special online learning platforms for Syrian students, establishing British learning centres for postgraduate studies in Syria and increasing the number of offered scholarships.

Syrian Students' Experience with Distance Learning

Basel, Ranim, Tala[1] and Ayoub are working at an international organisation and are studying online simultaneously. They were invited to participate in telephone interviews to which they responded and contributed their answers. The interviewees were chosen because they were doing an MA degree online in different British universities. They were granted the opportunity to pursue their studies online by the organisation they work for. After a certain number of years of employment in an international organisation, employees are given the chance to enrol in an online master's programme in order to improve their skills. In general, students apply to the desired programme and the organisation pays most of the tuition fees. A minor amount is paid by the employee. According to these interviewees, they applied through the university platform and the process was not complicated. Their studies are completely online through a specific portal and some of the materials are hard-copy. The exams are normally held in the British Council offices in Beirut as there are no centres for the universities they study in, either in Syria or in Beirut. However, since the outbreak of COVID-19, exams are conducted online.

The application and learning experience of these Syrian students who succeeded in enrolling in British online postgraduate programmes was not less challenging than the ones who aim to travel and study on-campus. Basel, who is doing an online master's degree in Global Public Health at Queen Mary University of London, talked about the challenges that he was facing before and after he started his studies. The extra challenges according to Basel are the following:

> The IELTS test tops the list of obstacles as it is not available in Syria so I had to travel to Beirut. Another is paying the tuition fees. Because of the US sanctions, I could not pay from Syria and I could not access the university platform without using a VPN. One more thing is the speed of the internet as it is needed for the live sessions in Syria.

Ranim, a student doing an online master's degree in Public Health at the London School of Hygiene and Tropical Medicine (part of the University of London) added:

> The challenge that affected my study timeline the most was the delay of sending the hard copy books. It took more than two months back and forth because they included a CD. I am not sure if the CD was the major obstacle that caused the delay, however; the material reached right after it was removed.

Unlike Basel and Ranim, Tala and Ayoub, who are also doing master's degrees in Public Health at the London School of Hygiene and Tropical Medicine, had to travel to Beirut in order to sit for an examination during the first year of their studies. However, in the second year, due to COVID 19, they did their exams online. Tala said:

> I had to travel to Beirut in order to take the exam in the British Council. It was quite difficult for me to find a place to stay at and the rent was expensive. Almost 90% of the tuition fees were paid by the organization I work for and the rest by me. If I had to pay all of the fees myself,

> then I would have definitely faced serious problems. The main issue was the inflation in Syria. The books shipment took a long time and some books were missing and I could not get some CDs because of the sanctions on Syria.

Ayoub clarified:

> I remember that there was one particular module where we had no hard copies of the material and the soft copy was not available as a link in the website of the university or the library so the only solution was having a Kindle account and I did not have one and I couldn't register for it so I asked the help of an Egyptian friend who had an account. It was not easy to find a solution. If I did not have this friend, it would have been much difficult to get the material. In general, the study experience was fair and good mainly because I have a backup system which is the organization. Other than that, I think I would have faced lots of obstacles.

Ayoub stressed the fact that the war in Syria affected the living conditions:

> It is a bit difficult as you have shortages in Electricity. Sometimes there is a bad internet connection. Unfortunately, every now and then, something happens in the country like water cuts and fuel cuts. So, your life is disturbed by these conditions and this includes studying. Studying online is a different experience from studying in-campus because you have to mitigate the living conditions in the country and you need to focus on your studies and your work.

Despite the aforementioned challenges, Tala, Ayoub, Basel and Ranim asserted the importance of the opportunity they were given to study online. Ranim explained:

> I am a wife and a mother so the dream of travelling to study abroad would have been difficult to reach if it wasn't for the online learning.

When Basel was asked if he had the choice of doing his master's degree on-campus, would he go for this option or he would adhere to the online one, he answered:

> I would definitely choose distance learning as I can't travel due to my work and other personal issues.

The results of the questionnaire conform with the interviewees' point of view.

Results and Discussion

Difficulties Expected in Online Programmes Enrolment

When asked about the difficulties students expect to face when enrolling in a distance programme at a British university, most participants in the questionnaire were concerned about their lack of English language proficiency and the slow internet connection in Syria. Other responses included high tuition fees and unavailability of language exam centres in Syria. The list of barriers facing Syrian students who wish to study abroad included not only academic but also logistic restrictions. The results of the questionnaire show that one of the most prominent obstacles is the English language proficiency test. It is commonly known that most British universities require an English language proficiency certificate. In Syria, the IELTS exam can only be taken in the British Council and in-person. Most foreign embassies and cultural centres among which is the British Council closed their offices in Damascus after the Syrian war broke out in 2011. The nearest place for a Syrian to take the test is usually Beirut. Students might also travel to Amman or Arbil. However, Beirut is the first option due to being the closest to Damascus Al-Fanar Media published an article explaining the costs the Syrian students face in order to travel to do the test, which states that the test itself costs \$205—the lion's share of an average monthly household income in Syria (Al-Fanar, 2019). A round-trip taxi between Damascus and Beirut is \$400. To enter Lebanon, Syrians need to show \$2,000 in cash at the border and proof of hotel accommodation. (They can 'rent' the cash and get hotels to provide proof of a reservation, but that also costs money.) The total cost of taking the IELTS can easily add up to \$1,000—the average income of a Syrian household for three or four months (Wheeler & Faek, 2018).

Depriving Syrian students of the chance to take the language tests inside their country contradicts Target 4.B of the UN SDG (Sustainable Development Goal) 4 which is to 'substantially expand globally the number of scholarships available to developing countries' by 2020. Being faced with such challenges, Syrian students resorted to online education. Nevertheless, the US sanctions imposed on Syria have also affected online learning as some online platforms have been banned. In 2020, Coursera, an open online course provider, was banned because of the sanctions and in August 2020 Duolingo which is a language learning service that offered an online English language test that is authenticated by many universities was also suspended. Consequently, some Syrian students who participated in the questionnaire have argued that international higher education is politicised and turned into a commodity that can be traded. According to Sylvie Lomer, 'International Higher Education reproduces "a discursive logic that distils human relationships, dreams, visions and aspirations into the language of value (which) is indicative of the tenacious hold of a market-based instrumentalism on the intellectual imagination"' (cited in Sidhu, 2006, loc762). What is more, some participants have stressed that Syrian youths who are living in the country are the ones who need education the most. While they are trying to improve their skills and develop their knowledge regardless of all the challenges they have in Syria, their exclusion due to politics is becoming normal worldwide. An example of normalising this exclusion, according to one of the participants in this study, is what the United Nations did recently. The UN has started the UN75 campaign to help youth around the world to have a voice in what are the main areas that the UN should work for in the next 25 years. The problem is, as the participant explained, that the UN who is supposed to be inclusive and supposed to actually advocate for inclusivity and equal rights used a link to their survey that doesn't load in Syria due to US sanctions.

Nevertheless, Syrian students have tried to defy this exclusion using different methods such as social media platforms. To be more precise, after a campaign was launched by some Syrian students under a nongovernmental organisation called The Syrian youth assembly, The Duolingo company was granted an exemption from the office of foreign asset control to reactivate its English proficiency test in Syria in December 2020. Thus, Syrian students could use it for scholarships applications at universities that are willing to approve its results.

Students' Suggestions

When asked about their suggestions for making distance learning at British universities accessible, students proposed making the programmes affordable and providing secure channels through which students can pay the tuition fees. This, according to the participants in the questionnaire, includes lifting sanctions on Syria, which would also allow the Ministry of Higher Education in Syria to collaborate with British universities and consequently offer joint scholarships. Participants also suggested opening centres and branches for British universities in Syria or at least reopening the British Council in Damascus so that students can have access to English language teaching and culture. If taken into consideration, students think that this step would solve lots of problems related to having English language proficiency tests and provide students with an official institute that represents the British universities in Syria.

Concluding Remarks

Being Syrian scholars, who live in Syria and who aspire to further pursue our postgraduate studies, it was our aim and mission to deliver the message embedded in this chapter on behalf of all Syrian students. Syrian students' chances of scholarly mobility have been diminished due to many circumstances and conditions, not least of which are the Syrian crisis and the sanctions applied to this country. Many dreams have been crushed deferred or put to sleep but, despite this, the Syrian youth has never stopped dreaming and will keep looking for new hope and opportunities.

Note

1 Tala finished studying and graduated in 2020.

References

Al Fanar. (2019). In Syria, the complicated web that sanctions weave. https://www.al-fanarmedia.org/2019/02/in-syria-the-complicated-web-that-sanctions-weave/

Becker, R., & Kolster, R. (2012). *International student recruitment: Policies and development in selected countries*. Netherlands Organization in Higher Education.

Brooks, R., & Waters, J. (2010). Social networks and educational mobility: The experience of UK. *Globalization, Societies and Education*, 8(1), 143–57

Higher Education Statistic Agency (HESA) (2016). Introduction—Students 2015/16. Retrieved February 2018, from https://www.hesa.ac.uk/data-and-analysis/publications/students-2015-16/introduction

Kemp, N. (2019). *Higher education's distance learning delivery dilemma*. University World News.

Leask, B. (2016). Internationalizing curriculum and learning for all students. In Jones, E., R. Coelen, J. Beelen and H. de Wit eds., Global and Local Internationalization, Sense Publishers, 47–53

Lomer, S. (2018). UK policy discourses and international student mobility: The deterrence and subjectification of international students. *Globalisation, Societies and Education*, *16*(3), 308–324. 10.1080/14767724.2017.1414584

Nada, C. I., & Araújo, H. C. (2018). When you welcome students without borders, you need a mentality without borders' internationalisation of higher education: Evidence from Portugal. Studies in higher education, 1–14.

Ploner, J. (2017). Resilience, moorings and international student mobilities: exploring biographical narratives of social science students in the UK. Mobilities, *12*(3), 425–444.

Sidhu, R. K. (2006). *Universities and globalization: To market, to market*. Routledge.

Syria Crisis Education Strategic Paper, 2016, London Progress Report, September 2016.

Taylor, G., & Ali, N. (2017). Learning and living overseas: Exploring factors that influence meaningful learning and assimilation: How international students adjust to studying in the UK from a socio-cultural perspective. *Education Sciences*, *7*(1), 1–25.

UK Council for International Student Affairs (UKCISA). (2018). International student statistics: UK higher education. https://www.ukcisa.org.uk/Research%2D%2DPolicy/Statistics/Internationalstudent-statistics-UK-higher-education

UNESCO. (2015). **SDG4-Education** 2030, Incheon Declaration (ID) and Framework for Action. For the Implementation of Sustainable Development Goal 4, Ensure Inclusive and Equitable Quality **Education** and Promote Lifelong Learning Opportunities for All, ED-2016/WS/28.

Waters, J. (2006). Geographies of cultural capital: Education, international migration and family strategies between Hong Kong and Canada. *Transactions of the Institute of British Geographers*, *31*, 179–92.

Wheeler, D., & Faek, R. (2018, November 16). Ambitious Syrian Students Often Enter a Maze—Al-Fanar Media. https://www.al-fanarmedia.org/2018/11/ambitious-syrian-students-often-enter-a-maze/

Author biographies

Ranwa Khorsheed was born in Damascus. She received her MA in Linguistics from Damascus University. She taught at different local institutes including Damascus University. She is currently a lecturer at the Arab International University. She is interested in cognitive and corpus linguistics and online education. She is a sworn Translator. She has published several papers on language teaching and co-authored a book on academic writing and research. She has recently got five certificates (Sustainability in higher education, digital skills, women empowerment, soft skills and gender equality), from UNED-sponsored by Erasmus.

Susan Deeb is an English Language Instructor at the Arab International University and Syrian Virtual University. She received her MA in Literary Studies from Damascus University's Department of English. Deeb has published several papers in different journals. Her research interest is focused on the integration of gender and ethnicity as roots and routes in African American women's road narratives. She is also focusing on how Distance Learning has reshaped language learning worldwide.

Rasha al-Dahhan is a BA English Literature graduate from Damascus University. She holds a master's degree in translation and interpretation. She has long been intrigued by pedagogy and teaching, particularly English as a second language. She has taught English to students of different ages, ranging from elementary to university. Also an advocate of applying new and diverse teaching methods, Rasha was fascinated by online teaching, introduced to Syria in 2002, and began teaching English as a second language at Syrian Virtual University. She later on became L3 English coordinator designing teaching plans and supervising exams and continues to be an active member of staff at SVU. She is also an English language instructor at Arab International University, the number 1 ranking private university in Syria. She has recently got five certificates (Sustainability in Higher Education, Digital Skills, Women Empowerment, Soft Skills and Gender Equality) from UNED sponsored by Erasmus.

Index

Note: Page numbers in *italics* indicate figures, **bold** indicate tables and page numbers with "n" indicate notes in the text.